RUNNING OUT
OF SATURDAYS

RUNNING OUT OF SATURDAYS

Laughs, life lessons and one larrikin's journey

Running out of Saturdays

First published July 2025 by
thatpeterbrewer.com

ISBN 978-1-7641114-0-9 PRINT
ISBN 978-1-7641114-1- 6 EPUB
ISBN 978-1-7641114-2-3 AUDIO

Copyright © 2025 Peter Brewer

 A catalogue record for this book is available from the National Library of Australia

All rights reserved. This publication (or any part of it) may not be reproduced or transmitted, copied, stored, distributed or otherwise made available by any person or entity (including Google, Amazon or similar organisations), in any form (audio, electronic, digital, optical, mechanical) or by any means (photocopying, recording, scanning or otherwise) without prior written permission from the publisher and the author.

Edited by Phaedra Pym - awaywithwords.net.au
Produced for the publisher by exlibris.com.au

*To my wonderful children:
You are the greatest gifts of my life.
The love in this book is my gift back to you.*

*And to my beautiful grandchildren:
Today, you look at your silly old Poppa B and fart.
Hopefully, one day you'll read my stories and smile.*

Foreword

How do you describe a man with as much personality as Peter Brewer (aka PB)? Many would describe him as enigmatic, a force of nature, a trailblazer and a whirlwind of enthusiasm. But to us, he's just Dad.

As Lauren, his daughter, I've had countless experiences at real estate events far and wide. "Is your dad Peter Brewer?" I'd heard asked more times than I can remember. In this book, Dad shares tales of his escapades and countless life lessons while creating a legacy in real estate based on decades of experience.

As Sam, his son, I've been privileged to have a role model like Dad. From teaching me how to pee on a 4WD tyre, how to fish, how to ride a bike and how to be a hard worker, to showing – not just saying – "I love you" and being a voice of reason and encouragement on life-altering decisions, he has guided me through so many life events. Now, as I embark on my own journey of being a Dad, I reflect upon my upbringing and strive to have a relationship with my children like the one I have with my best friend, Dad. Although I think I'll change a few more nappies than PB did on his journey!

Running out of Saturdays showcases a caring, ambitious man, ahead of his time, who challenges the norm and has always found a way to turn a shit sandwich into a footlong with all the trimmings throughout his life. We can all learn something from our dad, and if reading this book doesn't challenge your thoughts or perspectives, you are doing it wrong!

Dad's stories are barely embellished and almost always punctuated by his unique sense of humour. A word of warning, though – keep a box of tissues handy. You might laugh until you cry… or just cry. Either way, they'll make you reflect on your own life and maybe even challenge you to consider the legacy you'll leave behind.

Our dad has always encouraged us to chase our dreams, work hard, learn from our mistakes and never take life too seriously. He instilled in us a deep appreciation for the simple things – like a day at the beach or a yarn around a campfire. His belief in seizing the day and making the most of every Saturday echoes through every page.

This book is his gift – not just to us, but to anyone who's ever felt the pull of adventure or the quiet ache of time slipping away. So, settle in and enjoy the ride. You're in for a treat.

We're proud of you, Dad. Thank you for sharing your story with us and the world.

— Sam and Lauren Brewer
AKA "The Grotties"

A Little About Me and Saturdays

My life has been an absolutely magnificent journey. I've had the fortune to meet some incredible people and experience things beyond my wildest dreams. At 65, I can see the curtains on my life are slowly closing inch by inch, whether in one year or 20.

I don't know how history or St Peter will judge me. Frankly, over time I've learned to care less about the judgement of others. It's kinda been how I've approached the last 20 years of my life. I've become very comfortable in my own skin. I've learned to dismiss the detractors. It takes lots of self-reflection and self-affirmation to get to that happy place where you're totally comfortable with yourself.

On that journey, I met amazing people and shared some breathtaking experiences. I've also encountered more than my fair share of people who could do with a little more reflection and a whole lot less time stroking their self-affirmation! (Get my drift?) But isn't that part of life's beauty? Learning, forming your own views, finding your tribe and determining your niche and where you can make a difference through it all.

Life has been kind to me, and I think I've been kind to life.

I know that I've had an absolute blast every step of the way. Every win, however glorious, and every loss, however small, has taught me something. I'm thankful for those lessons and experiences.

My various careers have brought me incredible personal satisfaction. One of my mum's teachings as a child was, "It's nice to be important, but it's more important to be nice." I hope my life made her proud.

I do not claim to be a prolific author or a Gandhi-like figure. I'm just an ordinary boy from the "burbs" who gave life a good crack and who, through this memoir, decided he'd like to share a few of his stories with his grandkids in the hope that they might one day learn a little bit more about their silly old Poppa B and how he spent his days.

Why the title? While every day of the week has its own charm, there's something special about a Saturday.

Having worked on Saturdays for 30+ years in real estate, I learned to savour the rare free ones I had. There was so much anticipation about the freedom a Saturday offered.

Saturdays bring happiness. A gateway to week's end. The opportunity to lounge with friends, watch your favourite footy team do battle or loiter in a hardware store buying important stuff you didn't ever really need.

Saturdays are unique. Saturday draws its name from Saturn. Is it, therefore, blind coincidence we so often put a ring around a Saturday?

Even the word Saturday sounds friendly. In the 3,367 of them that I've enjoyed so far, I've never ever heard anyone refer to "Saturdayitis".

The life experience I share through a series of short stories in this memoir is that Saturdays are ours to be enjoyed. As a child, I remember shops closing at noon on Saturday. The banks and car yards were closed. Pubs, parks and beer gardens came alive. Theatres and clubs had matinee sessions to deal with the increased Saturday patronage. Streets came alive with the symphony of lawn mowers and leaf blowers.

Slowly, our society and demand for everything 24/7 has undermined the sacred time a Saturday has historically offered, when it should be a day to recharge the battery and fill your spiritual cup.

Ah, Saturday.

The message is abundantly clear, dear Reader. Savour your Saturdays. Inhale whatever they lay at your feet. They're totally yours to do with as you like.

But remember, we're all counting every day down together at exactly the same pace, and faster than you realise. Yes, we're all… Running out of Saturdays.

That Peter Brewer

Contents

Foreword — vii

A Little About Me and Saturdays — ix

PART 1 : This Is Me — 1

PART 2 : PB's Life Lessons — 131

PART 3 : Lessons in Leadership — 191

PART 4 : People Make the World Go Round — 211

Final Curtain Call…but the Show Goes On — 285

Acknowledgements — 297

Author Bio — 299

PART 1

This Is Me

The birth of Brewer Real Estate

Real estate wasn't always in our family's blood. However, Dad often shared with us the experience of him and Mum buying their first property.

Dad, a young motor mechanic at Hargraves – the local canned foods factory that went on to be Edgell's – described the scene of donning a suit and tie and making an appointment to see (cue deep bass music) "The Bank Manager".

In those days, the bank manager was a revered, god-like figure in the community with incredible superpowers. The seas would seemingly part as he eased his chariot along Manly Road and down into Cambridge Parade to his covered car park, the only covered car park in the village. His entrance was grand, almost royal, and his car park had the words "Reserved For The Bank Manager" inscribed on a Moses-esque stone tablet.

The bank manager of the 1950s/60s could either make or erase a family's dreams with the stroke of his lethally sharpened 2HB pencil.

In my mind, I'm picturing an undersized man in a dark suit seated behind an oversized teak desk peering over heavy, black-rimmed glasses, casting judgement and, ultimately, determining whether you'd walk out the door with tears of elation or with your dreams in tatters.

Dad and Mum were seeking the princely sum of 1,000 pounds to purchase their first home, a "cottage" at 58 Daisy Road, Manly, Queensland, which was no more than a converted, asbestos-ridden single garage adorned with a lean-to carport.

As an equal partner in the marriage, Mum – or as she was referred to back in 1957, the "little lady of the house" – was instructed to sit at home and wait to hear the outcome while "the men" sat to discuss business. (*Note: while it's a far cry from where we are today, much still needs to be done to support ladies equally in their property ventures. My friend Nicola McDougall writes more about overcoming this disparity in her book, The Female Investor. Buy a copy for your daughter, son and every female work colleague.*)

58 Daisy Road, Manly, Queensland

Dad endured the interview with the bank manager, explaining how he'd be using the new carport adjoining the cottage to service friends' cars at night and on weekends to help meet the house repayments.

True to his word, he did exactly that for 6 years until my brother and I were able to take Mum's place, grabbing tools and pumping brake pedals for hours, night after night, while Dad performed life-saving surgery on dilapidated old jalopies that had been entrusted to his restoration skills.

Dad had an incredibly strong work ethic and was tireless in providing us with what was, at that stage in life, a modest existence. He had ambition. Like me, he had no real idea what to do at that age. He just knew that standing still meant you would eventually get run over.

On reflection, that interview with the bank manager could well have been Dad's second clarion call that he had some burgeoning sales skills. The first was that he'd wooed Mum to be his Mrs

Brewer. Together, they forged a dynamic business and community partnership that would blossom and grow for 43 years.

Dad learned a few lessons when he met the bank manager that day. The idea of moving to a management role and becoming an "instructor of the work" rather than a "doer of the work" was born, and Dad was instilled with a drive to find a way up the corporate ladder. Crawling around under cars and trucks covered in oil and grease was probably now off his radar, and his interest in property was ignited.

Much has been written about empires that started as dreams in humble garages. Apple, Google, Amazon. Mum and Dad's purchase of 58 Daisy Road was no different. It was their dream, it was functional, and most importantly, it was affordable. Its basic, bare asbestos-clad walls are a wonderful life lesson that your first foray into property doesn't need to be a brand new 4-bed low set brick house with a pool, all the mod cons, and 2 new Toyotas in the driveway.

Tiny steps are just fine. They're a reminder to ignore the peer pressure of keeping up with the Joneses and their crippling mortgage and stress. There'll be plenty of time to overtake them later. And at speed.

As modest as it was, the free-standing converted garage at 58 Daisy Road became our home and a base from which the Brewer family and its real estate dynasty was born.

Summer holidays and first-degree burns

As a pre-teen, summer holidays at the beach consisted of 2 weeks in a friend's modest flat in James Street, Burleigh, a beach town in southern Queensland. Dad would fund that annual pilgrimage to the beach by being on call each night to assist the flat owner with his business as the local undertaker at Burleigh Heads. Yes, dear old Dad's nocturnal holiday work would consist of a random but regular knock on the door of our modest holiday flat. That knock meant Dad was about to be whisked away to assist in retrieving a corpse or two in various states of disrepair or decay, depending on the cause of the deceased's departure.

As I've grown as a father, I've started to appreciate what my dad had endured and sacrificed throughout his often tortured life so that we could enjoy many of life's luxuries.

Dad was a magnificent provider for his family, ensuring we had so many of the things he'd been denied as a child. He grew up in a large family with values steeped deeply in the Great Depression years and learned to make do with very little. One of my few late-in-life regrets is not showing him proper appreciation for his generosity during his days on this planet.

Despite the late-night knocks at the door and the devastation he'd witnessed, Dad would return in the early hours and be at peace, home with his family at the beach.

Our beach holidays were a daily ritual of 3 hours at North Burleigh Beach. It wasn't the closest beach to our flat, but it had "dumpers" – giant waves with a classic barrel shape – and Dad loved the energy of the ocean. It was when he seemed his happiest.

Like clockwork, Dad, Mum, my older brother and I would arrive at the beach at 9:30 am. No sunscreen, no hats, no water.

We'd take turns digging a hole in the sand to act as a safe anchor for the trendy rainbow-coloured beach brolly that would end up casting its tiny shadow across a patch of sand the size of Mum's left ankle. It looked fantastic. But in reality, it was a useless fashion accessory. It wasn't uncommon for that rainbow-coloured javelin to take flight in the slightest gust of wind across the crowded beach, spearing unsuspecting beachgoers on its path of carnage. My brother and I would take turns recovering this multicoloured missile and digging a deeper hole to embed it into the soft white sand. I swear we almost dug through to China!

A few minutes of digging holes and making sand castles, and then Dad would summon us to the rolling surf. He would take turns mercilessly throwing my brother and me headfirst into

North Burleigh's dumping waves. The result was always the same – bouncing around on the ocean floor, salt water filling lungs and nostrils, fearing whether we'd come up for air. Finally, we'd emerge, gasping for breath as we broke the surface, laughing and beckoning Dad, "Do it again!"

Beach holidays

Dad loved hardening us up and probably wanted to make sure he got full value for the swimming lessons he'd paid for. He was all about getting value from every dollar and, at times, had some interesting ways of making us feel loved. But we always did. I only ever felt the wrath of his disappointment twice, and I promise you, I didn't ever want to make it a trifecta.

Dad was a man of habit. His reprieve from the morning's beach frivolities was to bundle us into the sauna-like car, strap on the blistering metal seat belt and take us to the Miami Hotel, where he'd set himself up on a corner stool at the bar for some moments of reflection. At the same time, we'd patiently sit in the car outside for those 3 hours of reflection, wondering what mysteries lay hidden behind the walls of that sign: Public Bar.

On the really lucky days, Dad might leave his seat at the bar and venture outside to check that we hadn't died of dehydration or heat stroke. If we played our cards right and didn't die, he would sometimes bring out an icy double sarsaparilla with 3 straws to help us survive the blistering summer heat.

It would take another 10 years before I'd encounter the blokey mayhem of a noisy beer-swilling Australian public bar.

For many years, I struggled with his thought pattern of leaving us in a car without air conditioning, sweltering in the middle of an Australian summer, while he sat. And sat. And sat.

There may have been more unusual family bonding rituals in the 1960s, but this one was up there!

Fifty-five years later, I'm finally starting to comprehend what Dad endured when retrieving corpses each night of our holidays, and why he sat in that hotel bar for 3 hours while we fried outside. He weathered the confronting realities of tending to dead bodies and grieving families each night so we could enjoy our beach holidays. Those memories are a testament to his hard work, love and desire to provide the best for his family.

For all the complexities of his character, Dad had a genuine heart of gold. Sadly, such were the macho times of the 1960s, and he was often trapped by the weird societal norm of rarely shared emotions.

All complexities aside, did we love our holidays at the beach? Absolutely!

Did we feel loved? Absolutely!

Did we ever want for anything? Rarely.

Do I get flashbacks when I drive past the Miami Hotel now? 100% yes! My left eye started twitching as I typed the name of the damn place!

Did the blistering burns from the branding iron seat belt buckle ever heal? Nope.

Like cattle, we'd been forever branded as "Brewers", and we're bloody proud of it.

All the gear, no idea

Dad regularly used the expression, "Jack of all trades, master of none". He used it to describe some of his lesser-skilled work colleagues. But it was a more fitting description of my sporting prowess.

I've held a deep passion for various disciplines throughout my life. At primary school, I'd polish my much-loved footy boots and fantasise about Friday afternoon's footy comp all week. I'd picture myself, a not-insubstantial-sized child, proudly wearing the school's footy jersey and those immaculately polished boots.

Ah, Friday afternoon footy!

Each Friday, our team would be whisked across town in the back of Spud Murphy's dad's delivery truck. No lights, seats or windows. Each trip was perilous, and we prayed Spud's dad would remember his precious cargo of 13 smelly 10-year-old boys cocooned in the back.

It's one of life's true miracles that we all survived those Friday treks. Freighting kids to and from sporting events the same way today would be the catalyst for a Royal Commission!

They were simpler times.

To survive and thrive in the Manly West State School footy team of 1970, you needed a fair bit of skill, strength, muscle tone, agility and fitness, of which I had none. In short, I had all the gear, but no idea.

As my sporting career blossomed and I progressed to cricket, I earned accolades best described as "mediocre". I was never gonna be the kid who stood on the Olympic winner's podium, but I still had big dreams and stars in my eyes.

Each Wednesday, I'd anxiously await the local *Wynnum Herald* to see if I'd featured in the sports results. Reading "Brewer 3-15" or "Brewer 56 n/o" on page 76 of the local rag would ignite wild enthusiasm in me to head to the backyard for another 3 hours of batting or bowling practice. That simple recognition inspired me.

A Young PB

Through my time, I witnessed sports bring out the very best and also the very worst in people.

I learned much from the obsessive win-at-all-costs dads reliving their own sporting dreams vicariously through their kids and the never-sufficiently-recognised, passionate mums who sat for hours as scorers, ran canteens and washed smelly jerseys. I'm still in awe of those deeply dedicated parents chauffeuring their 10-year-old with dreams of Olympic glory each morning at 4:00 am.

And then there was that occasional natural sporting freak to whom you could hand any piece of sporting equipment, and they'd belt it out of the park.

Greg Padget, a friend of mine since grade 2, was that freak. A natural. Greg never fully realised his true potential of playing for his country. Greg, aka "Chogul", went on to be a mogul in the poultry industry and is still a great mate today.

I've never liked the often-championed quote, "Show me a good loser, and I'll show you a loser". To me, that win-at-all-costs mentality epitomises the ugly side of people unable to show appreciation and grace when your opponent plays better on the day.

To suggest that someone is a "loser" for showing respect for acknowledging their competition's skills reminds me of some of the vilest people I've encountered in business and on sports fields.

While the accolades reflecting my own sporting achievements were limited to page 76 of the *Wynnum Herald*, I'm grateful for the importance of the quality values that sport instilled in my life.

And while I donated my not-insignificant collection of trophies, medals, certificates and newspaper clippings to the local tip a few seasons back, I'm still proud of what I achieved, what I learned and where my competitive and representative endeavours with rugby boots, a snooker cue and a cricket bat took me.

Learning the art of being competitive while remaining respectful to your competition is a life skill that, once perfected, will take you wherever you want to go. I am forever indebted to the fact that I learned early on that it's okay to not be Don Bradman, Eddie Charlton or Wally Lewis. We can't all be freaks. It's totally okay to be a contributor to a team environment.

I learned that the mateship and life skills you gain from training, playing and socialising with people who share the same values as you will open your mind and doors to an incredible fountain of opportunities that will fill your cup forever.

While I never wore my state's sacred maroon jersey or pulled on my country's green and gold jacket, I was that ambitious and optimistic kid who sat on the sideline at every game with his footy boots or cricket bat. Whether it was local footy at Kougari Oval or The Gabba, I was forever ready for the coaches' call-up!

It's always important to look like you're ready!

If your religion requires you to manipulate someone, you probably need a new religion

Religion has played contrasting roles in my life.

I've witnessed the magnificence of a loving, uplifting congregation coming together as a fierce support group for those in dire health, lost on life's journey, in need of food or desperately searching for shelter. The power of a unified congregation is inspiring. But I've also experienced religion's darker side. Let's start with the good.

St Peter's Church of England at Wynnum was my first exposure to the Big Fella Upstairs via their Sunday school and as a rather reluctant choirboy who could hit the high notes with ease.

Mum was an integral part of the local parish and a voice of reason on the male-dominated parish council. She was a proud, card-carrying church member until she passed.

During my time there, St Pete's attracted some outstanding parish priests. An absolute stand-out was The Reverend Dr Keith Rayner, who subsequently became the Anglican Primate of Australia. Doc Raynor – or "The Doc", as he was affectionately known – earned every ounce of the respect he enjoyed through his engagement with the church and the wider Wynnum community. He was a wonderful friend to Mum and in turn, our family. He was warm and caring and empowered and encouraged her as a woman, often seeking her counsel.

The Doc was also kind to this pimply-faced kid, and kindness was a rare attribute in the churches of the 60s and 70s. His warmth and care left an indelible impression on me. There's probably a good lesson in that for all religious leaders – maybe for all leaders.

The Doc was instrumental in introducing the *Good News Bible* to the young people at St Pete's. The *Good News Bible* was a simple English translation of the original, rewritten and repackaged in a stroke of marketing genius. I won't go so far as to say it made religion sexy again, but it sure made it easier to consume and way more relevant to the flock of my young vintage. (*It was also an early lesson for me in how repackaging and relaunching an old product can be wildly successful.*) For weeks, I would studiously inhale passages of my psychedelically-coloured paperback copy, a treasured gift from The Doc.

If there was ever any chance that someone was gonna save my soul, The Doc was the man. Fifty-five years on and we're still swapping the occasional note. Even in his 90s, he's still trying! That's tenacity worthy of a reward!

Sadly, while there were (and are) some really good people in the church, others would benefit from guidance from their own scriptures. I'm not sure what happens inside the brains of certain people of faith that elevates their self-belief to the point where they believe they are above The Big Guy rather than simply carriers of his message. I guess just as some people lose their way, so do some church leaders. It was those people of misguided omnipotence at St Pete's who sadly drove this impressionable 14-year-old to search for a new church.

My new church of choice looked good. But as I discovered later, its leaders were deceptive marketers. They were the new cool kids on the block. I was easily seduced into their flock by the lure of their young people's Tuesday night music group, abundant with love and happiness. I bit hard on the bait they'd cast and swallowed it hook, line and sinker.

Within weeks, I'd had my ego sufficiently stroked by their heaven-sent hierarchy and had been elevated to the church's Youth Leadership Group. The clerical con men had grander plans for this gullible kid.

Using the influence I'd earned with a fairly wide network of kids in the area, our Tuesday night music group quickly grew and became a safe place for local teens to gather. We had guitars, music of our choosing, pizza and girls. In other words, they had created a teenage nirvana.

A few weeks of these Tuesday night musical love-fests ensued until, one night, the Church Elders took me aside for a chat.

Their edict? "Peter, with leadership comes responsibility."

An ultimatum was delivered: (1) Be baptised in the name of the Lord or (2) be banished from the leadership group.

At the time, option (2) wasn't that palatable for my over-inflated ego. The choice was either to bathe in a demonic demotion or an oversized baptismal font already conveniently filled. Which do you think I chose?

Yes, within 5 minutes, I stood in a cold baptismal bath on a winter's night, surrounded by an adoring flock and a few mates who couldn't stop chuckling at just how far I'd go for a free pizza.

With 3 quick immersions and the words, "Arise, St Peter", I can't say I felt "born again". I just felt cold. My shivering only increased when I realised I had to explain my desertion to the dark side to my steadfast Anglican mum.

I clearly hadn't thought through this whole "born again" baptismal thing.

There I was, 14, with wet hair and presumably sporting a shiny new halo. Telling Mum my religion was no longer Anglican was like a Queenslander suddenly barracking for the Blues – unfathomable, unforgivable and possibly grounds for excommunication from the family.

Walking into the house later that night I decided to play the "it was raining" card. *(My halo conveniently chose to wait outside.)* Mum bought it but I went to bed that night with the words "What the heck did you just sign up for?" racing through my brain.

When I arrived at the next Youth Group meeting, I was met by an immediate inquisition from the Church Elders: "We didn't see you at church last Sunday. Is everything okay?"

At this stage, I should have noticed a pattern forming.

Someone had neglected to mention that, by taking a free baptismal bath the previous Tuesday night, I'd also committed to reading bible passages to Sunday school kids every Sunday for the rest of my days. I apparently missed that in the briefing I'd received before my dunking.

This new adventure wasn't looking as sexy as I'd first thought. Maybe St Pete's wasn't such a bad option after all!

This was my first introduction to the wise saying, "The grass is brown on both sides of the fence. It's only green where you water it."

Things went from bad to worse Tuesday night. The group assembled, guitars fired up, pizzas arrived and assembled voices united in song. Swept up in the moment's mood, I leapt to my feet and joined one of the girls in a dance.

Boom! Instant offender of the Crime of the Century.

Chaperoned to a side room by the Church Elders, I was promptly admonished for my apparent moment of sexual depravity. I stood bemused: "What sexual depravity? What are you talking about? I was just dancing!"

Their quick retort? "Peter, the Bible says, 'Make a joyful noise unto the Lord.' That doesn't mean cavorting provocatively with the other sex, making sexual gestures and tempting the flesh in the house of our Lord Jesus Christ!"

Dr Bill Silcock - Still friends 50 years on

Clearly, things weren't going well.

I didn't return to the church that week. Or the next. Or the next.

And, like in baseball, I was about to discover that some churches have a "three strikes, you're out" policy.

While sitting at home on the fourth Sunday of my short-lived sainthood, I heard chanting coming from the footpath outside my parent's house. As I rose from the comfort of my lounge chair, my eyes bore witness to the entire church flock standing as one, chanting Biblical passages and announcing my excommunication while praying for the repose of my lost and misguided 14-year-old soul.

Fifty years on and their prayers for my soul have clearly fallen on deaf ears.

I do believe religion has an essential place in society. It's been a fantastic support to my family at times. But, like most things, extremists and opportunists taint its great work.

Many years later, in my real estate business, I managed a waterfront property that had been bequeathed to a local church by a recently deceased parishioner. The monthly rental income was used to help local families in distress. Donating the property to her local parish was a beautiful gesture from a lady with a philanthropic heart.

The day finally came when the property's value had peaked as a redevelopment site. It was the perfect time for the church to cash in their chips and maximise the proceeds to do even more of its good deeds.

Auction day came. Under clear blue skies and with a picturesque Moreton Bay foreground, we sold the property for an incredible price. The local church was ecstatic.

The following Monday, however, I received a call that still sickens me.

A lawyer acting for the church's Sydney-based HQ called with firm and concise instructions: "All future correspondence regarding the sale of that property is to be through the Sydney-based law firm representing the Australian HQ."

Sadly, the last will and testament of the local parishioner, whose clear intention was to bequeath her property "to and for the benefit of her local parish", didn't specifically designate The Wynnum Parish.

And so, in the blink of an eye and with the stroke of a pen, the sale funds made their way to bolster the consolidated revenue of the church's HQ rather than help real local people in real need.

It was despicable behaviour, and I wonder what the Lord they celebrate so loudly would think of this sad betrayal of the goodwill of a loyal local parishioner.

More recently, I witnessed first-hand how some men of the cloth have lost sight of their mission and inflated their self-importance. Sitting before me on a flight was a man of faith, swilling red wine and wearing a black cassock and an impressive collection of chains and crosses. At first glance, I wasn't 100% sure of his faith. It all became obvious when, after being addressed by a young flight attendant as "Mister", he corrected her to use his correct title: "Your Grace".

Need I say more?

It's one of life's tragedies that so much of the good offered by people of faith is undermined by people with too much self-faith. And it makes the decision to be agnostic simple for ye of little faith. People like me.

Mahatma Gandhi might have been onto something when he wrote the following:

"I like your Christ. I do not like your Christians. Your Christians are so unlike your Christ."

Toto, I've a feeling we're not in Kansas anymore!

Before I departed Wynnum High at 14, I set about securing a couple of references from the teaching team. My growing knowledge of the outside commercial world taught me that having some great references would assist in my hunt for a career. As someone with no tradie skills and zero comprehension of nouns, verbs, adjectives and algebra, I'd been led by experts to believe that my future career prospects would be pretty slim without some divine intervention.

I'd zeroed my sights on 6 teachers I thought would most likely respond with a paragraph or 2 to add substance to my limited resumé. And limited it was. One prospective employer had asked me to send him a one-pager. I was flat-out sending a one-paragraph! This was to become the first and probably the most important of the many thousands of pitches I went on to create. A pitch to sell me!

Ultimately, I sufficiently impressed 2 of those 6 teachers enough to get them to put their quills to paper. Or perhaps they felt sorry for me, and their benevolent souls thought their tomes detailing my scholastic achievements might increase my chances of not spending my life sweeping streets or packing groceries at Coles.

The first reference came in a sealed envelope from Mr Lee. Mr Lee was a short man with a pronounced stoop. Other kids called him Bernie B Buckle Back. I referred to him as "the single best chance I had at getting a decent reference, getting me out of the hell that was school and ultimately into a paying job".

From recollection, Mr Lee had experienced some medical challenges. Some unkind people suggested he'd successfully undergone charisma bypass surgery. That science and maths floated his boat probably should've been the first red flag. The fact that my reference was handed over in a sealed envelope should've been the second.

For several days, I agonised about steaming the envelope seal and taking a sneak peek. I hoped Mr Lee hadn't waxed too lyrical, and I was anxious to read how he'd summarised my many offerings with a particular focus on all that his 3 years of teaching had embedded into me.

It felt like those days past when they'd hand you an oversized envelope of sealed results at the x-ray clinic to pass on to your doctor at next week's appointment. I reckon that anyone who didn't sneak a peek is telling porkies.

Naturally, temptation got the better of me and I steamed the seal open.

To say Mr Lee's economical use of nouns, verbs and adjectives immediately underwhelmed me is an understatement. If I'd been marking his work, I'd have given him a 1/10.

The sum of Mr Lee's literary genius describing my mammoth scholastic efforts, including 3 years of his imparted wisdom and a summary of my personal character, amounted to:

> *"I confirm that Peter Brewer attended Wynnum High School from January 1975 to October 1977."*
> *Signed,*
> *B Lee*

Thanks for the inspiration and motivation, Bernie! Uplifting stuff. I still had one shot left in my quest – Mr Miles. Merv. Surely, Merv's words of endorsement would bring home the bacon and jet-propel my career prospects from "Average Checkout Chap" to "Teenage Marketing Sensation".

Thankfully, Mr Miles was a little kinder. I reckon his reference described me perfectly, albeit a tad too succinctly.

> *"Independent type of lad who has potential."*
> *Signed,*
> *Merv Miles*

Merv's parting words were economic in volume and uninspiring in tone to a potential employer, especially one looking for a team player. But those words were powerful for me and subliminally reinforced my continued position to pursue my independence, fertilise my own views of the world, challenge authority and pursue opportunities that others dismissed or avoided for fear of being labelled a trouble-maker.

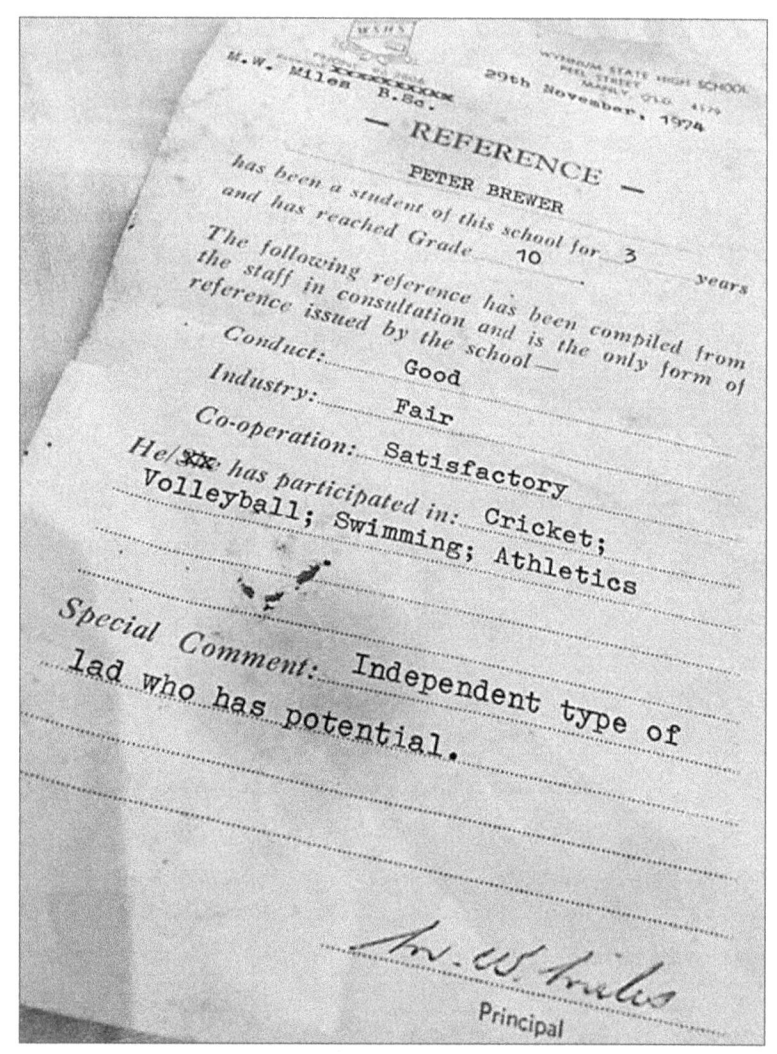

I wouldn't categorise myself in the resolute non-conformist column. Still, I started my journey by not being limited by societal norms, being happy to challenge convention and spending a fair bit of time asking, "Why?" Oh, also by being incredibly frustrated by mindless bureaucracy.

Right-brain creativity is where the stimulation began and where it still stands today.

Now armed with my exceptional references, it was off to the brave new world outside the boundaries of Wynnum High to pitch all that this 15-year-old dreamer had to offer.

But the shackles that school had held over my enthusiasm and free spirit were now ancient history. The time had come for this "independent lad" to unleash his potential!

Getting out of short pants

In 1974, there was no such thing as the SEEK website or employment agencies to streamline a job search. Finding a job meant scanning the daily newspapers or photocopying and stapling 50 copies of your resumé and references. Then you'd spend your mornings knocking on business doors, only to race home and sit by the phone praying your pitch might have appropriately inspired an HR department to summon you in for an interview. Sitting at home by a phone that rarely rang was a sobering and humbling life lesson to never waste an opportunity when it came.

In my quest for employment, I happened upon an advertisement in the *Brisbane Telegraph* afternoon newspaper for Waltons, a department store in Fortitude Valley, seeking the services of a Marketing Cadet. I submitted my pitch in writing, purposely omitting Bernie's and Merv's references. An interview ensued and, whether by good luck or a lack of other applicants, I scored my first job.

It was time to buy some long pants!

At the time, Waltons was an imposing upmarket flagship department store located on a prominent corner in Brisbane's "Valley". Today, it's an empty, graffiti-covered brick shell in dire need of rejuvenation. And like too much of Brisbane's history, it will likely be the subject of a middle-of-the-night demolition raid.

I don't mind sharing that my new gig had quickly added me to the list of Brisbane's high rollers. The whopping $38.88 weekly salary was paid in cash in a small yellow envelope every Tuesday after 2:00 pm.

Each week I'd divide my $38.88 cash windfall into $7.50 bus money and $15 board to Dad and Mum, leaving me $16.38 to party like it was 1949. I was living the high life!

A Marketing Cadet's daily duties varied. They included collating items to be photographed for our catalogues and newspaper ads, writing and proofing advertisements and, most importantly, going to the store's cafe at 8:15 every morning to get Mr Johnson a toasted Vegemite roll, a Bex powder and a can of Coke. Then, on cue at 2:00 pm, I'd prepare the board room/ping-pong table and shut the blinds in readiness for Mr Johnson to enjoy his afternoon siesta.

Peter Brewer Marketing Cadet at 15 years

Mr Johnson (KJ) was the office manager, a short man with a large, glowing red proboscis. He would sleep, racked and stacked, arms crossed in a "coffin-ready" position.

Our building was directly above the Valley Railway Station. This central transport hub shepherded 5 of Brisbane's finest old rattlers through its labyrinth of platforms every 3 minutes. Once KJ settled into his nap, it sometimes became a challenge to distinguish which roar came from a freight train 5 floors below and which were emitted from his engorged nostrils.

Waltons was instrumental in my early education in business. The department store's diverse environment and my wide and varied tasks fuelled my independence and challenged my already creative mind. I was honoured to work with some incredibly talented and free-thinking people. The Valley was an eclectic melting pot of Brisbane's weirdest and most wonderful people.

If Brisbane's misfits and creatives had a spiritual headquarters in the mid-70s, it was our level 5 rooftop bunker. Added as a contemporary after-thought to the traditional 5-storey art deco building, it played home to incredibly talented people with skills that sadly no longer play a part in today's retail world. Ticket writers artistically hand-drew every sign and ticket, window dressers transformed bland shop front windows on Brunswick and Wickham Streets into an enticing Christmas wonderland, and flamboyant fashion designers lovingly dressed mannequins that graced the store windows.

A favourite memory was seeing how long those devilish designers could freeze-frame in the store window posing as a mannequin, only to scare the living bejesus out of a poor unsuspecting window shopper with a cheeky wink or by blowing an air kiss.

Having fun at work at Waltons wasn't ever an option; it was 100% unavoidable.

Brian Hand was our photographer and my closest ally. Brian wore the most colourful shirts. Tall and trim with long, flowing locks, he was a 70s style icon and an absolute master behind the lens.

Waltons' monthly catalogue was the shopping bible for remote and regional Queenslanders. Brian and I were tasked with making it the New Testament.

Each week we'd truck mowers, lamps, fashion apparel, kitchen appliances, you name it to HB Green Studios at 26 Brookes Street, Bowen Hills. For days, we'd photograph item by item while adding stylish accessories like a plastic fern leaf or a pressed floral tea towel to make a basic kettle look like a piece of art that our readers wouldn't be able to resist.

Brian would weave magic with his trusty Minolta camera, while I busily crafted words of genius to entice customers into a buying frenzy. Yep, at 15, I was responsible for making a toaster, a kettle and a set of 6 tea towels irresistible to our catalogue readers.

Learning and crafting interesting words wasn't a skill taught at Wynnum High in the early 1970s. So, I loved the real-life learning and how success was measured by the sales my ads created. Those times ignited a passion inside me to thoughtfully use words to paint pictures and tell stories.

It was a magnificent life lesson that would translate perfectly to my later business pursuits. The beauty and impact of perfectly chosen words and smart storytelling need to create imagination in consumers' minds. Nail that in your marketing, and you're on the home straight.

Our loft at Waltons became home to many of the cool kids. One of our frequent guests was the delightful Delvene Delaney, Australian TV royalty and co-star to a life-long hero, Paul Hogan.

Delvene was dating one of our managers and became a regular visitor to our bunker. The always immaculate and striking Delvene would ascend the stairs to visit our top-floor haven heralded by a choir of angels. She was cool, down-to-earth and unaffected by the fame she'd quickly gained in the early stages of her career. Working with Delvene's unimpressive boyfriend at the time taught me a very important life skill – you don't have to be intelligent or good-looking to win the heart of a glamorous date. It's a life lesson that's returned me significant dividends!

Another Waltons brush with fame came when I worked alongside budding young actor and recording artist at the time, Mark Hembrow. It was clear Mark had his eyes on a career on stage, screen and in the studio. His mum, Sally, had carved out a career on Brisbane radio and TV, and Mark had caught the media bug. Mark's acting, producing and overall media career blossomed, and he went on to do some really cool TV and stage work. Mark also raised 3 daughters who Google tells me have made impressive names for themselves internationally.

My crowning achievement at Waltons, however, was the dubious honour of being responsible for the first-ever prosecution under Section 52 of the Trade Practices Act: False and Misleading Conduct.

I'd created an advertisement for a Victa Lawn Mower. Waltons had decided to include a cheap and cheerful BBQ flare on a bamboo stick as a bonus for anyone who bought the mower. Brian and I shot the mower with a BBQ flare attached to the handle, and I used the sub-headline, "Bonus – Free BBQ Flare!"

The ad appeared in the media the same week the Trade Practices Commission were seeking a sacrificial lamb to test their new laws. Creative advertising had its limits, they said, and some muppet in Canberra decided that a "free BBQ flare" couldn't possibly be free because in their world, *nothing* is free. The cost of the BBQ flare must be factored into the mower's price. In other words, they considered it false and misleading advertising.

A first offence fine started at $10,000. My mental calculations told me that, even with my amazing weekly salary of $38.88, paying any such fine would take me a while!

I was summoned to see Mr Anderson, the State Manager, who counselled me on the errors of my ways. He was firm and almost fair. My only bemusement was that Mr Johnson, the person responsible for proofing my creative wordsmithing, was never counselled. Perhaps Mr Johnson should have spent less time napping and more time coaching an independent young lad with potential!

After a year of the most wonderful business and life lessons, a mini apprenticeship in copywriting, photography, marketing principles and exposure to the most diverse of our society, I left Waltons. My experience was far from the cold, surgical classroom at Wynnum High. It helped shape my early acceptance of people who aren't cookie-cutter humans in a vanilla world.

I'll always treasure the learning and appreciation I received at Waltons. These days, whenever I drive by the now old and squatter-filled building, I look 5 storeys up and picture fearless, creative 15-year-old me dangling skinny legs over the edge of the penthouse floor bunker while marvelling at this huge world and the opportunities on the horizon.

And then, this boy from Manly who'd completed an express apprenticeship in the Big Smoke stepped back from that rooftop to take a leap of faith into the big bad world to make his own kind of music.

"It takes courage to grow up and become who you really can be."

E.E. Cummings

Food, glorious food

To suggest I've enjoyed a lifelong love affair with protein is an understatement.

I've had no loyalty to one particular species or protein. I'm equally at home at my BBQ with a slab of rump, a rack of lamb, a chunk of chook, a shish kebab of jumbo shrimp, a fork of pork or even a touch of tofu. Okay, no tofu. I'm an unashamed carnivore who wears his trusty tongs as a badge of honour.

Pork on the fork

At age 16, an offer came to lure me from my Waltons marketing career to my first brush with bacon at Dandy Smallgoods, a Brisbane institution in the 70s. The offer was good and I said: "Yes, I'll give it a try!"

My daily duty was to deliver fresh and smokehouse delicacies to corner stores, delicatessens and butcher shops across Brisbane. It was an opportunity that exposed me, literally, to some of the most wonderful people in retail and hospitality.

Each day, I was accompanied in the cab by my trusty sidekick, Wayne, while in the refrigerated back section, our trusty ally was a curiously-named companion called Bacteria Bill.

Full disclosure: Bill wasn't actually a person.

Bacteria Bill was, in fact, a rather large, rusty carving knife we regularly called on for help. His duties included:

- Cutting pigs and hams in half.
- Slicing a snack of sausage or a delicious smallgood for an impromptu lunch.
- Self-protection against some pretty crazy and eccentric European chefs in Brisbane's most salubrious restaurants of the 70s.

Wayne, Bacteria Bill and I were a formidable trio as we went to battle each day against arch-enemies KR Darling Downs, a competing smallgoods maker.

Those people and the personalities behind those delis, corner stores and suburban butcher shops gave me a peek behind the curtain of 1970s and 80s Australian food retailers. They were hard-working, multi-generational, multicultural families. No malls. No self-checkouts. Just places with fresh fruit and veggies, and where the local butcher or fruiterer knew you by name.

Sadly, the days of a dozen local delis, corner stores and butchers in every suburb are long gone. They were wonderful times. I'm not sure that today's families will ever truly understand how special those times were. I miss those colourful characters that would slice our meat to order and share a joke while they did it. Instead, we've sacrificed their smiles and personalised service in exchange for convenience and pre-packaged mush on cling-wrapped plastic trays.

Merv Butler's Butchery in Lota, Queensland

Of all the things I've done in my life, carrying freshly slaughtered pigs into butcher shops rates high on the "crazy careers" scale.

My enthusiasm for the pig gig was less about the money and more about the life learnings I gained from those cult-like characters of the 1970s and 80s, the quintessential larrikin, the Australian suburban butcher.

I can't name every one of those legendary characters I encountered. Their stories are all legendary and arguably deserving of a mention in this memoir. However, one of particular note is "Smiling Syd", the 2-fingered butcher.

A short, thin, balding man, Syd – with his missing 6 fingers and 2 thumbs – was a pretty average butcher by anyone's measure. He'd often try to blame the absence of those digits on the war, but that's a doubtful story. What Syd lacked in fingers and trustworthiness, however, he more than made up for in antics.

Picture this. It was 6:00 am on a Friday morning. I was a solo driver delivering 5 pigs to Syd's shop. It was the first of a few deliveries that day. On board were 20 pigs and several dozen cartons of associated smallgoods, all destined for the cold rooms of the other local butchers, aka Syd's fierce rivals.

As I hung the last of the 5 hogs in Syd's cold room, he thanked me and invited me to enjoy a cup of tea and a freshly cooked bacon and egg roll in his shop's make-shift kitchen.

Given my penchant for the finer things in life, I accepted his kind invitation. We chatted for 20 minutes about my life and sporting achievements. My fingerless friend's interest flattered me. Give me 2 minutes to talk about myself, and it'll be the longest hour of your life.

While waxing lyrical about my worldly 17 years, I was oblivious to the lack of the usual flurry of Syd's other butchers in the shop.

I thanked Syd for breakfast and bid him a fond farewell. A nice way to start the day, I thought, and I pondered what breakfast offerings the next 5 butchers might trot out.

Now, most butchers in the 70s had an arch nemesis. Syd's was Jimmy Stagg. Jimmy was a smooth talker and a hit with the local ladies. He was also my next delivery. I reversed my truck to Jimmy's loading dock, ready to transfer the next 5 life-sized pieces of crackling to his cold room.

Jimmy's welcoming wide smile was framed by his pornstar moustache – possibly an inspiration for my own facial fur later in life. He pegged open the shop's back door to allow me and my cargo unimpeded access.

I opened my truck door and was confronted with a moment of gut-wrenching horror that still haunts me today.

The back of my truck was empty.

Not a trotter in sight.

Not a sow to be seen.

Not one leg of ham.

Nada. Nothing. Zero.

The larder was bare.

Heart palpitating, I borrowed Jimmy's phone and urgently rang my manager. I explained my now-empty truck and started to recount my morning's steps. He stopped me part way through my panic and proffered, "You didn't by any chance partake of a bacon and egg roll and a cuppa at Smiling Syd's, did you?"

My jaw dropped. The phone went quiet. I fumbled my answer... "Yes?"

The raucous laughter coming from the other end was relentless: "Bloody Syd's gotcha!"

My manager continued, "Did he ask you lots of questions?"

"Yes."

"Did you see any of his other butchers in the shop?"

"No."

"Yep," my manager continued, "someone should have warned you. Syd gets all the newbies! Never leave your truck unlocked at Syd's. His gang will have it emptied faster than you can say 'flying pigs'."

I immediately returned to Syd's, searching for my 15 missing sucklers and 20 cartons of succulent smallgoods. Syd met me at the back door, wearing a wide grin. Before I could question the whereabouts of my precious porcine pallets, he uttered the words, "Dunno what you're talking about."

Vale my short-lived career as the Dandy Man and the amazing characters that were the suburban butcher of this great country.

And, as I bid a fond farewell to the bacon factory's front gates, the pearly gates to another dream job slowly opened.

Feathered friends

Having learned some valuable lessons about trust and doing my best to all but erase the trauma of my encounter with Syd the 2-fingered butcher from my memory, an opportunity to work with a different bunch of turkeys landed.

I was offered a gig to significantly increase poultry sales for Golden Cockerel, a small local business in Mount Cotton. The gig included a company car, which meant my trucking days were over. I'd hit the big time!

Sure, the company car was an ugly purple Renault, but beggars can't be choosers. Question is, would I be prepared to compromise my already low standards for a gig with a purple car and free fuel? Absolutely!

In my first month of flogging all things fowl, I created a new product called a "Raffle Pack". I designed it to compete with the traditional "Meat Tray", a standard fare offered at almost every club or pub's Friday night raffles. The age-old butcher's meat tray was a staple that badly needed a shake-up, and maybe I was driven to create competition by a hint of revenge against the dark deeds of 2-fingered Syd.

"Ladies and gentlemen, I announce the arrival of the 'Raffle Pack'. This tray of fine poultry boasts 2 delectable chicken breasts, 4 succulent wings and 6 mouthwatering drumsticks, beautifully presented with a sprig of rosemary on a colourful tray that puts the boring and humble meat tray to shame."

Pubs and clubs across Southeast Queensland couldn't get enough of my roosterly revolution!

Orders came thick and fast, and chicken production numbers went through the roof. Our trays of fabulous fowls flew out the door faster than the company could grow chickens to fill the orders. Management was ecstatic at my innovation and creative marketing. I was rapidly becoming the Sam Kekovich of chicken. (*Note for non-Aussies: Sam's a huge proponent of Aussie lamb and fronts our Lamb Day ads. Check them out on YouTube.*)

The humble hen was back on the top of Queenslanders' menus.

Each day, I'd navigate my now-trademark purple Renault through Brisbane streets, amassing orders from new clubs, pubs and even butchers wanting to get their hands on the prized "Raffle Pack". (*I don't mind sharing that I, too, was shaking my tail feathers and had eyes firmly affixed on the soon-to-be-retiring sales manager's seat!*)

Unlike most fairy tales, however, this one was in a crash course towards an unhappy ending.

While I'd amassed excellent marketing skills, at 20, I hadn't quite gained a proper understanding of the anatomy of a chook.

Everyone at the chicken plant was singing my praises… except one. Whinging bloody Kelvin, our production manager!

I don't think it's just me. In my experience, there's a bloody Killjoy Kelvin in every business! Am I right?

I arrived at the monthly management meeting where everyone was clucky at our sales numbers. Well, they were until Kelvin, a very formal chap, dropped this clanger:

"Congratulations on your new item and its success. But I have 2 questions for you, young Peter. Firstly, how many legs does a chicken have?"

Not being an authority on the topic (*I mean, how is a 20-year-old steak eater supposed to know the anatomy of a chook?*), I took a wild, uneducated stab at the answer.

"Four… ?"

(*In case you are also unsure, I can reveal here that 4 is apparently the wrong answer.*)

Kelvin shook his head and followed up with his next question: "As the Production Manager, what am I supposed to do with the rest of the carcasses of these now legless chickens?"

I did have an off-script answer to that question, which again was the wrong answer and, when shared, brought my career in all things poultry to an abrupt end.

As quickly as the "Raffle Pack" weaved its way into the social fabric of Southeast Queensland, it was plucked into obscurity by my lack of chook knowledge and Killjoy Kelvin.

Later that morning, I returned the keys to the ugly purple Renault and immediately felt my dignity lift 4 levels.

What was next on my career menu?

I hurriedly checked which food groups were left and quickly confirmed that fish don't have legs.

Teach a man to fish

Aged 20 and still bruised by Syd and Kelvin, I decided it was time to put my entrepreneurial skills to the test and back myself in a business of my own.

With the help of a couple of mates over a thirsty long weekend, we collectively built a mobile cold room. I say collectively because I opened the beers and cooked the burgers while they built the cold room. I call it effective leverage and good delegation.

A cautious winching and guiding onto the back of my blue Holden ute and Australia's newest fresh mobile seafood business was born. Introducing *Peter's Seafoods*.

A quick scan of the White Pages of 1979 showed a business with the same name already existed. It had a fleet of 20 trucks and a sizable warehouse in 4 regions across Queensland. I figured 2 Peters is better than one, and I wasn't about to change my name. I also wasn't going to change the impressive signwriting on the side of my fleet of one, which I cutely decorated with "Unit 21". I figured that if you can't beat them, you may as well join them!

My rig looked amazing! The world was now my oyster, pardon the pun.

As I mapped out what my new epicurean enterprise would resemble, someone I took an immediate dislike to mentioned corporate structures, council health inspection requirements and food safety certificates.

As a budding entrepreneur, I didn't need such negativity or added overheads in my life. I decided to leave that bureaucracy for the other Peter's Seafoods. I figured they probably already have that part nailed.

On my first day in business, I convened a key stakeholders meeting, including the CEO, Head of Strategy, Chief Procurement

Officer and the Janitor. In a bid to keep overheads low, I'd elected myself to each of these roles unopposed. The minutes of that first meeting will reflect that I shared that I was honoured, humbled and grateful to have received the unanimous support of my entire team.

Onwards to Launch Day for Peter's Seafoods!

As usual, I woke around 9:30 am and decided to embark on creating a simple 2-part business plan, albeit from the comfort of my own bed:

Part 1. Find some seafood to sell.

Part 2. Find some customers to sell it to.

While others might think those 2 things would be fairly central to the success of a start-up seafood business, I regarded them as minor hurdles to navigate.

Fortunately, I've always prided myself on the relationships I've been able to build and sustain. I've (thus far) been blessed with an exceptional memory for people and places. One of my early lessons was mastering a self-invented game called "Who do you know who… ?" It's served me well throughout my entrepreneurial career, especially in real estate. Through it, I've developed an exceptional "little black book" of people I trust. It's rare that I can't facilitate a warm introduction when someone asks me, "Who do you know who… ?"

So, given my contacts, I didn't foresee finding some seafood to sell or people to sell it to as a major challenge.

Day 1 of Peter's Seafoods was a tiring day of planning and sleeping. By noon, I needed a beer and more sleep. I was quickly learning that bootstrapping a start-up business can be taxing.

Day 2 arrived. I knew a guy who worked in Brisbane Fish Markets. I got my usual early start and headed off at 10:00 am to chat with him about filling my amazing new mobile icebox with a veritable smorgasbord of Queensland's finest *fruits de mer*.

Our meeting quickly revealed 3 major stumbling blocks that would prevent me from being Brisbane Fish Markets' brightest new customer:

1. I needed money,
2. I needed to pay for a licence to be able to bid at the daily seafood auctions, and
3. The auctions actually started 4 hours before I was used to getting out of bed.

I knew there had to be a better way.

As luck would have it, I'd previously shared an ale or 6 at the appropriately named Fishers Hotel with a couple of fishermen who had trawlers moored in Wynnum Creek. We shared a deep passion for 3 things:

1. A cold beer on a hot day,
2. Starting work after 10 am, and
3. A tax-free economy.

Isn't life so much sweeter when you find your tribe?

We agreed to terms that I'd take as much seafood as they could fit into my truck on consignment in exchange for saving them the bother of filing those troublesome annual tax returns.

Now, with a truck full of seafood, I needed to find some customers.

I once read a book that said: "Build it, and they will come." It may have been the Bible. It might also have been a reference to the new Wynnum Tavern, but I liked the general concept.

I set about discovering who had built something that people were coming to and quickly learned that the biggest, newest building in Brisbane at the time was the Australian Taxation Office.

Perfect, and so very appropriate.

I set about finding a nice, free, cool parking spot in the basement car park of that ATO where, for 3 days a week, I'd peddle the freshest of fare to a delighted customer base.

What better place to launch a cash-only, tax-free business? I'm hopeful that a statute of limitations now exists. In my 2 years in that basement, not once was I ever asked to provide a customer receipt or file a tax return. Again, I figured that the other Peter's Seafoods probably had that annoying bureaucracy under control.

Not my logo. Not my truck.

After surviving the rigours of toiling 10 am to 2 pm 3 days a week for 2 years I decided there must be other fish to fry, pardon the pun. A call came to join a mate selling real estate on the Bay Islands off the coast of Brisbane. More about that soon…

Today, I still have friendships with people from each of those career tangents. Each opportunity opened more doors and gave me some amazing insights into a wide range of people and businesses. They also offered me some interesting (to say the least) life lessons and experiences, including:

- Being locked in a cold room with an amorous mid-50s Greek woman who was determined to introduce this innocent 16-year-old boy to adulthood.
- Attempting to butcher a pig with a steak knife and a pair of scissors in a bid to impress a girlfriend's parents. (*For the record, I failed at both goals.*)
- Discovering that too many seafood shops delight in selling their product's wet weight. $49 a kilo for water makes them pretty profitable!
- Learning that an imam actually does go and bless each chicken before they meet their makers at the poultry abattoirs.

I also found that selling salad had zero appeal to this fully fledged carnivore, and that the world is full of colourful characters and incredible experiences you'll treasure for all of your days if you open your eyes and dare to say, "Yep, I'll give it a go."

Most importantly, I learned that:

"If you fish and catch nothing, you have still caught a lesson."

Matshona Dhliwayo

We will remember them

When I hit the legal age to enjoy an ice-cold frosty, Dad pulled me aside and told me he didn't want me drinking in pubs. He believed an impressionable 18-year-old might end up mixing in the wrong circles and could run off the rails. I didn't have the heart to tell him that this particular train had derailed 18 months prior. Still, I admired and appreciated Dad's ambitions and intent for the youngest and thirstiest of his progeny.

On the morning of my 18th birthday, I was sitting at the bar of the Manly Hotel at 10:00 am, waiting to collect my free birthday beer. The then-pub owner, Sandy McDonald, a local icon who knew me well as a regular customer, poured me my free birthday beer, wished me happy birthday and kindly asked which birthday I was celebrating. The look on Sandy's face was pure gold when I told him I turned 18 that day!

Dad's goal of encouraging me to drink in classy clubs rather than grotty pubs was perfectly timed. Around the late 70s, our local RSL, Football Club and Fifty-and-Over Leisure Centre were, for a short time, offering "Life Memberships" for around $200 each in a bid to raise capital.

And so, I found myself blessed with 3 life memberships that have thus far given me 47+ years of awesome benefits. My Dad sure did have an eye for value.

Dad was also wicked smart. His strategy of encouraging me to drink in clubs exposed me to a diverse cross-section of society and the opportunity to gain real-world skills.

I was excited that I'd finally been introduced to a learning environment where I felt at home and respected. Real-world teachers talking about relevant topics that I had a thirst for – bliss.

There was no talk of nouns, adverbs or adjectives, no algebra, no abuse, no belittling from impotent teachers, and no sounds of a chalk duster whistling past your ear. As my friend Jim Walberg would say, "Real conversations with real people all just walking each other home." Real life learning doesn't get any better.

I especially loved the companionship of amazing and diverse friends at Wynnum RSL. As those afternoons wore on, the circle of tables and chairs grew wider as the cavalcade of characters returned to the fold to wind down and share their often diverse views after a hard day "working for the man".

You could set your watch to Westy, a mid-50s abattoir worker arriving at 4:00 pm on the dot, having spent the day carving up cattle.

Dessy, another character, would silently slide in at 4:15, sporting a trademark flannel shirt and a jet-black bushy moustache, a frosty 10-ounce "sandwich" firmly affixed to his left hand. He'd nod and politely muffle the word "g'day". Des's volume of words and level of audibility would increase in direct proportion to his consumption of additional 10-ounce sandwiches.

My dearest mates, father and son, Keith and Gary Baker (Spot and Gaz), would make their own grand entrances.

At 4:45 pm, Spot, a passionate smallgoods man in his late 50s, would appear. He'd make a beeline to the bar for his refreshment of choice, which, on payday, included a bonus shot of Bundaberg's best export.

Spot was a delightful man of whom I became very fond. Married to the tolerant but never shy Marjorie, he was the envy of club members, and not just because of his friendly and calm nature. He only had to walk 26 steps from the club bar across the street to the comfort of his lounge chair. Another 4 steps, and he'd be at his kitchen table where, like clockwork, Marj would serve his evening meal just as the music cued for the evening news at 6.

On the rare occasion Spot might overstay his welcome at the club, it was inevitable he'd be paged to the front entrance by Marj with the firm words, "I've put your dinner in the oven for you, you old bastard... It's a salad."

We adored Marj and Spotty. They were a wonderful pairing, and there was no doubt about their love for each other and their 3 sons.

Spotty had thick skin. He needed it with a son like Gaz, the oldest of his 3 boys. Forty-five years on, I still rate Gaz as one of the most generous and true humans I've encountered on my journey.

Each night, I'd eagerly await his entrance through the club's front door any time between 4 and 6. His arrival time depended on whether he was enjoying the benefits of flexitime or hard at work administering the secretarial and financial affairs of the snooker club that bonded this crazy gang of magnificent misfits together.

One of the most refreshing things I enjoyed about our friendship was how diametrically opposed our political views were, often debated passionately. However, ultimately, we could still share a hundred beers and be good, respectful mates.

That's the measure of real mateship. Some lessons for modern society there.

Today's world of poor debate skills, unwillingness to listen to opposing views and faceless keyboard warriors resorting to abuse could take lessons from Gaz. He would look you directly in the eye, hear your position and analyse every word while mentally crafting a brilliant framework for an alternative.

He might nod and pose some open-ended questions. But then he'd use his impressive power of persuasion, combined with a healthy dose of laughter, to prosecute an alternate case. He'd deliver the facts and data with so much precision and conviction that he'd have you questioning whether night really does follow day or whether the chicken actually did come before the egg!

Gaz would've been a brilliant barrister had he been prepared to compromise his high moral values.

Every evening from 4 to 6, our gang would grow. As each person entered the bar, they'd be greeted across the room with a welcoming yell, "Hey, stupid!" Despite its negative wording, this was actually an affectionate greeting from Vince, a retired public servant who'd been warming his seat at the club since 10 am.

Vince was a loveable larrikin who never strayed an inch from his prized perch at the bar. You could pinpoint a theodolite on his bar stool's latitude and longitude. It sat 4.5 feet to the right of Alex McFarlane's stool and 2 feet in front of the standing position of Vince's doppelganger, his son Clive. (*I was never sure if Clive stood 2 feet behind Vince to catch him should he fall from his stool pissed or if, on Vince's instructions, he was to grab that stool before some other envious bastard grabbed it if Vince popped off the perch. I have a sneaking suspicion Vince had actually bequeathed his position at the bar to Clive.*)

Vince's 1.5 square metres was sacred turf. Woe betide anyone who infringed on this prime Bayside real estate, with commanding views of the snooker tables, a sweeping aspect of the 6 dart boards, and a birds-eye view of every unsuspecting victim who entered the front door.

You knew you were "home" when you heard Vince's trademark welcome ring out.

At 5:15 pm, Maurie the whinging Pom would arrive, usually moaning about "cheating Aussies" or whatever his pet peeve of the day was. We often told him to shut up or row his boat back to England. We didn't really want him to, but watching his face turn crimson as his blood pressure went through the roof was fun.

Maurie was a steady and fiercely competitive snooker player who despised losing, and few could beat him. Three things Maurie hated with a passion:

- Third on the list – all Aussies.
- Second – paying for his own beer.
- First – his nemesis on the full-sized billiards table: a

polished, full-time gentleman and part-time hustler by the name of Aubrey (Aub) Bannah.

Aubrey Bannah was the head of fundraising for the Queensland Cancer Fund and a highly accomplished and celebrated statesman, who later went on to be honoured with an OAM by Queen Elizabeth II.

Aub would enter the club calmly, handmade English ash cue in hand, his aura almost levitating him above the sticky carpets. Seeing him weave his magic around a billiards table was like witnessing a man in perpetual motion. He'd address the billiards table like a surgeon, tilting his frameless glasses to allow him a perfect view of the table. Shot by shot, he'd clinically destroy anyone gullible enough to wager $20 against his skill. His control of the billiards table was unmatched.

Having lined his pockets with $20 bills, Aub, only momentarily flicking his poker face, would offer me a sly wink and a wry smile as he departed the building in the same graceful style with which he arrived. Left in his wake would be an adoring crowd and the mumbling of "cheating Aussies" from a yet again defeated and deflated Maurie.

Our daily meeting of minds could sometimes grow to 20. Often, the discussions of the day's topics could become heated and loud. Fortunately, Vince was always on duty. His simple 2-word call-to-order would settle the discussions.

While the conversations raged strongly with countering opinions each night, we'd unite and stand at 6:00 pm as the lights dimmed and the flame on the wall ignited for a minute of silence and a recitation of the Ode of Remembrance. Lest We Forget.

And just as we all arrived between 4 and 6 pm, like clockwork, we'd depart between 8 and 10. Out we'd march, single-file, cups filled literally and philosophically, fuelled and ready to do battle with our own worlds the following day.

We left in comfort, knowing that in less than 24 hours, we'd be welcomed back "home" by Vince's traditional greeting: "Hey, stupid!"

The only violence I was ever involved in at the club was needing to take one disrespectful loudmouth car salesman to the car park for an overdue appointment in the club's dumpster for being a dick. Not my usual method of negotiation, but highly effective nonetheless.

I recall my actions prompted cheering and loud applause from my fellow members. Unfortunately, those actions also scored me a one-month suspension from the club. But hey, sometimes you gotta do what you gotta do.

My days, months and years of working on my "Life MBA" while enjoying the camaraderie of this cavalcade of crazies came to its finale with the toll of wedding bells and fatherhood.

A wonderful chapter closed. Another was about to be written.

My dad's strategy of wooing me from pubs to drinking in clubs paid dividends in ways I'm sure he'd never contemplated. Those

3 x $200 life memberships may have been the most unorthodox but best investments he'd made in my personal and professional development.

I was with smart people 2 and 3 times my senior. I created amazing personal connections and some life-changing business opportunities. But most importantly for Dad, he knew his wily youngest son was safe in a good environment.

In fond memory of those who paid the ultimate sacrifice.
Lest We Forget.

Moses and the Eleventh Commandment

Before her passing, Mum requested that her eulogy convey the impact that the Ten Commandments – as taught to her as an impressionable 6-year-old by Captain Daphne Evans of the Wynnum Salvation Army – had on shaping her life.

Growing up in a poor family and as the youngest of 8 ruggies, Mum lived in hand-me-down clothes. She desperately craved the feel of a new pair of shoes and admired the other girls at Sunday school with their new dresses. She wished she could be the proud wearer of a brand new, bright white Sunday school dress that hadn't already done the rounds of the other church kids over the previous 10 years.

Mum said the temptation to steal money to fund the purchase of shiny new shoes or a pretty pinafore was almost overwhelming. But she stayed true to the lessons of the Ten Commandments Moses brought to the people of Israel.

Most things that shape us go way back to early life events and learning right from wrong. For example, you only put your hand on the stove hotplate once. You only ever backchat your father once if you're smart. You only ever drink Fosters once. You know what I mean.

All important lessons come from making a mistake once. You must make mistakes before understanding the pain of making poor choices. And most of us have built-in values based on what we learn early in life.

In 1980, the newly built Wynnum Tavern had some comparisons to Mum's Church of St Peter. Both had plenty of cheap wine, rows of uncomfortable chairs, no shortage of souls in need of saving and were the home to many of my poor life choices. Unfortunately, Moses had a different impact on me.

Join me at the bar. It's a usual Saturday night. I'd spent the afternoon not unrefreshed. You *could* say I was in the very firm grip of the grape.

Saturday nights at the Wynnum Tavern had a reputation of being epic. It was a lively pub. Clean and new furniture. You could walk through the bar and not feel your best Julius Marlows stick to the carpets. The bar staff were under 70 and didn't call you "Love" or "Darl", and the bar wasn't littered with barflies standing on a carpet of the days losing betting tickets.

These attributes meant the tavern attracted a young audience ready to rock their socks off to the beats of live local bands. It quickly became the new Mecca where we youngsters conducted our form of weekly worship.

Now, I acknowledge I'm not the best dancer. My dance floor moves have been described as resembling an oyster on opioids. Put simply, I'm not known for rhythmically tripping the light fantastic. Although, in fairness, I did have some secret signature moves that carved up the dance floor after a dozen or so beers. My Whippersnipper was a special hit with the crowd. Fortunately, my dance floor days pre-dated mobile phones with cameras. So, I'll leave you with your imagination to picture my version of The Worm and The Pop-up Toaster.

If I'm honest, my intentions on a Saturday night were far from noble. They had less to do with impressive dance moves and more to do with pickup lines and the backseat of my Holden Commodore.

Hey, I was young!

Saturday night at the Wynnum Tavern wasn't just an opportunity to carve up the dance floor and pick up girls. You could also demonstrate your vocal genius to the adoring masses. It was a fun way to finish the night with a talent quest that, on most nights, was totally devoid of any identifiable talent. Talk about the pot calling the kettle black!

One particular Saturday night, I decided that the masses in the mosh pit would ascend to a frenzied level if I were to volunteer the gift of my magical melodies from the elevated stage.

Let me set the scene:

The band welcomed me on the stage: "All the way from Manly, ladies and gentlemen, please welcome… Elvis the Pelvis!"

Yep, I had a stage name that stirred the masses into frenzied anticipation.

The Pelvis had entered the building.

The band struck up my tune – "Suspicious Minds".

And, with those magical opening chords, I launched into one of the most amazing dedications to the man with the blue suede shoes anyone had ever heard.

I let my tonsils loose, and the crowd rallied to the cause. I'm still not sure why they all had their fingers in their ears as they danced, but the dance floor remained full, the band was on fire, disco lights were strobing and the big man was feeling goooooood.

This song was a new addition to my repertoire, so I felt a little unsure about how this award-winning performance would end. What would be the crowning crescendo?

My eyes glanced down and saw the mosh pit going wild. (*My eyes might also have been blurred from an afternoon of far too many beers.*)

I suddenly knew how to bring this home: I decided on a stage dive to end all stage dives.

I visualised myself launching from the stage into the outstretched arms of the devoted crowd on the dance floor, who'd crowd-surf me to the bar for final drinks. It would be a Hollywood ending.

I was all in.

And so, at 11:59 pm on that fine Saturday evening at the Wynnum Tavern, I propelled my not insignificant frame from the 2-metre (6+ feet for you Yanks) stage into that crowd.

An event of Biblical proportions occurred.

Somehow, Moses must've been part of that mosh pit crowd because, just as the waters of the Red Sea once parted, the seething mosh pit on the Wynnum Tavern dance floor also divided neatly in two, leaving me to land face first on the dance floor.

My alcohol-fueled, rocket-like launch into the air resulted in me firmly meeting *terra firma*, prostate on a now-empty dance floor, left with a concussion and a right knee sitting at 90 degrees.

The show must go on, but not for Elvis.

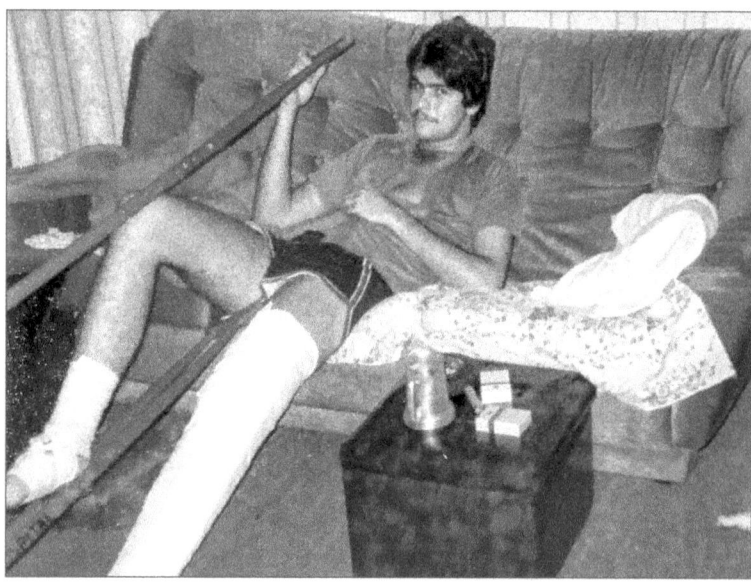

Elvis has left the building

You've never seen 200 people exit so quickly from a bar. The band went home. The staff closed up, and the manager, Frank Shaw, sat with me, shaking his shiny head, mopping my sweating brow and awaiting the arrival of an ambulance. That emergency surgery began my lifelong affinity with stupidity and hospitals.

Hopefully, that'll give some further depth to my caution around biblical figures. As promised, I did honour my mother's love of the Ten Commandments in her eulogy, albeit with my fingers crossed behind my back.

Because on that fateful night, Moses had the chance to ensure my dreams of dance floor greatness and a dalliance in the back of a Commodore were realised. Instead, he delivered a good lesson in trust. That night, at the Wynnum Tavern, Moses taught me the Eleventh Commandment:

"Thou shalt not put your trust in a mosh pit of drunken dancers to prevent you from landing face first on a dance floor."

There endeth the lesson.

Mr and Mrs Baklava

My mate Winston Marsh is the original source for many of the wiser words I might occasionally mumble. One of Winno's finest lines that resonates with me is, "Starvation focuses the mind."

So, at about 20 years of age, I was (barely) surviving on Russell Island, just off the Queensland Coast, selling people their island dreams.

It'd been a particularly lean time in business, and one Friday morning, I found myself with just one egg to last me until the last taxi boat back to civilisation on Sunday, when I'd be heading back to the mainland to replenish clothes and food.

Now, those who may also have found themselves in a cash-strapped quandary over 40 years ago will empathise that in the 1980s, there were no such luxuries as an ATM or EFTPOS. Banks closed at 4 pm on Friday and wouldn't be frequented again until 10 am on Monday.

Being a budding masterchef with zero other options, I planned how to make that one egg last me until Sunday: eat the white on Friday, the yellow on Saturday, and chomp the shell down on Sunday to keep my roughage intake up.

By 10 am Sunday, it's fair to say the worms were biting, and I'd also taken more than a couple of passing glances at the roadkill up on Wahine Drive. Fortunately, I managed to elude the diet of bitumen-fried wallabies that Sunday morning as I repeated Winno's wisdom to myself: "Starvation focuses the mind."

Freeze frame: It's 1980s-ish. There's no internet, email or mobile phones. It's a miracle we did business. Our modus operandi for selling land 40+ years ago was simple—sign-written "island cars" on each of the 4 islands we sold land on. (*I'll leave "island cars" to your imagination. Let's just say they'd been moved from the mainland for good reasons.*)

The weekly land special was handcrafted onto a chalkboard on the roof of each car, e.g. "Waterfront Block – $4,500. Last one." I reckon we sold that "Waterfront Block – Last one" 40 times that year. We seemingly had an endless supply of them!

They were island cars for a reason

With our mobile marketing machines ready for action, we'd park at the jetty and meet each incoming taxi boat in the hope there'd be a genuine buyer looking to buy their dream block on one of 4 islands: Russell, Karragarra, Macleay and Lamb.

With my 3-day, one-egg diet complete, my stomach and I were almost desperate to board the last taxi boat home later that day to find some sustenance. I had only one appointment left for the day: an old Greek couple – let's call them Mr and Mrs Baklava – from West End in Brisbane, coming over to (hopefully) buy an investment for the family.

On cue, they arrived on the 11:00 am taxi boat and took their chances by climbing inside my island car. We made light conversation as I toured them around Russell Island, pointing out all the "opportunities" and trying to inspire an early purchase so I could get closer to a T-bone steak on the mainland.

No dice!

Nothing inspired them on Russell. Their thoughts could be summed up as, "Too many hippies and weirdos with 3-legged dogs and kombis." I couldn't argue with them.

Bugger.

Plan B saw us get the noon taxi boat from Russell to the much smaller Karragarra Island. A quick tour of Karragarra in the next island car and again, "No. Nothing." The island's flatness worried them. It could go underwater sooner than later. (*I may have shared a similar thought.*)

We are now 50/50. Two islands down, 2 to go.

We arrived at the "Karra" jetty just before the 2:00 pm taxi boat taking us to Macleay Island, the jewel in the crown and a 10-minute boat ride away.

I took that time to check my breath, review some of my closing lines and focus on selling my new Greek friends their dream block on Macleay Island so that I could get on that 3:00 pm boat back to food, any food.

The next boat delivered us to the Macleay Island jetty welcoming party, which, on this day, consisted of a drum circle of pot-smoking flower people. This was probably not what my new Greek friends had in mind as a homecoming for their family investment.

After a quick dusting of the red dust from the car seats of the island car, we embarked on my brilliantly scripted tour of Macleay Island. I reckon I'd delivered that script 150 times that year with an 80% success rate.

Was this to be my finest hour?

In my mind, I was already bringing home the bacon. Mmmm, bacon… My stomach had started to consume itself.

We toured as I expended all my zingers. We ended up sitting at the end of the island, marvelling at the view back to the mainland, then walked the one sandy beach as we borrowed fresh passionfruit off a vine at the church hall. I slipped in a trial close I'd been taught at real estate school. Still, I couldn't raise a hint of interest from my new baklava-consuming friends. Mmmm, baklava…

We did a second tour round in case I missed something. Nup, zero interest. No dice. No cigar. Nada. Not one buying signal. Drats.

Things were looking crook.

Now, to be clear, they were a delightful couple. He was a greying, short, round man, probably in his 60s. She was a lovely lady of similar proportions, with jet-black hair, a wicked smile and a deep, raucous laugh. They had a fruit shop. We'd had a fun day. They were ready to either adopt me or marry me off to one of their 5 daughters. We'd had fun, but still no sale.

Desperation loomed.

Three islands down, one to go.

I could see our next taxi boat from Macleay to Lamb Island approaching the jetty.

Lamb was a charming, green and well-treed island. It was my final chance at salvation. The island was well-advanced, with good housing, and its residents took pride in their ownership. There were no 3-legged dogs, kombis or drum circles of pot-smoking flower people in sight.

I really needed this sale, and the options were running slim. I was determined to make this last show count. I anticipated a comfortable taxi boat ride, some light conversation and a nice walk along the jetty to the waiting island car to carry us around the island and me to victory.

Much has been said about real estate agents who remove the internal door handles and lock people in the car until they buy or die. Well, dear Reader, the thought did cross my mind. My empty belly and I convened an urgent committee meeting. We decided all options were on the table that afternoon.

We climbed inside this last island car. I found the keys under the floor mat. It turned over at first click.

Mr Baklava was seated beside me on the bench seat. Mrs Baklava was perfectly positioned in the middle of the back so I could gauge her reaction to the blocks via the rearview mirror. The scene was set.

Quick check of the mirrors. All safe.

Select D on the steering column. Nup. It's stuck. I pull down harder.

It won't move into D. (*I don't mind saying that the "F" word was mumbled several times under my breath, but ever mindful of my newly adopted parents, I retained my decorum.*)

No matter what I tried (or mumbled), the bloody car would NOT go into Drive.

HELP!

Lamb isn't a big island; it's a long island. And at 4:00 pm on a Sunday afternoon, with the last taxi boat for the day due at 4:45, walking Mr and Mrs Baklava around the island was definitely not an option.

Winno's words floated through my malnourished brain: "Starvation focuses the mind."

I focused hard and quickly pondered my limited options. And then? A stroke of brilliance!

I told Mr and Mrs Baklava, "Turn around."

They looked at me dumbfounded and repeated my statement as a question, "Turn around?"

"Yep," I said, "Turn yourselves around and face the other way."

And in what should go down in real estate history as a stroke of genius and a prime lesson in never saying die, I selected R for reverse. With an almighty jolt of the gearbox, we embarked on an epic tour of Lamb Island in a car *in reverse gear!*

100% honest truth.

With my left arm draped over the front seat, I craned to look through the back window. Mr and Mrs Baklava were on their knees, fully facing out the back window and joining me in this rather unique experience.

Mrs Baklava's deep, raucous laughter started to build. She started rolling around on the back seat, convulsing in laughter as I described each block to them:

"The block on my right, which will be to your left, is a gently sloping 600sqm allotment down to the water's edge. Asking price $4,500."

Onwards, the tour went. Block after block, booming laughter, driving up and down the streets of Lamb Island, locals standing in their front yard incredulously sharing in the hilarity of their local real estate agent brilliantly navigating the roads like Peter Brock at Bathurst, *but in Reverse.*

I'm unsure if I wore the Baklavas down into submission or if they felt sorry for me. Either way, in a moment that affirmed my belief in doing whatever it takes to get a deal done, I heard these glorious words emanate from my captive audience locked into the 4 doors of our rear-facing roving rustbucket: "We'll take it!"

And so, my Friend, we sat on a beautiful spring afternoon, handwriting a land sales contract on the bonnet of that backward-facing bucket of bolts for the Baklavas to purchase a delightful 600sqm piece of island paradise for $7,500.

We managed to catch the last boat back to Redland Bay. That night, I savoured a much-needed and definitely-deserved T-bone steak, chips and salad at the Cleveland Sands Hotel.

It was a defining moment I've treasured my entire real estate career. It taught me that you do whatever it takes (assuming it's legal) and that:

It ain't over 'til the Baklava lady laughs!

Ship happened

It was around April of 1981.

I'd been selling land on the Bay Islands and living in the Black Swan Chalets. (*The name gives the establishment a much more exotic flavour than it deserves.*) My very modest and compact room included nothing. It was a single bedroom with a toilet in the corner and a shower over the toilet – literally over the toilet. Whoever designed this compact feature clearly fixated on 2-for-1 efficiencies.

While a land sales career on the Bay Islands was entertaining, selling blocks of land for a few grand wasn't as rewarding as the drinking and partying habits demanded of a 22-year-old. I had one final weekend to serve out of my island hopping escapades as an island sales real estate agent.

I was a front-seat passenger in a taxi boat returning to the islands for my final weekend. It was a Friday night, mid-winter, around 6:15 pm. It was dark and cold. Around 30 of us were on board chatting, laughing and teasing out what the weekend would bring.

Ours was the last scheduled boat back. However, a last-minute overload of people meant another was summoned to ensure everyone made it home safely.

It was overcast, with no moon. Our skipper was navigating the tight channels on the 30-minute trip back to serenity. If you make one wrong move, you could easily run aground on the mud banks. Focus was important.

Radio communications were normal, with our skipper, Chris, chatting periodically to Allan, the captain of the otherwise passenger-free boat. Captain Allan was heading back for the stragglers who'd shifted their mood to island mode.

The boats were powerful twin-prop Shark Cats. Our boat, named "BITS" after Bay Island Taxi Services, was heading east. The other boat in the fleet rocketing west was ultimately and sadly christened "PIECES".

In the dark waters and at high speed, these two powerful Shark Cats collided head-on in the icy black waters of Moreton Bay.

In the craziness, BITS, at high speed, had sliced across the top of the other boat, PIECES. As we spiralled high into the air and then plunged, I was catapulted from my front passenger seat out of the crippled boat, face-first through the windscreen into the bay.

The scene was utter carnage.

My face and skull were littered with glass fragments, my frozen body in deep shock and disoriented.

I frantically searched the surroundings for any sign of a device to help keep me afloat. Fortunately, within minutes, our skipper was able to limp his smashed boat over to drag my freezing bones back on board.

PIECES was now without a captain and was spotted doing small concentric circles of Moreton Bay, ultimately finding a resting place on a nearby muddy mangrove bank.

We miraculously managed to get everyone from our boat who had gone into the water back on board.

I sat beside Captain Allan's daughter as our damaged vessel limped its way back to the mainland to a crowd of ambulances and media. I could do nothing more than hold her hand and wrap a warm coat around her. Sitting in silence, we both knew that the news of her dad's prospects from the high-speed impact was unlikely to be good.

Tragically, Captain Allan Robb, a true gentleman, lost his life, and his family lost a great father.

It's a trip that still haunts me today.

It was also a time that gave me some early perspective about the fragility of life and taught me to truly enjoy what I've been gifted with each day. Time for this island party boy to get serious about his real estate career.

An interview with a friend

In all aspects of life, my dad saw great importance in dotting your i's and crossing your t's. He struggled with half-hearted efforts and fiercely argued the value of doing things correctly. Dad came from a world where only tightening 3 wheel nuts or not filling the brake fluid to the brim could have serious consequences.

Which brings me to the "interview".

After a stint selling land on the Bay Islands and in the Redlands, I'd returned to the mainland. For reasons that defy logic, I'd been working in a real estate office 22km from home, even though Dad and Mum had a successful real estate business only 2km away.

With the rising cost of fuel and what seemed like a loss of valuable drinking time spent driving, I suggested to Dad that he might consider employing me. I knew I had lots to offer, but I struggled to elicit what that was.

Dad was a stickler for due process, and I was highly confident in my interview prospects.

An invitation to attend an interview came via a phone call. A time was dictated, and I prepared myself for what should have been a pretty pedestrian affair.

It began with the usual stuff: name, address, phone number and religion. Tick some boxes and get a nod to start next week. Pretty simple, I thought. But, as we know, the best-laid plans rarely end that way.

To describe the interview as interrogation would be an understatement. Dad was in fine form, and had it been legal to ask for a DNA sample as part of the process, I suspect he would have.

I somehow survived his grilling and filled out the papers he'd handed me. Dad delivered his parting words with a weird smile, "Give me a call tomorrow."

With an ample degree of cockiness, I made my way to the Wynnum RSL to celebrate. It would take just 16 hours to learn that those celebrations were a tad premature.

In a bid to not show too much desperation, I left my call to the grand patriarch until after noon the following day. I figured I'd let him sweat a bit.

The ensuing phone conversation went a little like this:

Me: "G'day, Dad. Just checking in to see when you'd like me to start."

Dad: "Pete, when you filled out that application form yesterday, did you fill it out completely?"

Me: "Absolutely! Um. Well. I think so."

Dad: "Well, based on what's in front of me, I think not."

He continued: "Had you taken the time to properly read the paperwork, you'd have seen a place for 3 referees' names and contact details on the back of the application form. And, as I'm looking at that application form, I don't see anything in those boxes. So, if you'd still like to be considered for a position at *Don Brewer Real Estate – The Professionals*, you need to pick up that paperwork, fill in the details of your 3 missing referees and return it to me for further consideration."

Me: <*Gulp*>

I returned to his office that day with my tail between my legs and filled in those 3 missing names and their phone numbers.

Dad called those referees to determine my good character. Yes, I called him the next day, and yes, he finally confirmed a job offer.

It was the birth of a respectful and profitable business partnership that prospered and grew for 20 years. (*That experience also taught me to check the paperwork twice on every transaction.*)

And while this young bull gained an enormous amount of Dad's business brilliance from working together, I'm also incredibly honoured and grateful that the old bull eventually acknowledged he'd learned a few things from this young buck.

Dad had historically sweated the small stuff, which caused me enormous frustration and often stifled decision-making, resulting in missed opportunities. Where I'd be keen to make what would seem an obvious decision to do something, Dad would sometimes overthink and miss a golden opportunity.

I remember when Mum repeatedly asked him about spending a few of their dollars on a holiday and some luxuries.

Dad replied, "No, I'm saving for a rainy day."

To which Mum responded with her usual trademark marketing gold, "Don, it's raining *now*."

Dad was a very conservative businessman. As a team, though, our combined yin and yang made for some absolute magic. We became a dynamic team who played to each other's strengths. Dad: analytical and strategic. Me: flamboyant and enthusiastic, with an eye for maximising an opportunity and a lasting reminder to read the paperwork and take nothing for granted.

Let the games begin!

P.S. I love you

As life progresses, you go from getting invitations to 18th birthdays, engagements, weddings and a few christenings to – now at 65 – being invited to my kids' places to babysit while *they* go to 18th birthdays, engagements, weddings and a few christenings. Talk about the circle of life!

As I hit age 35, the one anomaly to the above was I found myself spending more and more time at funerals for the dads of mates who had been prematurely lost to heart attacks, cancer and strokes. I suspect it's no coincidence that 35 is "half time" of the 3 score and 10 years that influenced the title of this book.

Some of us get to play the full game, others miss out on the second half.

Life can be really unfair, and if seeing a mate in his mid-30s struggling to read their dad's eulogy or carry their dad's coffin through the church doesn't soften the hardest of men, then I'm not sure what does.

I was chatting with a mate in his 60s last year. Trevor was headed overseas to see his ageing dad after 5 years apart. His dad was unwell, his Saturdays all but gone.

In our exchange, I imagined aloud that he was looking forward to hugging his dad.

His stony-faced response sent chills through my veins:

"Pete, in 62 years on Earth, I've never received a hug from Dad. Our only physical contact has been shaking hands. Throughout my entire life, he's never called me anything other than Trevor. It's never even been truncated to Trev, Love or Mate. Very occasionally, the word 'Son' is offered if Dad expresses his displeasure."

I find it unfathomable that in 62 years, they've never said "I love you" or expressed any emotion beyond a formal "Good morning/night" and a handshake. I could see the pain and sadness in Trev's eyes from the walls surrounding his stiff-upper-lipped father's inability to share emotion.

So sad.

As they say, something good usually comes out of something bad. A common denominator seemed to recur at my mates' dads' wakes. On almost every occasion, as we would be reminiscing over beers later, their shared regret would pour out in trembling voices that they had never told their respective dads they loved them.

Those moments cemented in me an absolute determination to say those seemingly simple 3 little words out loud to *my* dad before he made that final journey.

I started mapping out a plan for how to do it.

Saying "I love you" to Mum was always easy. She was soft and warm and open to giving and receiving affection. Dad? Not so much. It's just how blokes of a certain era were raised.

So, after reflecting a little on my plan to tell Dad that I loved him and appreciated all he'd done for me in life while also trying to mitigate the possible risk of him being absolutely horrified at the son he'd raised, I realised this was gonna be a tougher task than I'd first thought.

How would I go about ensuring I get those 3 life-changing words out?

One of the things Dad taught me in negotiations was that the best way to disarm the other party was to get them on your turf, to remove them from the comfort of their surroundings. A simple strategy.

I loved fishing, camping and beach driving, and I spent hundreds of hours on the beaches of Noosa, Teewah, Double Island Point, Inskip Point and Fraser Island (now K'gari).

The plan was hatched to take the old bugger beach fishing on Fraser!

On my terms, in my happy place. How simple it all will be.

Well, maybe not so simple.

Our conversation was wide and varied on the 2-hour drive from Brisbane to the beach access road at Noosa North Shore. We covered interest rates, property investments, favourite cricketers and the usual regurgitated battle stories of our best sales. Traffic was kind, but my brain was racing as the conversation continued. When would be the right moment? I repeatedly practised the 21 words in my mind, "Dad, I just need to let you know that I love you, and I really appreciate all you've done for me."

Easy to type, bloody hard to articulate.

Should I start the trip with these words? Or would they be the perfect words to end the trip?

All I knew was that the first 2 hours had me choking every time I went to voice them. This wasn't gonna be a cakewalk, but I was determined I'd get those words out. Somehow. Somewhere. Sometime. I had 3 days.

The access track to the beach at Noosa North Shore is rough, ungraded and has soft sand that claims a dozen or more inexperienced 4WD enthusiasts each day. A whole new economy has developed based purely on fellow 4WD enthusiasts towing others stuck up to their axles on the perilous track, in exchange for a 6-pack of whatever the beer of the day might be.

This was Dad's first foray into being in a 4WD on a beach. I was determined it wouldn't include the humiliation of digging our way out of axle-deep sand, waiting for rescue. Besides, Dad had bought the beer, and the thought of asking him to part with one beer, much less a 6-pack, to pay our way out of trouble wasn't overly palatable.

We stopped the car atop the sand dunes and dropped the tyre pressure to 18 PSI while inhaling the warm, salty sea air. I could hear Darryl Kerrigan embracing the serenity.

The sky was an incredibly deep blue, the waves benign and unthreatening. A flock of around 150 seagulls were lightly dancing on the wet sand as the waves rolled gently further up the beach with the incoming tide.

Over the years, one of the most incredible beach driving experiences I've had is driving alongside massive flocks of birds and watching them launch themselves from the sandy shores and sweep across the skies in fantastic formations. It's a beautiful sight, and I marvel at nature and man sharing and playing together in their natural habitat.

The setting was perfect.

Even Dad marvelled at the magic and nodded his approval at this first stage and the ensuing next stage of the journey, an 80-kilometre comfortable beach drive on the hard sand at low tide – north via Double Island Point, Rainbow Beach, Inskip Point and on to our final destination, Fraser Island.

The mood was right.

The setting was perfect.

No time like the present, I thought.

I inched my faithful Landcruiser onto the beach access as I'd done a hundred times before – second gear engaged, good revs, excellent traction – and slowly and successfully meandered our way across the soft sand onto the beach proper.

Dad was smiling. I was in my element.

Now, one of my (many) flaws is my impulsive nature. I often go with my gut. This trait has served me pretty well. I'd give it a 90% success score (thus far).

So, I went with my next impulse. Let me recreate the feeling of being at one with nature for Dad as a precursor to delivering those 21 words.

My trusty Landcruiser gathered momentum as we moved down the beach towards the birds. They frolicked. My heart smiled. Dad was about to experience magic.

We inched closer and closer, the birds firmly in our sights.

Momentum gathered. Man was about to be at one with nature.

And in a heartbeat?

Instantaneous avian annihilation.

Not one of those frigging seagulls did what their clearly much better-educated cousins have done for decades. Not one of them moved. At least a half dozen oversized, squawking chip-stealers met their premature graves that day.

In a second, the mood turned.

You see, Dad was a bird lover. And his next task, on this beautiful Australian beach day, was to prise seagull remnants out of my car grill and wheel arches with an umbrella he'd hastily retrieved from the back seat of the instantly remodelled hearse.

Over the next few minutes, we salvaged what we could and covered the crime scene with the help of the incoming tide.

The next 80km drive was pretty quiet. I'm not sure what was going through Dad's head. As I tried to repeatedly explain what had happened, I think the last words I heard him mutter as we drove off were, "What the eff was that about?!"

For the record, we also caught no fish and it rained for 3 days. The only saving grace of that adventure was that the RSPCA was never called.

Needless to say, I didn't get to tell Dad how much I loved him and appreciated all that he'd done for me on that trip. That would have to wait for another, less bloody, day.

The gaps that people leave in our lives can never be bridged.

Step up or shut up

One of the most fulfilling periods of my real estate business career was from the early 1990s until my first attempt at retirement in 2009.

My real estate business was a proud member of The Professionals in Queensland, a larger marketing collective that my father had been an inaugural member of 20 years prior. Over time, as a fee-paying member, I'd become increasingly frustrated with a procession of CEOs who many believed had taken our members for a ride. To see my dad's legacy and valuable resources being wasted and its fee-paying members' goodwill disrespected by overpaid corporate flunkies was no longer tolerable. For me, it became personal.

My entire life, it's been drummed into me that "if you're not part of the solution, then you're part of the problem". So, I was left with no moral option but to be part of the solution. But how? I had a growing business, a young family, and I was working 7 days a week. I had zero experience running 95-member strong real estate groups.

I'd read somewhere that if you want something done, you should give it to a busy person. I definitely ticked that box! I also knew I had the motivation and energy. I just needed to find the extra time.

So, with some encouragement, I offered myself for election to a Board position.

Thankfully, it's now way outside the provisions of the statute of limitations, meaning I can confess that I actually became privy to a sneak peek of the poll result of that vote. I'd absolutely romped into office, securing 94 of the 95 available votes! Surely, that was a ringing endorsement worthy of celebration. But was I celebrating? Nope, I found myself drowning in bitter disappointment that I'd failed to get the support of one of my colleagues. Seriously! We humans are a strange lot.

After serving an apprenticeship as a Director for 2 years, I served 9 years as the Executive Chair of the organisation. In my time in the Chair, raw passion led me to miraculously find the time to plan a corporate restructure that included not re-engaging a CEO. (*Shock horror!*) Instead, I designed a role for an Executive Chairman who would work alongside a superb management team. Their entire focus would be returning the business to its core *raison d'etre:* delivering marketing, training and support services to help every one of our members run more profitable real estate businesses. Pretty straightforward stuff.

Changing the corporate structure of any business comes with inevitable obstacles. Men of a particular vintage can become strongly wedded to certain ideas and be incredibly unyielding to change.

(Exhibit A: Watch the turmoil unfold after 7 mature men are asked to sit in a different seat at a meeting. The ensuing mayhem and shift in dynamics can be flabbergasting.)

I was one of the first of the second generation of this real estate brand. An unavoidable generational standoff loomed between the conservative old guard and me, the young buck with a bushy moustache and big ideas ready to challenge the old-timers. Some had scant regard for this Johnny-come-lately with insufferable enthusiasm.

Fortunately, others on the Board inhaled the fresh winds of change.

Having now committed to leading the brand's transformation, I set about creating a presentation to the Board on the looming behavioural changes in the industry, their own members' expectations, where they'd been duped in the past, and why they needed to display some courage and take a leap of faith or continue with the status quo and be banished to the history books as dinosaurs who failed in their duties.

Around the same time, I'd been reading about the little-celebrated history of Brisbane's Story Bridge. It had just turned 75. Today, it's a critical structure joining North Brisbane to South Brisbane. But in the 1930s, it wasn't a popular concept when first presented to Kangaroo Point pork farmers residing on the Southern riverbank and the New Farm poultry farmers on the opposite bank. Their farms sat smack-bang in the middle of the proposed 6-lane highway, seemingly from and to nowhere.

Unsurprisingly, the farmers loudly protested that a 6-lane bridge wasn't needed. People could row their boats across the Brisbane River if they needed to venture to the City or the south! All true and logical, but seriously lacking vision. Apply the same logic, and we'd still be sitting in horses and carts on a dirt track for a day trip out of our capital cities.

The government of the day was relentless and undaunted by the detractors. They continued to deliver their vision of what a Brisbane of the future required.

I decided the history of the Story Bridge was the perfect metaphor for the moment. I built my Board presentation on that story, laying out the Board's options of being either the insular-thinking poultry and pig farmers or bold visionaries.

I still remember walking laps around the corporate HQ building where I would deliver my vision, before the meeting. Anxiety levels were high. I tried to take deep, calming breaths. This presentation would either see me elevated to the penthouse or banished to the outhouse.

Time to roll the dice. I entered the room to encounter a silent, stony-faced Board. In business, I'd previously encountered some tough negotiations with hard-nosed home sellers, so I was match-fit for the moment. My presentation was delivered with my trademark passion. While I had some detractors, I also had amazing supporters in the room who might buy into that passion and endorse my proposed changes.

I rejoined the meeting after being momentarily excused to enable the Board to deliberate my vision. I stood anxiously awaiting the jury's verdict. Would our members still be rowing their boats across the Brisbane River in the ensuing decade? Or would we invest in building a tunnel to deliver on our charter to make their businesses more efficient and profitable?

Looking across the top of his wire-frame glasses, with his unwavering straight face, my mentor Les Thornton delivered the verdict in his trademark calm monotone: "Yes, Peter, the Board accepts your proposal. You'd better get to work."

There I sat, both elated and petrified at the enormity of what I'd so passionately pushed for.

For almost 10 years, I was humbled to have been allowed to lead the company my dad was a proud founder of in 1976. People I respected, who, aware of my lack of academic qualifications, sensed that my deeply ingrained passion trumped a framed certificate any day. They took a leap of faith and fell in behind me to help steady the ship. Along with an incredibly devoted and gifted management team, including Marilyn, Kathlyn, Kimmy, Binny, Flicky and many more, we became laser-focused on doing things that mattered to our members, to their resounding delight.

There were no boozy international junkets. No creative accounting. No spin doctors. Our objective was to return to the business' roots by ensuring that every dollar of income was spent on delivering extraordinary marketing, relevant training and services that helped our members remain competitive.

Our success didn't go unnoticed. Like many successful businesses, our attackers came from unexpected places.

During our 10 years of impressive growth, my team continually fought off relentless coups from misguided counterparts obsessed with controlling our proven model for success. It's a weird, sad preoccupation that some Southerners seem to have with successful Queensland businesses that I'll never comprehend.

Rotary has an ethos, "There's nothing more past than a past president", is simply a nice way of saying, "After you've had your day in the sun, nick off and let a new president get on with adding their flavour."

It's advice I'll take after making one final observation supporting the incredible work my amazing team did for a decade:

Since my team's departure, I've been saddened to witness some history and people being erased and the narrative rewritten to massage the egos of fragile freeloaders. Others I still hold as close friends today have continued the fine work my team built on. Overall, it was a very special time in my life working with a magnificent group of people. Our mission was simply to ensure that our members had access to the best marketing support and training available to the profession and to build a strong culture across the brand. I'm immensely proud that we delivered on that promise.

In the meantime, like the Story Bridge, my little celebrated team still stands proud. Their work in revolutionising the brand, growing membership numbers, embracing the digital world, passionately endorsing the work of the National Breast Cancer Foundation to the tune of 3 million dollars (over 10 years) and strengthening the brand's culture – while Southern counterparts continued on a misguided path of self-destruction – continues to inspire me.

The Story Bridge is still fit for purpose as it approaches 90 years. New leaders across all brands are charged with the responsibility of ensuring the businesses they lead are the same.

I know that my accomplishments during that period choked my dad up. That his vision as a founding forefather of that organisation ultimately provided a platform for his rebellious son to shine personally and professionally is something I'm forever grateful for. There are few greater feelings in life than receiving your parents' approval.

I'll close with one of my favourite quotes:

> "A society grows great when old men plant trees in whose shade they know they will never sit."
>
> Greek proverb

My Professionals Team

Who's on your bus?

I've received some heartwarming kindness in life. A warm embrace or kind smile on a crappy day can turn a Titanic.

Like most of us, there was a time when I was skippering my own Titanic inch-by-inch closer to an iceberg that had the capacity to take my passengers, ship and me to a watery grave.

For a period of time in the 1990s, I became dangerously engrossed in a passion project: growing a business that paid me nothing and that I had no commercial interest in.

To keep the metaphor going, I focused on the starboard side, with zero focus on the rapidly approaching refrigerated rocks on the horizon.

There's nothing wrong with committing to passion projects. They're great for the heart. As I was about to be reminded, however, the banks of Australia don't accept "passion and heart" as legal tender when it comes time to pay people's wages, bills to keep your doors open or the mortgage on the home providing shelter for your family.

Over my career, I've seen some incredibly generous, community-driven people pay a massive price for their passion.

Of particular note, I knew a local builder – let's call him Bill – whose community club work appeared endless. If a family was in crisis, he was there with an envelope full of cash. If a family lost a roof in a storm, he was there with a tarp. If a dear old lady needed a new chicken coop, he'd be the first to build it and then be back in an hour to stock it with half a dozen of Rhode Island's finest reds.

Bill's kindness lit up everyone's face. He inspired a community. His generosity of time, money and spirit was legendary. He became a local hero. The more Bill did, the more he was asked to do, fuelled not by ego but because he saw more people who needed help. He just gave more and more to help them.

I often wondered how Bill could show such incredible kindness and be "Eddie Everywhere" while maintaining a successful local business and feeding a family of 5.

The answer to that question came with a brutal dose of reality when I received a phone call from a repossession agent exercising their power of sale on Bill's unfinished 20-year-old family home due to an unpaid mortgage.

Their instructions were for me to contact Bill to retrieve the keys to his home, finish the construction of the home so that it would be saleable and then sell the property for whatever I could achieve in a less-than-kind property market.

The sickening chills through my body at what was happening to Bill and his family caused by the distractions of his passion projects was the start of an epic awakening for me.

The cold look of defeat on Bill's face as he handed me his keys was devastating. He left his home with his only possessions being a rusty ute full of well-worn tools and a torn heart. A kind heart that had helped so many was now homeless and penniless.

I won't draw parallels between Bill and me. There aren't any. But there are parallels in our journeys, and learning from witnessing his tragic fall started me on a course to check for leaks and icebergs in my own Titanic journey.

The property markets of the 90s had been mixed. I'd always had strong cash reserves to draw on to keep the ship afloat during the occasional storm.

For better or worse, my then-wife and I believed that we didn't just employ a few staff; we saw that we were responsible for many *families and associated tradespeople.* Our people looked to us to provide the fundamentals for survival through secure employment and ongoing trade jobs. We took this responsibility seriously and never shirked it.

With the spectre of Bill's story still haunting me, I had a chance encounter with my bookkeeper Gwen, my dad's sister. Gwenny was a perfect administrator of our financial affairs. Everyone and everything got paid on time. Like clockwork, Gwenny would call by our office each Tuesday to pick up a yellow milk crate of the week's bills, timesheets, chequebooks, etc. She'd then head to my home office to ensure all the cattle were fed and the wolves kept well away from the door.

The chance encounter I mentioned came with a throwaway comment from Gwenny as she handed back that well-worn yellow milk crate one Tuesday afternoon.

"Hey, Bozo, you better top up that number 2 account this week. It's looking a bit skinny."

(*Yes, Gwenny's nickname for me was Bozo. I'm optimistic it wasn't derived from a particular TV circus clown with the same moniker. But, I guess, if the orange wig fits!*)

I was a bit taken aback by Gwenny's comment about the need to top up account number 2. It had always held significant reserves.

I thought, "She's obviously made an error. That's a bit unusual. But hey, I'll forgive her. We all make mistakes."

And yet.

Something about our conversation niggled me until I decided to address it at 2:30 am the following morning.

Troubled, I ventured downstairs to my home office to find the error so I could give Gwenny some peace of mind about our profitability.

And yes, dear Reader, you've picked it already, haven't you?

As she'd always been in her 50 years of precise and forensic bookkeeping, Gwenny was right. The financial *faux pas* was 110% my fault. Like Bill, the distraction of saving other people's bacon meant I'd lost focus on protecting my own business.

I hurriedly dug deep into our accounts, debtors, creditors, cash flow projections, unconditional sales and even how much we were paying ourselves.

The sobering and sickening summary kicked me where I deserved to be kicked at around 3:30 that Wednesday morning:

I had $36,000 of bills due. I had $9,000 to pay them.

I busily started researching the Bible story about loaves and fishes. But as much as I had a strong sense of self-confidence, I wasn't optimistic I could perform a similar miracle.

I quickly realised that if I didn't get back into the wheelhouse of the Titanic and change its course, we were about to have access to as much ice as we could have ever dreamed of for our impressive liquor collection.

Some words of wisdom shared years earlier with me by Les Thornton, one of the most astute people I've encountered in my personal and business life, echoed in my head. Now, Les is the master of the one-liner of wisdom and incredibly economical with his words, but each one is jam-packed with wisdom.

"Peter, the first thing to do is not panic."

Easy to say but much harder to do, especially when your heart is beating out of your chest while sitting at your desk at nearly 4 in the morning, contemplating the futures of the people you're about to fail. In a week, you won't have the cash to pay them, and there are some very difficult conversations with at least half of them about to happen.

Early in business, I learned that when you're stressed by tough decisions, very few things give your thinking clarity more than taking a long, head-clearing walk. The combo of exertion, clean air and no distractions, with just you and your thoughts, is priceless.

Nothing that's ever been written in any textbook would solve the problem I created. After all, if you point one finger at someone, there are 3 fingers pointing back at you. It's an important reminder to accept your mistakes, learn from them and fix them so they never happen again. They're called life lessons for a reason.

My predicament had nothing to do with a soft property market. The interest rates of the day were irrelevant. The swanky BMWs in my driveway hadn't arrived unannounced under their own diesel. Our lack of stock was because someone else was doing a better job attracting new listings.

There's something liberating when you're completely honest with yourself and own your mistakes. It makes it easy to move forward when you own it.

I created this problem. I needed to fix it. Fast.

As it happens, while on my head-clearing walk, I ran into one of my loyal team members. Let's call her Sally.

Sally and I exchanged waves as I wandered by. This particular morning, she gave me an extra wave and, with a hand gesture of tilting a teapot (or wine bottle – I was open to either at that point), motioned me into her impressive home overlooking the harbour.

I don't know much about Sally's formal education, but she was street-smart. And by now, you'll be patently aware of my appreciation for people who've actually done the hard yards and have smarts far beyond academics whose only exposure to running a business is through the prism of an outdated textbook advancing impractical and untested business conventions. I guess I'm implying that if you haven't experienced the real-life pressure and pain of running a small business and having people's futures in the palm of your hands, your manufactured hypotheses mean little to me.

Sally could read a room. She knew body language and could read the signs, from a nose scratch or earlobe twist to crossed legs or arms. They were all signals she'd studied and perfected in her years of negotiations.

After several sips of our "tea", Sally could tell that something was niggling me. She dug deeper to turn my frown upside down. Since Sally had been a good and loyal friend, I felt I owed her the courtesy of explaining the predicament in which I found myself.

I gave her the abridged version. I had nothing to lose, and I needed to improve my ability to deliver bad news to good people.

She heard me and nodded. She knew me and my capabilities. We travelled some rough roads together and also celebrated some wonderful successes. We'd been good to each other.

But what was to follow still moves me as one of the most amazing gestures I've experienced from anyone in my life.

Aside from the gift of letting me have the last glass from the bottle of chilled breakfast Chardy, Sally went on to offer that she had an account with $50,000 and no immediate need for it. She was happy to give that money to me for as long as I reasonably needed it to solve my woes.

What a kind offer!

Did I take her up on it?

Of course not.

What I took from Sally was worth much more than $50K.

From Sally's mind-blowing offer, I took renewed energy and

vigour to steady the ship, chart a new course and navigate us back to safe waters. I trusted myself anew. I realised others believed in me. I knew exactly what needed to happen. Time was of the essence.

By 10 that morning, I was back on the phone talking to prospective clients, following up with former clients to check in on their needs and writing my monthly newsletter for 3,000 people I already had relationships with but had stopped communicating with.

By 7:00 pm, I'd hand-delivered 2,000 letterbox flyers to my dedicated farm area.

80 Cambridge Parade, Manly, Queensland

From that point, my focus shifted to the core activities that had been the foundation of our business's success. Sally's kind offer delivered me the dividend of a life lesson I can never repay.

Sure, I could have taken the $50K and bought my way out of short-term strife using her money. Or, as I did, use this incredible offer as a driver that amazing people believed in me so much that they'd literally hand over their life savings to support me.

As a leader of people who believed in me, I owed them the courtesy of being the best possible version of me. I owed it to my family, and I definitely owed it to myself.

Within 3 months of laser focus, the number 2 account again blossomed. My passion project still lived; it just had to take a step to the side of my priorities.

Overall, I'd dodged a Titanic moment and emerged with no casualties and a captain steadfastly vigilant again at the helm.

It was a valuable period of learning.

I learned the importance of surrounding yourself with good people and being 100% transparent during both good and bad times.

I learned that whenever I started making excuses, I needed to check how many fingers were pointing in which direction.

I was reminded about priorities, personal responsibility and being completely honest with myself.

Most importantly, I was humbled and buoyed that someone believed in me enough to back me with their life savings and, in turn, be reminded that the hard-working and loyal people sitting in my office could have chosen to work at any of 20 other agencies in my town. That they put their faith in me was something I would never take for granted again.

"Life is a succession of lessons
that must be lived to be understood."

Ralph Waldo Emerson

From little things, big things grow

While this chapter refers to my passion for boobs, it's less about admiring them and more about saving them.

I'm not sure when my love affair with breasts began. Truth be told, it probably goes back to 1959 when they first fed me. Anyone who knows me knows I deeply appreciate anything or anyone that feeds me.

Along with colleagues from a real estate brand I was working with, I was fortunate to meet some amazing people from the National Breast Cancer Foundation.

We learned that one in 11 Australian women would be affected by breast cancer in their lives. A staggering statistic. We were honoured to meet some survivors and others who, ultimately and tragically, would not beat the insidious disease.

I knew we had the capacity to make a difference by raising critical funding to assist the important research that could reduce the horrendous loss of life. I knew we could raise large chunks of cash from generous people who were part of the brand I represented.

Ultimately, we set a voluntary levy on every sale we transacted nationally. Properly managed, we could raise extraordinary money for a great cause while protecting some of my favourite body parts.

Most members across the nation rallied and embraced the initiative. It was eye-opening just how much breast cancer has impacted so many lives. Our social initiative inspired our people to take positive action, and donations from fundraising activities rolled through the National Breast Cancer Foundation's door.

You'd think introducing an optional levy to raise funds for a program to help save our ladies' lives would be an absolute no-brainer. But I learned quickly from one vocal member, a father to 4 daughters, that not everyone has a charitable side. His abusive protestations and loud public dissent at supporting our initiative were astounding.

(It's noted the Lord works in mysterious ways, and I can only ponder whether the cancer that soon riddled his own body wasn't a gentle karmic nudge from the heavens.)

So, *sans* the support of the inevitable village contrarian, we raised some significant cash. Our Australia-wide teams were relentless in their efforts: nationwide morning teas, levies on sales, a breakfast radio broadcast from Central Railway Station in

Brisbane and charity dinners with fundraising auctions were only some of the events sponsored and run.

Fund raising with Ross Davie 4BC - Iris Brewer - Peter Brewer

At our events, we heard the deeply personal stories of amazing ladies (and men) who shared their battles to beat the ruthless bastard that is breast cancer.

In the emotionally charged environment of a fundraising event we held on Sydney Harbour, someone suggested that, as a sign of support for our special guest speaker who had lost their hair from chemo, I too should have a bald head.

At that time, I had impressive jet-black locks of which I was pretty fond. Those locks had disguised a fairly unattractive watermelon-sized skull for 3 and a half decades.

To dissuade the idea of shaving my melon, I promptly set a reserve of $10,000, confident my locks would join me intact on the flight home to Brisbane the following morning.

But we all know what they say about the best-laid plans…

Considering I'd earned a certain level of respect from my professional peers, I figured there was no chance of anyone finding one person who disliked me enough to meet the $10K bounty.

What I didn't factor in was the likelihood that 20 people would have sufficient desire to see my pale, bald watermelon in all its glory in exchange for a $500 donation each.

And so, with the promise of $10,000 now secured in favour of the National Breast Cancer Foundation, a razor was summoned. In just a dozen strokes, I became a card-carrying member of the "Conehead Club".

A $10,000 haircut

A quick #protip in the event you ever find yourself in a similar position: unless you have a strong desire to resemble a massive pumpkin, do not, under any circumstances, attempt to disguise a lily-white head with fake tanning solution!

One of the greatest honours afforded me as a leader of this fundraising group was being asked to help realise the final wishes of a mother riddled with cancer.

Annie's wish was to fly from Sydney to Brisbane to see her 10-year-old son Bill train with the Australian Cricket Team before her imminent passing. We made Annie's wish come true in a heartbeat. Annie and Bill flew to Brisbane for a morning of training with his Australian cricketing idols, who made the occasion heartwarming and special.

I returned the mother-and-son duo to Brisbane airport 4 hours later, armed with an almighty swag of personally autographed cricket gear. Bill's smile was wider than the Story Bridge, and Annie's was priceless. I will hold that memory forever.

Another of Annie's dying wishes was to sing backup vocals for the Australian band Human Nature. They quickly obliged and invited Annie to join them on stage in Newcastle. She wasn't just doing "doo-wop" backups either. No, for one very special moment, the Human Nature Fab 4 transformed into a Fab 5, with Annie singing lead on their cover of "Every Time You Cry". Annie's performance while fighting for her life and suffering from late-stage metastatic cancer was an inspiring moment that would melt the hardest of hearts. She was magnificent.

I shared a recording of Annie's performance on YouTube, more as a memory and for personal inspiration. Eight years later, I was alerted to a comment on that video that said, "Hey, that's my mum". It was signed "Bill". Knowing we had helped Annie's son Bill find a rare video of his mum realising her dream was special and proof that for all the ills of social media, it can also facilitate plenty of goodness in this world.

Raising cash for the National Breast Cancer Foundation became part of my DNA in the 1990s and 2000s. By the time I moved on from my commitments with that real estate brand around 2014, we'd raised around 3.2 million dollars to fund research for a cure and significantly raised awareness of the insidious disease. More importantly, we'd helped amplify the deeply personal stories of Australian women fighting for their lives daily. Giving those ladies a voice was incredibly fulfilling.

A humbling honour I received in that era was an invitation to break bread with the Governor General of Australia and his wife at Admiralty House on Sydney Harbour to acknowledge our fundraising achievements. It was one of the few times I willingly wore a suit and tie. This special afternoon also allowed me to demonstrate to a broad audience that, despite the volume of uneducated pile-on criticisms thrown at the real estate profession, behind the industry beats 10,000 hearts who care deeply about the people and the communities they serve.

With Governor General of Australia Michael Jeffery and Lady Jeffery

What still fills my cup today is that the initiative has raised $4.2 million (as of 2025) to fund researchers' efforts to find a cure for breast cancer. It's one passion project I'm incredibly proud of. I look forward to the day we don't need to fundraise for this cause anymore.

Many business and sporting heroes have inspired me in my time on this planet for their courage and wisdom. And I've met some amazing titans. But my friendship with Annie and the honour to share in helping fight her battle and gain deep personal insights into her strength, will to live and care for those around her is the most memorable and inspiring.

Wash away the tears.

My proudest sporting achievement

Someone once noted, "Golf is a good walk spoiled."

It's hard to argue.

I was a loyal patron of Wynnum Golf Club for a brief period. *(The reason for my short-lived membership was that I discovered other golf courses offered electric carts adorned with eskies and stubby holders.)*

It was a middle-aged man's Nirvana.

I could command a chariot laden with a dozen of Milton's iciest refreshments – Brisbane's (in)famous XXXX beer – and be let loose to chase an oversized white pill, only occasionally stopping to readjust my ball's location with the aid of my size 11 Julius Marlow shoe or to crack open another cold one.

Now, the indisputable fact that underpins my genius at golf will come later, but suffice to say, I haven't always been a revered master of the game.

I recall a charity day when I was invited to play with my mate Greg. I believe it was for the Poultry Growers Association of Queensland. Who even knew the Poultry Growers had an association, let alone a golf day? Life continues to deliver knowledge bombs!

As we approached the first tee, one of the organisers asked what my handicap was. I quickly learned that "a crook knee and no ability" is not an appropriate answer to tournament officials who take these things rather seriously. The correct answer is apparently 27, the maximum for a novice with borrowed clubs and zero ability.

Now, before tee-off, our assembled playing group had taken the opportunity to survey the impressive bounty of prizes on offer for the day's winners.

As our day on the course wore on, 2 things became apparent:

1. Our inadequacies as hack golfers were frustrating the living bejesus out of the deadly serious players behind us.
2. None of our group legitimately stood any chance of winning any of the impressive prizes on offer. *(I said "legitimately"…)*

I'm unsure what the statute of limitations is on golfing crimes, so I'm not prepared to tender a full confession. Let's just say a good scorer always beats a good player. So, late on that warm autumn afternoon, our team walked away with a car full of impressive prizes acknowledging our miraculous golfing prowess, with 120 golfers scratching their heads in total disbelief at our clean sweep.

In what must be sheer coincidence, Greg wasn't invited to the Poultry Growers Association Golf Day the following year, nor for any subsequent years.

I ultimately retired from golf on a balmy Sunday summer's afternoon in 1998, having perfected the 18-hole game. Men in their late 80s are still chasing their dreams and a little white ball, but at 39 I'd scaled my golfing Everest, been lauded by the Masters and celebrated by my colleagues for my achievements. It's a rare feat for someone of that tender young age and one of which I'm very proud.

Many have remarked on the circumstances that led to that retirement. I prefer to categorise any negativity as professional jealousy and envy from others whose lack of equivalent skills has left them pondering their inadequacies.

Here's the abridged version of events that culminated in me hanging up my trusty Callaways:

It was Sunday afternoon, around 3:00 pm. My wife of the time, Michelle, and her son, Brendan, agreed to join me for a cheeky 9 holes at Wynnum Golf Club. On arrival, we ran into a former schoolmaster of mine, Steve Paul. Steve, also then a real estate client, agreed to make up a friendly group of 4. Being summer and a Sunday, we chose the back 9 for its shade and distance. *(The choice might also have been mildly influenced by the proximity of the final hole to the bar.)*

Our first 8 holes were pretty vanilla. None of us hit the ball particularly well, but the company and conversation were nice, and the beer was cold.

The 9th and final hole at Wynnum is around 135 metres. A slight dogleg to the left, tall trees on both sides, with the clubhouse in the distance.

On my march to perfection, I'd won the previous hole, so I would tee off first.

Two seasoned locals stood near the 18th hole ahead of us. They waved me up to take my shot. With my 3 partners observing from behind, me and 2 veterans judging from the target green, I'll confess that a little voice whispered the ever-comforting and reassuring words, "Don't fluff this up."

I approached the tee with my trusty 5-iron in hand and minimal trepidation. This was my moment to shine, the culmination of endless hours striking thousands of balls at the practice range all compressed into one shot at glory.

Unfazed by the pressure of the moment, I swayed my cute arse back and forth. *(Hey, it was cute in 1993!)*

I found my sweet spot of balance. My back was suitably arched, knees floating perfectly, grip and arms in sync, eyes, like a tiger, singularly focused on the red flag set to the left of the green 135 metres away.

I rocked gently back and forth, arching my back as I slowly raised that 5-iron above my shoulders. With one deep breath, I floated a perfectly timed stroke into the heavens to be kissed by angels.

For seconds that seemed like minutes, the ball sat in the skies before gracefully falling back to earth, exactly 134.95 metres from where it first began its journey. A gentle roll towards the flag ensued, followed by a bellowing cry with much animation from my 2 new best friends standing on the 18th: "It's in the hole! It's in the hole!"

Yes, on that balmy Sunday summer afternoon, in the presence of 5 of the best witnesses one man could ever wish for, I scored the perfect shot in golf. A hole-in-one.

I'd perfected the royal game. I'd reached the pinnacle. There was no higher mountain to climb. The time had come to stand aside and give others the opportunity to shine.

There was no media conference or fanfare to mark the momentous retirement. Instead, we adjourned to the bar to celebrate.

(Side note: I have no idea where the stupid rule came from, which says the person who hits the hole-in-one has to shout for drinks at the bar. But let me just share that I think it's stupid.)

Game perfected – Time to sell the clubs

Now that this field has been conquered, where would the "independent type of lad who has potential", as described by my school teacher, chance his luck next?

"Golf is a game whose aim is to hit
a very small ball into an even smaller hole,
with weapons singularly ill-designed for the purpose."

Winston Churchill

A bridge over troubled water

Earlier, I wrote about Brisbane's Story Bridge and the turmoil between the chook pluckers on the Southside and the pork producers on the Northside arguing the need for its construction around 90 years ago.

Their logic? Why try to fix what was arguably not broken? It's a reasonable argument if you're a pig or chicken destined for an early date with a rotisserie.

Ninety years since that failed barnyard brawl, and Brisbane has an iconic bridge that fulfils 2 important purposes:

1. Sheltering the front bar at Howard Smith Wharves from the blistering morning sun.
2. Adding an hour to a Southside-to-Northside commute while Brisbane drivers continue their struggle with the concept of merging.

Its origin isn't the only story of the grand old dame, which some cruelly refer to as "Sydney Harbour Bridge-Lite".

I have a personal story. The Silver Arches and I haven't always boasted an 8-lane love affair.

There was a period that, for reasons I'm only now starting to rationalise, I had more interest in taking my chances swimming across the bull shark-infested "Brown Snake" (aka Brisbane River) than putting myself through gut-churning feelings of fear, despair and paralysis I'd encounter whenever my trusty Commodore approached the grey gangplank.

The heart-pounding terror I felt for a time in 1999 crippled me to the point where I found myself stopping short of the bridge. For a few moments, I'd have to give myself a pep talk Wayne Bennett (a famous Queensland NRL coach) would be proud of. It's the only way I could beat the crippling fear of driving across that bridge.

I'd never been paralysed with fear of such proportions before. Not on a sporting field, not in a business negotiation – speaking on a stage to several thousand people – and not even meeting my partner Tara's parents for the first time.

The basis of my trembling trepidation was that the ageing aqueduct was waiting for my arrival so it could crumble into a million pieces, swallow me up into a pile of twisted steel and concrete and dump me head-first into the tidal torrent of turds below.

What was the rationale for this sudden paranoia?

This beautiful bridge was hardly new to me. It had been the route home from the hospital as a newborn baby! It was part of my daily commute for my first job. I'd traversed it weekly for 40 years.

How did it come to this?

Well, I'm no Freud, but here's my take on my cross-river fail.

The year was 1999. I'd just turned 40. Until then, life had been very kind to me. I could have been nicknamed "Koala". I definitely had been a protected species.

I'd had a dream run in my life: limited responsibility, a secure role in the family business, low debt, good equity and high income. My wife of the time had blessed me with 2 amazing children, aged 9 and 5, and a stepson, aged 15. I had my health and great friends, nice cars, a caravan, and I'd experienced some incredible holidays. In retrospect, I was living a Peter Pan existence and was probably unappreciative of the amazing ballot I'd drawn in life.

Life was a highway, and I was riding it all night long.

Then, as the age-old saying goes, life randomly jumps out from behind a vase of daffodils and smacks you in the face with the back of a heavy timber chair for a sobering reality check.

Okay, maybe that's not the saying, but I think it's a pretty apt visual.

Because there, amid cartonfuls of booze, buckets of jumbo king prawns, kilos of T-bones and as much gravy on my potatoes as I wanted, BAM!! The jar of daffodils fell off the table and the back of a heavy timber chair embedded itself into the middle of my forehead.

Wednesday, around lunchtime, I received a phone call from my distraught mum, who was drowning in devastation.

After 43 years of loyal and devoted marriage to my dad, her worst fears had been realised: Dad had strayed in a way that left

Mum with no option but to call time on their marriage. The trust underpinning their relationship was in tatters. His gaslighting was soul-destroying. By Mum's high standards, the betrayal was unforgivable. There was no turning back.

Such was the impact of the betrayal on her beautiful soul that, within a matter of days, she was committed to psychiatric care at the New Farm Clinic, which was unfortunately located on the northern side of that damn Story Bridge.

The wheels had suddenly fallen off. Life had kicked my Peter Pan world squarely in the nuts with size 16 steel-capped boots.

The state of play was this:

- My amazing mum was experiencing a totally understandable but incomprehensible meltdown.
- Concurrently, my brother was fighting some demons *and* a judge, resulting in being an invited guest at Her Majesty's pleasure in one of her more down-market secure facilities. *(He and poor life choices were constant companions.)*
- Dad had been banished to the Gold Coast, where he was licking his wounds and coming to terms with the ramifications of his sustained indiscretions. It was painful to watch Dad living the hell that came with crossing lines he'd spent 40 years imploring me to stay on the right side of. Our own relationship was understandably fractured. The bonds between mums and sons are special. What else can you say?

Within days, I'd been elevated to my newly fractured family's "leadership" role. With the other 3 team members out of action, I had suddenly become the captain, coach and sports psychologist charged with getting my injury-ridden team fit for play again.

I hadn't campaigned for this job. I didn't see the ad for it. I had no intent on applying for it. And frankly, I was seriously underqualified for the task at hand of managing the trail of devastation.

It was time to be a big boy, step up as a responsible adult and triage the situations.

My focus became simple: save Mum.

She'd been the bond that had selflessly glued us together for my 40 years on the planet. She'd not transgressed an inch but was suddenly the victim of a horrific betrayal. She was reduced to a shell of a human prone on a psychiatric ward bed in the foetal position, questioning every person she'd put her trust in. The internal destruction I witnessed is indescribable. It's the most gut-wrenching pain I've ever witnessed a human endure. As I type this piece, I'm shuddering at reliving the trauma Mum experienced.

When you're from a proud family with a high public profile, who do you turn to for guidance when the storyboard suddenly turns ugly? How do you seek help while wanting to protect your mum from the pain, indignity, invasion of privacy and scuttlebutt of a small town? There's no step-by-step manual you can buy to guide you through.

I figured that love conquers all. Unconditional love is what Mum had gifted me my entire life, and I had to repay her in spades and quickly.

She was heavily sedated and in a quickly declining spiral. Time was of the essence.

While my Peter Pan world was up in flames and my days crept longer as I kept the family business alive, I dealt with the growing local gossip mill and fielded calls from well-meaning friends. I also attempted to rationalise why Dad was somehow hosting his own pity party. I decided that giving him a self-awareness lesson could wait until later.

Each day, for 6 weeks, usually at breakfast or morning tea, I'd visit Mum in her highly secure New Farm Clinic, hoping that a loving, friendly face and some positivity might give her reasons to fight for life. I have never encountered anyone as low as she was. Ever. Mum was in supervised care in a drugged, zombie-like state for 3 of those 6 weeks. Anything was possible.

And each day, I fought the demons that plagued me so I could drive across that bloody Story Bridge so she wouldn't be alone.

Many moons later, I reflect that my intense, crippling fear came from a place of not knowing what I'd experience when I got to the other side. Would Mum have made some progress? Would she have lapsed deeper? Would she be awake and mildly lucid?

Every trip was, to borrow a metaphor from an interesting colleague, a "wheelbarrow full of surprises".

I'll acknowledge that this may appear to be a self-serving comment, but it was bloody tough. I had no skills in this department. Each night, I'd depart Mum's room and head back to my own home, trying to process the devastation she was encountering and somehow try to compartmentalise my own trauma so I could be a father, husband and businessperson.

Every time I crossed that bridge, I knew my emotions would be torn. I could be elated at some small progress or devastated and feeling helpless on the dark and lonely trip home.

What I did know was that it would take a long time for me to look forward to once again traversing that frigging onramp to uncertainty.

Bridges of various sizes and spans have become monuments for the challenges and exciting journeys of my lucky and privileged life.

Bridges are wonderful life metaphors.

Most of us drive them without knowing we're even on a bridge.

Many of us walk them for enjoyment and to marvel at the rivers, creeks, caverns and beauty below.

Some photograph them for their architectural magnificence.

Sadly, some jump from them when love or life feels lost.

Some even ceremonially burn them and everything in their paths as parting gifts to businesses and relationships.

Some become so vindictive that they add more fuel, even when nothing remains but a pile of unidentifiable rubble smouldering on a riverbed below.

Bridges come in all forms. We all approach them differently depending on who we are and the challenges we face in our journeys.

But I've learned that despite the protests of chook and pig farmers, there will always be new bridges to cross. We will all face bridges in our lives. There's no other option (unless you plan on doing a lot of rowing). It's how each of us crosses them that matters.

And know this: Although we all have faced gut-wrenching fear in some shape, it's how you deal with that fear and who's on your team to help you arrive unscathed on the other side that matters.

How did my "Battle of the Bridge" pan out? Thanks for asking!

My fear resulted from being unprepared for and not knowing the challenges on the other side.

Would it be wine and roses? Or would it be grief and drama?

I'd tied myself up in knots and multiplied the enormity of the moment. Because in the scheme of life, most challenges are just moments on the journey. They're inevitable and often uncomfortable speed bumps on a very long highway. But they shouldn't be life-defining.

Mum and Peter 2000

I'll accept I'm generalising. Some of the cards we're dealt are simply unfair. But I'll hazard a guess that, for many of us, the default reaction to anything left of centre is that we tend to catastrophise it. Fight or flight kicks in.

I've learned to not let those mad moments consume or define me. As I wrote in another story: You can't wait until life isn't hard anymore before you decide to be happy.

Mum was out of psychiatric care after 6 weeks. Then, in true Mum style, she returned to New Farm Clinic as a volunteer just a week later, helping new patients through the early stages of their own trauma.

Mum went on to live a magnificent life, free from the shackles of a controlling partner and completely on her own terms. She found a new loving partner and spent the next 6 years living in luxury and almost delirious happiness on a boat in the canals of France.

Dad and I rebuilt our relationship within 12 painful months. Acknowledging his transgressions helped him become less rigid and more accepting of the fact that life isn't simply black and white. His very public fall from grace taught him a brand of humility he'd never felt before.

From the entire experience, I learned the importance of forgiveness and letting go of the stuff that can eat you up inside, perpetuate needless anger and ultimately define and poison you and the people around you.

I learned that the deep love I'd concentrated on Mum to help her heal and rebuild her trust in the world and people around her was equally well-received and impactful with my dad. I also learned that there are 3 sides to every story and that life is full of challenges.

Simon and Garfunkel say it so well in the final verse of their classic, "Bridge Over Troubled Water":

> *Your time has come to shine*
> *All your dreams are on their way*
> *See how they shine*
> *Oh, if you need a friend*
> *I'm sailing right behind*

Like a bridge over troubled water
I will ease your mind
Like a bridge over troubled water
I will ease your mind
I'm sailing right behind

When you're crying you bring on the rain

Around 2007, I was sitting with some mates, sharing our inflated wisdom and reliving our past glories over a few beers. We often spent time slapping each other on the back and reflecting on "the good old days". There's no question that the older we got, the better we'd been.

We'd been mates for a long time and had humoured each other's ever-inflating achievements and theories of life a thousand times over. Having great mates who endlessly tolerate listening to your bullshit is a wonderful gift.

In Ricky Nelson's hit song, "Garden Party", he sings, "If memories are all I have, I'd rather drive a truck." It's an important reminder to create and celebrate new memories rather than continually reliving past glories.

Having great mates means there's no filter when it comes to telling you how it is. Often, usually without prompting, they'll happily slap you squarely in the face with a cold, wet, smelly fish of reality without giving it a second thought. If someone else were to share that kind of feedback, you'd probably smack them in the mouth. But good mates have an unconditional licence, even a responsibility, to call it as they see it.

Then, there are your special cradle-to-the-grave mates. You might not see them for 5, 10, 15 years, but you can still pick up the conversation as if it were yesterday. In part, social media has increased that connection.

They're your tribe. They know where all your skeletons are

buried. They've held your hair back when you've vomited on the boss' shoes. They've offered you a mint when your breath could maim a camel. They've discretely motioned to you about that bat that's dangling in your left cave. They're warm, special, unconditional friendships.

And just as in *Survivor*, you sit up and pay attention when the tribe has spoken.

Some mates will wear their honesty as a badge of honour. Some will tell it like it is to keep you grounded. Regardless of the motive, if it's offered by a good mate, it's probably got some credibility and is a cause for some self-reflection.

This particular day, I found myself in a random conversation with my "brains trust" about the wonders of world travel. I shared photos of a recent trip I'd taken to various parts of the world, including me atop the London Eye, another savouring the view down the Champs-Élysées from the Arc de Triomphe, another on the steps of the amazing casino in stunning Monte Carlo, and another in Japan with mighty Mt Fuji as a backdrop.

There I stood at some of the world's most recognisable landmarks. They were travel opportunities many people only dreamed of and experiences I should have been doing backflips over for having experienced.

My boisterous band of boofheads scanned my travel pics, and the predictable fluff talk ensued about Pommies being whingers, the French being arrogant and the Japanese being incredibly hospitable at home. We've had those conversations 100 times over… And I pray that life offers me the fortune of having them another 100 times over.

As we sat perusing my travel pics and waxing lyrical about the world, one of the assembled tribe had been quietly observing the pictures of my jet-setting lifestyle and decided to pull that cold, wet fish out to slap me back to a thunderous reality:

"Hey, dickhead, how come you're in all those fancy places, but you're not smiling in any of the photos… ?"

BAM!

I hurriedly scanned the pictures. He was right! There was not a glimmer of a grin to be seen. My usually wide smile had clearly travelled to a separate holiday destination from the rest of me.

Time to turn that frown upside down

How could I be in such exotic places yet have a face that looked like someone had announced that the bar had run out of beer? It was unfathomable in both regards.

I obviously needed to do some soul-searching. Everyone who knows me would agree I was among the world's luckiest people. And let me be crystal clear on this. I 100% was, and I still am.

Supportive people, partners and amazing children surround me. I have had profitable businesses. I've held prominent positions in national organisations. I enjoy the respect of people who matter. At that time, I was in excellent health, had healthy bank balances and freedom of choice.

Life was good.

So, what was stopping my face from telling the same story as my privileged life?

I sought some counsel from my local GP, a wise and decent man. I shared with him that, at times, I would find myself a little faint or dizzy. Three or 4 times a week, I'd find myself wide awake at 2:30 am, staring at the ceiling, mulling the previous day's activities over, kicking myself over missed opportunities and planning what I wanted to achieve the next day.

I shared with him that sometimes frustration would overwhelm me. I'd find myself driving to the office at 3:00 am to catch up on whatever was troubling my mind so I could clear my brain and go home to get back to sleep.

The passion for business ran pretty deep in my veins.

The good doctor's advice was considered but simple: "Peter, you need to slow down. If you don't, the only way we'll fix you will be with tablets."

Dark days

Doc was smart and, as history was to prove, also a visionary. Because almost 5 years to the day, I walked back into his surgery at Wynnum with chest pains, shortness of breath, anxiety and a touch of paranoia.

The clinical diagnosis? Well, I can't recall the exact wording he used, but knowing I'm a fan of nice cars and a student of relatable metaphors, he said, "Peter, your engine is stuffed. You failed to get the scheduled servicing done on time, you filled the tank with the wrong fuel, ignored the knocking noises in the gearbox and now your warranty is stuffed." Essentially, I was suffering from a severe case of burnout.

Doc continued, "Remember 5 years ago when I said that you need to slow down because if you don't, the only way we'll fix you is with tablets?"

Looking up with puppy-dog eyes and ears, I gave him a knowingly guilty nod.

He shook his head and reached out with a small bottle, uttering, "Congratulations, here are the tablets."

Lesson learned. Slow the heck down. Smell the roses.

I had to remind myself that my business success had been built on helping people, providing for my family, following my passions and funding my lifestyle.

Maybe I'll get bashed by all the 4:00 am hustle-and-grind people and lambasted by business owners who've forgotten their kids' names, are in toxic relationships and never take a holiday.

Trust me. It's not a race to see who can collect the most toys before they go toes-up. That's just macho business talk you've been suckered into believing at expensive seminars.

When I walked out of the doctor's surgery that day, I had two really important things:

1. A bottle of Clonazepam, and
2. A passionate goal to ditch the need for that bottle of Clonazepam as quickly as possible.

Things needed to change. And it started and ended with me.

The road to redemption would take a while, and truth be told, I'm probably still on it. Discipline isn't one of my more impressive traits.

I studied where I was letting myself down. What was missing in my world?

Self-taught business boneheads like me aren't typically good delegators. Harvard Business School was never on my radar. Hell, almost completing Year 10 at Wynnum High stretched the limits of my academic capabilities.

But street smarts are completely different, as I was to learn later in life.

Many of my real estate clients had completed 7 years in uni and boasted academic qualifications with nicely embossed certificates and impressive titles. I've learned that those years at uni did little to teach street smarts and common sense to people I'd ultimately design and implement significant wealth strategies for.

I'm buoyed by my finding that career academics might know a lot about academia and theory. But, to coin an urban dictionary acronym, SFA about the stark realities of life outside a classroom or textbook.

No textbook can prepare you for the challenges of leadership in business. It can be incredibly lonely. Often, you're flying by the seat of your pants on a wing and a prayer.

I knew that success in my former business required me to carry a certain level of self-confidence. It was important to the team and community that I looked like I knew what I was doing. I'd worked damn hard, literally day and night, on building an encyclopaedic knowledge of residential real estate. I was very proud that people of substance would seek my counsel on matters of law, compliance, sales techniques and client management.

The more people wanted my thoughts, the more I obliged. It became a self-perpetuating machine that gained impetus with every revolution. The more people sought help, the more I helped.

If, like me, you've got a mildly compulsive or competitive streak, it's easy to get caught up in the flurry of life, business, self-importance and an overwhelming desire to do the next deal, delight the next client or solve the next problem. We're people-pleasers. The brain quickly moves into troubleshooter mode whenever you get thrown a curveball or hear of someone you or your little black book can solve a problem for. It's a rare and admirable quality that can come at a tremendous personal cost.

It can become intoxicating. You start to mix your priorities, sacrifice your social life, set unrealistic expectations of yourself and create expectations that others rely on you for. It's not too long before you're carrying the weight of 20 other people's worlds on your shoulders.

And in a short time, I could see it was detrimental to everything I was meant to be focusing on. One minute, I had life by the balls; the next, the tables and grip turned before I could blink.

Saying "no" doesn't come naturally to some people. It certainly didn't for me back in those prime years. It still doesn't come naturally today, but I know I'm getting better at it, and I've become much more selective about who my tribe is.

As I reflected on that question from one of my mates:

"Hey, dickhead, how come you're in all those fancy places, but you're not smiling in any of the photos… ?"

And with my doctor's words ringing in my ears, I set myself on a path of creating a business that worked for me rather than me working for a business.

I needed to make time for myself.

I needed to learn to say no.

I needed to realise that I couldn't single-handedly save the world.

I needed to be less tolerant or completely dismiss my world of toxic people.

I needed to learn to delegate.

I needed to understand that hearses do not have luggage racks and you can't take your money with you.

Easy to say. Fricking hard to do.

But it's funny how life sends you signals…

I was driving back to the office one Saturday afternoon around

4 after an open home on a sweltering summer's day, sweating to death in a suit and tie, with about 2 hours of client callbacks ahead of me plus 2 salespeople in the office spitting their dummies about which one of them owned a particular buyer when something caught my eye on the side of the road. It's as vivid today as it was then.

Off to my left was a guy about my vintage sitting on a camping chair in his garage. He was wearing a baseball cap and cream T-shirt. He had what I presume was an ice-cold beer sitting on the garage floor beside him. There was a transistor radio beside the beer, and I assume he was listening to the footy or maybe the races. He was tinkering with a fishing rod leaning on the side of his chair, seemingly oblivious to anything else going on around him. He looked like his biggest worry in the world was having to get up to get another beer.

That simple image that afternoon became ingrained in my head and the poster that replaced Pamela Anderson and Sharon Stone on my vision board.

I wanted to be that guy, and I gave myself 12 months to do it.

With the help and support of what I believed to be a well-credentialed business mentor, we put an optimistic plan in place:

- Exit the family business.
- Bank a sizable cheque.
- Retire by the age of 50.
- Put the suits in the cupboard for a year.
- Travel.
- Contemplate a comeback as a part-time consultant.
- Start charging for the advice I'd been freely dishing out for the previous 25 years.

In meeting after meeting, my business mentor and I designed the perfect exit strategy. With each meeting and another action ticked off, I could see myself inching one step closer to the goal of being that guy in the garage.

Fast forward 12 months from the first seed being planted, and there I was:

- ☑ Adult day care centre sold.
- ☑ Mortgage paid out.
- ☑ Bank balance with more zeros than I'd ever dreamed possible.
- ☑ An empty diary on the following Monday.
- ☑ A new camping chair in the garage, a stubby holder and a new transistor radio.
- ☑ Ample time to dust off my fishing rod and oil up the Alvey reel.
- ☑ No staff egos to manage or placate.

I love it when a plan comes together.

The incredibly rewarding real estate business life of Peter Brewer 1.0 was over. Would there be a Peter Brewer 2.0? Only time would tell. But if I have 2 pieces of advice on exiting a business, they would be these:

1. Find highly skilled business mentors to help you actualise your dreams.
2. Make sure that none of them are high on lithium to treat their bipolar… *(But that's a story for another book!)*

"When you're smiling, the whole world smiles with you."

Louis Armstrong

I've seen sunny days I thought would never end

James Taylor and Carole King are my 2 musical inspirations. Their humility and magnificent ability to tell stories are inspiring. I'm blessed to have seen them both in concert. They fuelled in me a desire to develop the skill of capturing an audience's imagination through song or words. In writing this memoir, I'm hoping I might have captured your imagination as I've shared some of the real and raw stories of my own life.

Throughout this book, I've compiled a balanced summary of whether I was half decent at my craft. The fact that I survived the wrath of the local firing squad at dawn for 30+ years, which claimed the careers of so many others, should say enough.

Our family business lived in an era of an analogue form of "Rate My Agent". People didn't go online to read reviews. After all, there was no such thing as "online". If you wanted honest feedback on almost any local business person's performance, there was no better source of critique than the local pub, footy club or mates' BBQs to get the tea on someone. In a small town, there's never a shortage of people ready to spill it.

Even today, 16 years after I turned the key on our office's front door for the last time, I still hear people speak in glowing terms of our business. Our service ethic makes me proud of the values we unwaveringly stood for. I'm very proud of our longevity and unrelenting commitment to doing real estate business professionally. We served our sellers and investors without compromise and our buyers and tenants courteously.

Was it all wine and roses? Of course not. I wouldn't be honest if I didn't share some of the lighter moments.

I've long believed that if your chosen career on this journey of free trips around the sun doesn't bring you happiness, it's probably time to go with the job your School Career Guidance Officer suggested. After all, that gig at Woolies might have been your real calling.

During my early sales career, it wasn't uncommon for me to spend a Friday night with a couple of close mates. The first was a quiet, tall, dark Scotsman named Johnny Walker and another poisonous pair known as Benson and Hedges. We were constant companions until closing time on a Friday night at several local establishments.

It wasn't uncommon for festivities to continue at our real estate office until a slither of morning light would crack the window blinds, bringing with it a stark reminder that I had 2 hours to get home, get showered, get sober and get back to work. Fortunately, I was pretty resilient in those days – sharp as a tack and able to sell my way through most situations.

One particular Saturday, I had a busy afternoon of open homes. By the last one of the day, I was rapidly fading. My overindulgences had finally caught up with me, and I was limping to the 5 o'clock finish line.

I prepared the final property on the list for the last showing of the day following my usual routine: signs out, welcome mat at the door, lights and air conditioning on, visitors book ready on the kitchen table, cold bottles of water on the bench, some property brochures and some modest self-promotional material.

This particular home hadn't been a hit with buyers at previous open homes, and it was unlikely today would be any different. I anticipated a long, lonely 30 minutes ahead of me.

It was a Saturday in December in Australia, so I knew there'd be cricket on the telly and a comfy chair from which I could see out the final 30 minutes until my own stumps were drawn.

On this last open home for the day, I'd made the rookie error of being seduced by a very comfortable recliner perched under air conditioning in front of a telly instead of my usual sentry, standing guard at the property's front door with my buyer registration clipboard.

I'm sure you've already figured this story doesn't end well.

The combination of a hangover, fatigue, TV and a comfy chair under air conditioning got the better of me. In one of the most embarrassing moments of my real estate career, I was startled awake as I heard roars of laughter and 3 car doors slamming outside the property.

I quickly woke from my afternoon slumber and jumped back into real estate agent mode, ready to greet these giggling visitors. You can imagine my horror when I realised they were departing rather than arriving. As I shook my head with embarrassment,

I discovered 2 things that swore me off my boozy Friday night rituals for the next 2 years:

Proudly inscribed in the visitor's book on the kitchen table were the names and contact numbers of those 3 people.

In my once-empty top pocket, I found the business card of one of my fiercest rivals in the local real estate industry.

Yes, my Friend, while I lay comatose in that comfy chair, cricket on the telly, I'd had not 3 but *4* visitors. I can only be thankful that the days of social media were still a decade away!

And speaking of open homes…

Mad dogs and roundabouts

Running open homes can be challenging for a real estate professional. Not every home occupier presents their prized possession in its best light. Little things like picking up dirty clothes, emptying stinking ashtrays and removing Fido's "land mines" camouflaged underneath 8 inches of unmown grass are just a few that gain my ire.

Some of the simpler things might be to not make a fish stew 30 minutes before an open house or to consider vacuuming the pet hair off your carpets and taking your unmuzzled mutts with you while the open house is going on.

#ProTip: Not everyone loves being slobbered and knocked over by your rottweiler or relentlessly barked at by your crazed chihuahua while they wonder about the possibility of fleas.

One sunny Sunday afternoon, I found myself running an unusually long (2-hour) open home at a property on busy Wynnum Road.

The sellers, an old English couple, loved their 2 corgis. They also believed everyone else would hold the same love for their snotty-nosed canines, and, despite my protestations that they please not leave the replicas of the Queen's mangy mutts behind, they fired up their Tardis and, I assume, disappeared into time.

One secret my sellers hadn't shared with me was that their corgis, curiously crowned Lizzy and Phil, were runners. Escape artists. Canine Houdinis. If they got a sniff at a sliver of daylight through a slightly ajar door, they'd wobble their ample posteriors through that gap faster than you can sing "Rule Britannia".

Bereft of the benefit of that tightly-held wisdom, I made the rookie error of leaving the front door unguarded for a microsecond. And yes, you guessed it, those hairy mutts made a dash for freedom and a beeline for busy Wynnum Road.

I'll assume that you, dear Reader, are not a traffic engineer, so let me provide some insight. On a Sunday afternoon, Wynnum Road carries around 2,000 cars per hour, all travelling at speed. It's a lot of cars to dodge for our 4-legged friends. Double that challenge for an old bloke with 2 dodgy knees.

Having achieved their dash for freedom, Lizzy and Phil sat briefly surveying the world at their paws, finally setting their sights on the wide open spaces of Primrose Park about 400 metres away across the Wynnum Road racetrack and a busy 4-way roundabout.

I stood at the front door in shock at what had just happened. My heart was palpitating, my brain was racing, and I was terrorised with fear over how I'd break the news to the owners that Lizzie and Phil were more than likely now furry speed bumps for the 304 Bayside bus or any number of trucks on the busy 4-lane thoroughfare.

I had 2 choices:

1. Stay at the house, do my job and earn the commission I'd come out on a rare Sunday to work for and leave the rest to Darwinism.

2. Down tools, lock up the house and spend the next 2 hours chasing those damn dogs around the streets and parks of Wynnum North, risking life and limb and testing out just how far I could push my newly acquired atrial fibrillation before collapsing on the dirt praying for my final forgiveness.

Did you guess it?

Yes, I chose the latter and spent the next hour and 58 minutes using every means known to man to catch those death-defying dogs as they crisscrossed the park and dodged traffic. It's a miracle I wasn't carried away in an ambulance after almost 2 hours of trying to catch those mangy mongrels.

With just minutes left until the sellers' return, I wrestled the mutts to the turf and marched them back behind the royal gates, where they promptly assumed the sleeping position in their kennels.

At 3:00 pm, the sellers returned in their Tardis, anxiously awaiting the success of the afternoon's Open.

Covered in sweat and grass, gasping for breath and fearing I was about to expire, I momentarily regained my breath and shared the feedback, "It was pretty quiet today."

Anyone who tells you that the day-to-day life of a suburban real estate agent truly reflects the glitz and glamour of today's tits-and-teeth "reality" TV shows is pulling your leg. I promise you, reality is *way* more fun!

Why did we do what we did?

"Why did we do what we did?"

It's an interesting question we should all ask of our own businesses or careers.

In our case, our business gave us a healthy return on our time and monetary investment. It gave us a great lifestyle and the freedom to make choices not afforded to most.

But a broader purpose drove us.

Almost every one of our interactions was driven by people's fundamental need for security and safety and a place they could call home, whether that was a place they owned themselves or a shell they put their personal touches on and rented.

Good people entrusted us to help them realise their property dreams. They willingly handed us the keys to their single largest investment. We were gifted a unique honour and afforded the privilege of seeing inside their lives, finances and relationships. We helped our clients and customers move on to the next stage of their lives. It's a special feeling and exchange of trust when someone hands you the keys to their home and confides what's happening in their lives with you.

I often reflect on one of our most loved sales professionals, Patrick (aka PRK). PRK loved his work, and we loved PRK. He was diligent, caring, methodical, process-driven and deeply committed to his wife, Marjorie, and his faith. PRK earned around 80% of what most agents of that time were earning. What he lacked in earnings, he doubled up on in customer satisfaction and generating repeat and referral business. People trusted PRK to do the job ethically, morally and without fanfare.

I once made the mistake of sending PRK to an auction school run by a cocky and overconfident presenter with an overinflated opinion of his own abilities.

Following day 1 of training, a morose PRK walked into my office brandishing a white envelope. *(Any employer will know where this is going. I hate where those white envelope conversations are usually headed.)*

PRK asked if he could have 5 minutes of quiet time with me. I immediately obliged and we sat quietly as he gathered his thoughts, selfishly feeling like I wanted to vomit at the thought of losing such an important member of the team for whatever reason.

PRK felt like he was letting us down. He went on to say that the previous day, the trainer (let's call him Motormouth) had said he wouldn't get out of bed for the kind of money that PRK was generating.

Motormouth went about pumping his own tyres up and slowly but surely eroded the confidence of every attendee who'd given a day of their time to learn the skills of great auctioneers.

However, Motormouth neglected to mention that he was earning less than half of PRK's wages. How did I know? Well, I was the chair of that organisation and signed the fortnightly pay cheque for each staff member.

With much reinforcement of our belief in and appreciation of him, I was able to entice PRK to tear that white envelope up and rescind his resignation. In no uncertain terms, I made him aware that our shared values of looking after the customer mattered most to us as a company. PRK went on to enjoy a comfortable career as a much-respected real estate professional. Marjorie loved him, his clients loved him, and we loved him.

Motormouth eventually got out of his bed. Fortunately, it was to go to the airport to return to the USA to see how many other careers and dreams he could destroy.

Lesson: The world needs more Patricks and fewer Motormouths.

Like PRK, I've always believed that the best way to attract more business is to surprise and delight your clients. It's not a difficult concept.

Since we sold the real estate business in 2009, I've not spent a dollar marketing my services, yet the phone still miraculously rings.

Hopefully, that explains a little about what drove us then and what still drives me today. It's never been with a focus on a fancy watch collection, a tricked-up BMW, a wall of perspex trophies or some misguided pursuit of celebrity status. Business has always been driven by the opportunity to help another human. I believe that if you get that bit right, the world is your oyster!

Without customers, there is no business.

Peter Brewer 2.0 – My sliding doors moment

Having sold the real estate business with little public fanfare at age 49, I had arrived at a point where I'd decided that my working days were done and dusted. The time had come to put my feet up on the teak and enjoy the fruits of my labour.

As my friend Winston Marsh and I often joked, "I plan on retiring and spending my ill-gotten gains while sunning my glorious body on the most beautiful beaches of the world." Winno would continue, "And by the way, if you don't think I've got a glorious body, I want you to imagine it with oceans of money washing over it!"

Effectively, the burnout from business had poisoned me. My attitude to people stunk. My "get up and go" had "got up and went". I'd worked my socks off, almost 18 hours a day, 7 days a week for the previous 25 years, and the rewards were in proportion. While my attitude sucked, my bank account had blossomed and afforded me the freedom to do whatever I wanted. It was a great place financially, but far from an ideal place mentally. Being miserable and toxic definitely wasn't part of my life plan.

For reasons I can't explain, I've always had a dark feeling that mine would not be a long life. *(This premonition may ultimately become reality, depending on how you define "a long life".)*

Either way, the moment's mood reinforced that I had much living to do before my number was called. Being a financially comfortable guy with a bad attitude wasn't what I'd worked hard to achieve. I had to fix that before it became terminal.

It can be confronting changing life patterns from working 18/7 before lying awake and worrying about unappreciative people for the remaining 6 hours, to suddenly having zero responsibilities and days of absolutely nothing to do.

In all my master planning to build a perfect exit strategy from the real estate business, I'd failed miserably by neglecting to build a "keep myself occupied" strategy for whatever I'd do beyond the business sale.

Now officially retired, I found you can only vacuum the house or the pool so many times each week. Morning walks along the Manly Foreshore were pretty, but watching cars and businesspeople heading off to solve a problem or contribute to society left me feeling I may have peaked prematurely. I knew I still had plenty to give to the right cause. It just became a question of finding that cause.

You may have already read about me perfecting the game of golf. Maybe making a comeback to the fairways could be my saviour?

After 3 weeks, I realised this idea might have been a tad misguided.

For a game meant to bring out the best in people through regular physical exercise and healthy competition, it brought out the worst in the people I played it with. Mature adult men obsessed with winning and attaining perfection had somehow forgotten what it was all about in the first place. Some scared me with how angry they'd get after a misdirected drive or a putt that lipped the hole. Clubs were bent and twisted in anger. Full sets of clubs rattled as they were hurled through the sky to land in their final resting place – the murky depths of Wynnum Creek.

It didn't take long to learn that the much-revered game wouldn't give me the calming and relaxing hobby I sought. Plus, I realised I actually sucked at golf.

I bid the golf club a fond farewell and wished those frustrated golfers all the best with their stomach ulcers and high blood pressure. The search for an interest continued.

As I approached 50, I decided a party to celebrate the milestone was in order.

Our family has a history of putting on cracking shindigs. We've perfected the recipe: add music, merriment, awesome friends, select relatives, liberal doses of booze, a great venue and stir. It works a treat every time.

And so, about 100 of the most dubious characters you could ever meet assembled at the Royal Queensland Yacht Squadron's home for a Sunday afternoon of feasting, fun, frivolity and amazing music delivered by my wonderful friends Greg and Laura Doolan. Greg had provided the entertainment for my 21st birthday, so an encore for my 50th was in order.

We had an outstanding afternoon. One old radio friend, Ross Davie, delivered a sensational version of "New York, New York", and my brother sang an emotional rendition of "He Ain't Heavy, He's My Brother". I'm still unsure if his song choice was a piss-take on my not-insignificant girth, but let's just run with it being a lovely tribute.

Friends and former business colleagues travelled far and wide to join the festivities. The bar tab stretched, as did the boundaries of truth. It was a cherished afternoon celebrating a milestone birthday with love and amazing friends in comfortable surroundings – a much-needed bowl of chicken soup for my soul.

Conversations were had; my brain was revitalised. My energy returned, networks were re-established and "my people started talking to their people". Within 48 hours, I found myself gainfully employed heading up a start-up digital marketing business specialising in the real estate profession.

A new dawn, a new challenge and a new set of skills to learn – Peter Brewer 2.0 was born.

Elsewhere in this *magnum opus*, I talk about my amazing "work wives". These incredible ladies know my darkest secrets and where the skeletons are buried. Should they ever get together to compare notes and go public, I'll likely serve somewhere between 20 years and life.

But it would be remiss of me to not mention my co-conspirators, Kath and Kim, in the rebirth of PB 2.0. True story! Kath and Kim. Both were a major inspiration in the growth of that business. Together they gave amazing spreadsheets, could sushi anyone under the table, shared my love of a cold Corona and for 2 years, did the seemingly impossible job of making me look good.

Working to grow that business on behalf of an international real estate company afforded me the opportunity to study and develop an encyclopaedic knowledge of the digital media space by attending amazing industry-specific events across the United States.

Whether I was at mind-blowing events with 22,000 attendees at NAR conferences in Las Vegas, New Orleans, Anaheim or San Diego, or at Proptech/Martech industry-specific "boutique" events of 4,000 people run by Inman in New York or San Francisco, or beaming in a webinar from the USA at 1:00 am to my laptop propped up on kitchen table, I was under no illusions that I'd been afforded a rare opportunity to prove myself in a new career.

At this point, it's appropriate to introduce the man solely responsible for deepening my passion for that new career and creating incredible opportunities for me in the USA.

The year was 2009. A colleague had told me that Jeff Turner, based in Santa Clarita, California, was the emerging world authority on the effective use of digital media in the real estate profession.

Naturally, I followed Jeff online and soaked up the wisdom he shared. The dude was smart, clearly respected and definitely skilled. He had a multifaceted knowledge of all things digital and real estate that was underpinned by a very apparent warmth as a good and decent human.

I was keen to meet the man in person. As luck would have it, I learned he was moderating a panel of USA real estate all-stars called "Agent 2.0" at an NAR conference in San Diego.

Now, it's a big stretch for a start-up to stump up the cash to send a bloke to San Diego for an hour. Still, the learning opportunity was what both the business and I needed. Fast forward a few weeks, and I found myself sitting in the back row of a rapidly filling 2,000-seat auditorium in San Diego.

I could see Jeff Turner, surrounded by adoring fans. His rock star persona held true in real life. I sat for a few minutes, checking I had sufficient paper to take notes and that my digital recorder's batteries would capture the infinite wisdom that would be imparted by Jeff and his all-stars when they hit the stage.

In the moment of growing anticipation, I had a rush of blood. I thought, "Big Fella, you've just flown 10,000 miles across the globe. You've burned a bucket load of cash for this moment. Are you just gonna sit here, take copious notes and fly home, or will you walk the extra 50 metres and introduce yourself to this apparent icon?"

Of course, the natural fear when meeting one of your heroes is that they might say, "Piss off and leave me alone, mate!"

Caught up in the moment, I found myself walking past 2,000 other swooning fans to the stage. I reached out and nervously extended my hand to Jeff across a noisy room and said, "G'day, Jeff.

My name is Peter Brewer. I've come from Australia for this session. I'm really looking forward to hearing what you have to share."

To my delight, Jeff completed the handshake with warmth and, accompanied by an equally warm smile in an almost apologetic tone, said, "Welcome, Peter. I need to facilitate this panel now, but let's catch up afterwards. Is that okay?"

I quickly grabbed a seat and inhaled every word of the wisdom he and his stellar panel shared. Probably the most important thing I learned came as an answer to a question from one attendee who asked, "What do we need to do to make this digital media stuff work for us?"

The candid but weirdly reassuring response was, "We have no idea." I suspect, 17 years later, it's probably still the most honest answer given in the ever-changing landscape of digital media.

Peter and Jeff Turner at San Diego 2009 NAR Conference

After that session, of which I still have the recording, I waited outside the room for Jeff's multitude of adoring fans to dissipate and approached him again to thank him for sharing his wisdom. His handshake grip was again warm and firm, his eye contact engaging, and his interest in what I was doing back home in Australia apparently genuine. We chatted, laughed and captured a selfie for posterity and to prove to my Board that I'd actually attended the event.

This was my sliding doors moment.

Jeff and I have now become very close friends. We've stayed at each other's homes and holidayed together. We've flown across hemispheres to literally have a beer and a laugh with each other. We've shared stories of love and loss.

Taking those steps in San Diego in 2009 to introduce myself to Jeff was one of my most life-changing and career-defining walks.

Blessed by Jeff's generosity and some amazing introductions, I worked hard to build an international profile and relationships and to squeeze every ounce of information I could to better our business back in Oz.

It was common to find me up at 3:00 am working to a US clock, attending meetings with generous people happy to further enhance my knowledge and reputation.

That commitment to supercharging my knowledge and building relationships saw me recognised as an Ambassador, first for the 1.7 million-member National Association of REALTORS® and then for Inman News. I'm immensely proud to have been the first International Ambassador either brand has appointed.

I went on to hold my Inman International Ambassadorship for 9 years. It took the cruel blow of a pandemic and the cessation of international travel to ultimately close the curtain on a role I'd performed with deep conviction.

One of the challenges of being first to the market with any new concept, particularly in the real estate industry, is the industry's apathy and resistance to change. In 2009, it was a hard slog introducing the concepts of blogging, video, websites, lead generation, SEO and almost anything deemed "different" to agents who'd become addicted to letterbox-dropping recipe cards to market their skills and services.

Peter with Brad Inman

Generally speaking, real estate agents are a challenging mob when asking them to embrace new concepts. For far too many, it's become easier to sit back and moan about portals and other third-party websites over the last 17 years than it is for our profession to get off their arses to embrace a new world of opportunity and changing consumer behaviour.

I probably should be thankful. It was that apathy at all levels that spawned the further evolution of Peter Brewer 2.0. Invitations began to arrive to speak at industry events across Australia, New Zealand and in the USA as a thought leader on the topic of digital media in the real estate industry. Practitioners who had brushed it aside as a passing fad finally saw an opportunity… about 3 years after the horse had bolted!

It was the frustration of watching industry leaders blissfully ignoring the opportunities of the emerging digital landscape that fuelled my drive to seek member endorsement to run for a position on the Board of the Real Estate Institute of Queensland (REIQ), the peak industry body in my home state.

I strongly believed that some had served beyond their "Best Before" date, totally blinkered to a changing world and refuting new concepts. They had much to answer for. My life experience tells me that too many Directors occupy valuable seats at Board tables, either denying or completely and blissfully ignorant to the changing world happening around them.

It seems inappropriate to acknowledge their lack of vision. But it's only because of it that I've enjoyed the honour and privilege of serving 9 years on the Board of the REIQ, 7 as their Chair, helping our extraordinary management team modernise and digitally transform a 106-year-old organisation steeped in tradition.

My friendship with Jeff Turner, the knowledge he gave me and the networks he introduced me to back in 2009 created opportunities and a rebirth that propelled me into an exciting new chapter of my life that I'd never dreamed possible.

Life works in mysterious ways. Doors open and close. Choose which you walk through wisely.

Man down!

My favourite conferences are held in New York City and Vegas (formerly San Francisco) and run by my friend Brad Inman. Brad has been incredibly generous and given me some golden opportunities.

One such opportunity was an introduction to the real estate marketing team at Facebook in San Francisco. My impressive new Facebook friends were good people who extended a warm invitation to me to host a private tour of the Facebook campus for some of my Australian colleagues.

Facebook HQ is appropriately located at 1 Hacker Way (I kid you not), Menlo Park, about an hour south of San Francisco and a far cry from the office of my Year 10 School Career Guidance Counsellor, who'd pigeonholed me to a life of collecting trolleys at Woolies.

My colleague Steve Carroll accepted the chauffeuring duties to drive us to Facebook HQ. While Steve's choice of sporting teams leaves a lot to be desired, he's still a bloody good bloke and a genuine giver, and not just to the real estate profession. Steve has founded a charity focused on supporting and creating career and educational opportunities for young orphans in Thailand. He's a remarkable and passionate human who has already raised over 3 million dollars for his charity. So, it was no surprise that he was first to raise his hand to accept the driving duties to Facebook HQ.

The Facebook campus is impressive, and the tour shared many inner workings and the culture that drives the business. For example, the ceilings have never been completed to signal the team that the job is never finished. Also, Zuckerberg fronts a fully transparent "anything goes – no holds barred" town hall meeting at 3:00 pm every Friday.

Some may say it's all smoke and mirrors, and having a sense of cynicism about the FB behemoth is okay. I can only report on my own first-hand experience, and it's an impressive behemoth up close!

As we completed our tour de Zuck, I felt a painful click in my left knee. I brushed the twinge aside, figuring that Tara (my partner) and I had enjoyed a 15km bar crawl across the San Francisco wharves district the previous afternoon sharing a few margaritas. Maybe I'd twisted my knee doing a tequila-fueled signature dance move?

A few more steps towards the famous Facebook sign, and BAM! Man down!

My left knee locked and spasmed. The pain was crippling.

Steve Carroll suddenly went from being our chauffeur to quickly becoming my emergency paramedic. With lights flashing and car horn wailing, the whinging Pom expertly navigated us through crazy traffic back to my San Francisco hotel, swapping lanes like a drunken swimmer. It's a bloody miracle that we survived. I don't know how Steve got his driver's licence, but I have a feeling that it may have involved the back of a Corn Flakes box.

Special mention should be made of Steve's impressive 4-wheel hand brake slide performed in our makeshift ambulance across the driveway of my hotel. That's something you wouldn't have seen in a self-driving Uber!

Against all odds, Steve, the makeshift medico, had successfully delivered his pain-ridden patient back in one piece. Thank you, Steve.

On that character-building drive back, I was hit with a sinking feeling that I may have neglected to take out travel insurance.

Not wanting to publicly admit my stupidity, I quickly Googled the cost of hospitalisation and emergency knee surgery in the USA. Those searches made the solution to my quandary patently clear.

Dr Brewer preparing for an amputation. But first, lunch…

Yes, that fine Monday afternoon in San Francisco, I decided I would be performing a world-first self-amputation of my left leg under lethal anaesthetic of tequila, Starbucks eggnog and an endless loop of Andrew Bolt or Fox News political commentaries guaranteed to put anyone to sleep.

Once settled back in the room, I asked the concierge to send extra towels, 40 buckets of ice, an extra sharp cheese knife and 7 sewing kits. I then awaited the return of my trusted Nurse Tara to this impromptu operating theatre. We had much work to do.

As luck would have it, Nurse Tara arrived with a zippy mobility scooter she'd kindly hired for me. Tara said we'd been invited to a free lunch.

I quickly weighed up my options: stay in the room and cut off my own leg? Or enjoy a free lunch?

Lunch was fantastic!

I was two spoons into a delicious tiramisu when I caught the eye of fellow Aussie Peter Schravemade. Pete is a seasoned world traveller and a fount of knowledge. I embarrassingly whispered my uninsured status to Pete and sought his knowledge in the art of self-amputation.

Sadly, he knew nothing about the latter but was encyclopaedic on the former. Pete enquired who I booked my travel through. I shared that it was the card company you should never leave home without, American Express.

His response: "Mate, if you booked the whole shebang through them, you'll have cover."

I immediately heard angels sing.

A quick zip back to the hotel room on my mobility rocket, and I was on the blower to chat with my new best friends at Amex to experience the most amazing customer service.

After a quick ID and location check, I was connected to a most delightful Nurse Julie back home in Australia. She, too, was unable to provide any tips on self-amputation of a left leg. However, she did have a questionnaire that, based on the right answers, might see me repatriated to Australia on the opposite end of the aeroplane to which I'd arrived.

Nurse Julie launched into her questionnaire: "Peter, can you tie your own shoe laces?"

"I think so."

"Are you able to look after your own toileting?"

"I probably could."

"Are you able to manage getting yourself from a chair to a wheelchair?"

"In a pinch."

"Can you put on and remove pyjama pants on your own?"

"What are pyjama pants?"

After a couple more questions, Nurse Julie gave me news that caused me to start sweating bullets. A cold shiver went up my spine, and I felt nauseous.

I'm sure she's told people lots of bad news before, but this one hurt. Even today, her words wake me in fright.

Friend, brace yourself. Feel the terror as I repeat her heartless response:

"Peter, based on your answers, I can arrange for you to be repatriated to Australia in a flat-bed Business Class seat this Saturday night. Unfortunately, however, based on your answers, I'm unable to provide Tara a seat in Business as your carer. She'll need to fly in Economy."

WHAT????!

Clearly, my longevity was not at the top of Nurse Julie's priority list.

I promptly considered my options:

A. I could either walk back out to the hotel lounge room and tell Tara the news that I was flying home in the pointy end but that she was still sitting in 77K, or
B. I could proceed with the self-amputation option.

Any person who honestly thinks that Option A was ever a viable and survivable option is braver than me.

My mind was racing. What should I do? How had life dealt me this card? Where could I buy a surgical knife at this time of day? Because I sure as hell wasn't delivering Option A to Tara!

With Nurse Julie still on the line and probably sensing the terror rushing through my veins, she asked, "Are you okay?" In a second of self-preservation genius, I muttered to Nurse Julie, "Do you mind asking me those questions again?"

I'm sure I could hear her smile down the phone…

"Peter," she asked again, "Can you tie your own shoelaces?"

"Not a chance!"

"Are you able to look after your own toileting?"

"Nurse Julie, I think I may have soiled myself already!"

"Are you able to manage getting yourself from a chair to a wheelchair?"

"I'm actually calling from the floor and can't get up."

"Are you capable of putting on and removing pyjama pants on your own?"

"What are pyjama pants?"

Nurse Julie's next words opened the heavens. Angels sang, harps played and trumpets heralded out a victory tune.

Peter with Nurse Tara on the repatriation flight

"Peter, Tara can join you in Business Class as your carer on Saturday night's flight home to Australia. I'll email you the tickets shortly. Will there be anything else today, Peter?"

"No thanks, Nurse Julie, you're a lifesaver. Literally!"

I never got to use the knowledge I'd gained from watching that YouTube video series on self-amputation of a left leg. But I'm quietly confident it would have been a successful procedure. Enough tequila fixes most broken things.

Everyone needs a Nurse Julie. And a Steve Carroll.

Father and he/him/she/her/they

In life, I've accepted the responsibility of 2 roles with equal parts deep appreciation and significant trepidation.

I wouldn't trade number 1 for anything, and I had no say in it, and I wouldn't trade number 2 for all it's given me.

Of course, they are the roles of "Father" and "Son".

Having been anointed with those roles, it's probably no surprise that the Cat Stevens song "Father and Son" from the legendary *Tea for the Tillerman* album has been a frequent and welcome visitor at various intersections of my life.

In 1970, Stevens, or as he later came to be known, Yusuf Islam, crafted the now-iconic music and lyrics to tell the story of a father trying to guide his son through life using the benefit of his wisdom and a son trying to find his own way, not ready to heed his father's lessons.

My relationship with my dad was like most other young men. Dads of my era had strong views on how you should live your life. At various times, for which I can only now enter a plea of stupidity, I'd combine fluctuating testosterone levels with being an obnoxious, disrespectful teenager. The result invariably meant that one of Dad's trademark "attitude adjustments" was soon headed my way. In our house, an "attitude adjustment" meant a swift kick in the arse.

Finding your way as a youngster can be bloody hard.

My life experience tells me it's probably similar for both boys and girls. Having now been on both sides of the fence as a father and a son, I can share that it's equally frustrating regardless of your lot.

Being a father comes with no instruction manual. I literally turned from being a self-absorbed boozehound with a selfish view of my "entitlements" to being handed a 7-pound bundle of joy on November 4, 1990. Fittingly also a Saturday. Along with Michelle, our son Sam's wonderful mum, the responsibility of feeding, teaching, changing, counselling and nurturing this amazing bundle had just been thrust into my nervous, unskilled arms.

The lack of relevant qualifications to carry out any significant role would be a constant companion in my various careers. Fortunately, I'm an eternal optimist, and I've successfully pursued each life role with passion, belief and exuberance.

I've experienced euphoric moments, but bearing witness to the birth of my 2 beautiful children is the most magical of my life. The care and support in the hospital after birth is comforting. Nurses and midwives at your beck and call. Doctors check in every hour. Your partner and baby are safe and cared for.

Then, suddenly, someone in a lab coat shoves a discharge form under your nose and points you in the direction of the door to the real world outside. No more doting nurses or doctors.

Congrats! You're a father. Have fun. Enjoy that nerve-racking drive home!

As fathers, we fumble through the role and give it our best shot. Sometimes, we nail it; sometimes, we stumble short of the winner's post; and sometimes, we fail our responsibilities miserably.

The responsibility and the pressure to suddenly be a provider has its challenges, but I found myself willing to do anything to protect my bundles of joy. Thirty-four years later, the same feeling. Never stand in the way of this father and his flock.

There are 5 people you never want to disappoint in life: your mum, your dad, your partner and your own kids. *(And, of course, Wayne Bennett. I'd never want to disappoint Wayne. That disapproving glare from the veteran coach is gutting.)*

No father of sound mind ever purposefully seeks to disappoint their children.

By virtue of not owning my life actions, I can attest that the intense pain of feeling the disappointment and wrath of 4 of the above 5 is deeper than any physical torture one could impart on another. Losing the respect of the most important people in my world, the people I'd dedicated half of my life to supporting and living for, took me to some very dark places.

There was a period I won't dwell on that earned me the wrath of my trusting children. I failed their expectations of me, and I created hurt for them and their wonderful mum.

I've found that when "outsiders" hurt you, it's expected and easily gets brushed aside. But when those close to us create the hurt, the cut is 10 times deeper, 100 times more painful, and can take 1,000 times longer to heal.

Those self-inflicted tough times provided me with a wake-up call that, while incredibly painful to endure, reset my focus on restoring their faith in me and fulfilling my responsibility of being there for them rain, hail or shine as their dad.

As fate would have it, the aforementioned Yusuf Islam was levitating his way to Brisbane on his magic carpet to perform a stage show.

The song "Father and Son" was to tap me on the shoulder again as it had with my dad and me. It was now with my son and me.

There's something special about this song.

The master musician's words of wisdom, delivered in his trademark tone of a blend of equal parts storyteller and soothsayer, set a scene.

> *It's not time to make a change*
> *Just relax, take it easy*
> *You're still young, that's your fault*

There's so much you have to know,
Find a girl, settle down
If you want, you can marry
Look at me, I am old
But I'm happy
I was once like you are now
And I know that it's not easy
To be calm when you've found
Something going on

No words need to be spoken between a father and son when Yusuf's strumming guitar strikes up. It's a silent nod, a unifying virtual acknowledgment that I'm picking up what you're putting down, even across a sometimes awkward generational divide.

Yusuf's decision to come to Brisbane left me with 2 predicaments: would my Sammy want to come along, and if so, how quickly could I secure tickets?

As if a sign from the universe, I received a text from Sam telling me he'd seen an ad that Yusuf was coming to Australia and, heartwarmingly, asking if I wanted to go.

That text sorted out predicament number 1, and I sorted out number 2 in a heartbeat. We secured seats with a commanding view of the artist formerly known as Cat Stevens sitting mid-stage before us on a set that resembled a warm and homely family living room. It was just Sammy and me, casually gathered around the master storyteller's living room for an intimate chat with him and 12,000 new friends.

He played his way through his impressive repertoire that transcends generations, song by song, pitch-perfect, with a voice that's gained added wisdom in its soothing tone as the years ticked by. In the dim concert light, I saw my Sam singing along. I, too, was subjecting the intimate gathering to the torture of my less-than-tuneful tones. Anticipation built as each of his hits ticked. 11,998 of us became a bit more excited as we got closer to the banger hit we'd come to experience.

The room lights dimmed. You could hear a pin drop.

And then Yusuf struck the first magical chords that heralded the ageless classic, "Father and Son". His melodic genius delivered soul-soothing goodness to enamoured, entranced and now enchanted souls.

In an emotion-filled auditorium, 12,000 people united in voice for 4 minutes and 21 seconds of love. Each exuded their unique story of pain, love, loss and happiness they've lived over time in their cars, lounge rooms or at family events, be they sombre moments, moments of success or moments of peace and reflection.

I could feel the glow of Sam's smile in my periphery as he mouthed the song's opening lyrics. Deep in the moment, tears welled in my eyes. And in a moment I will carry in my heart for the rest of my days, I felt Sam's light, warm, reassuring touch. A kind of "check in" that all between us was okay.

Sam is an incredibly impressive young man who, I believe, if DNA-tested, would show an abundance of his mum's kind and caring genes and a very small dash of mine. He's a wonderful husband, loving dad, tireless worker and highly respected for his business and people management prowess.

Lauren, Sam and Peter Brewer

He's a humble and reluctant but very capable leader. He's a team player who will step up if required, but he's not one to pursue the limelight. He's a considered thinker with great perspective. In fact, it's not uncommon for me to bounce various personal or business concepts past Sam in a bid for a balanced, objective, contemporary perspective.

He was my closest confidant and sounding board through the emotion-charged challenges of administering his nanna's (my mother's) estate and demonstrated maturity beyond his years. I'm incredibly proud of the human he's become.

Fatherhood to a wonderful son is one thing. Fatherhood to a daughter is another.

My daughter Lauren was named with some solid influence from the beautiful Betty Joan Perske. Where does that connection come from? How does Betty Joan Perske provide any possible naming reference to Lauren Anne May Brewer? You might even be going to Google right now to find out who Betty Perske is!

Well, my Friend, if you can't answer that question, you'll never be a partner of mine at a trivia event.

Betty Joan Perske was the birth name of one of Hollywood's most magnificent leading ladies, Ms Lauren Bacall. Therefore, it shouldn't take long to work out that my son Sam's moniker is derived from Lauren Bacall's partner of many years, the wonderful Humphrey Bogart, a pairing of Hollywood stars described as the central cast of Hollywood's greatest love story.

Clearly, we would never saddle Sam with the name Humphrey, so "play it again, Sam" became a very simple choice. Sam shares one of his middle names with me because I'll never let a chance go by, and the other, Thomas, as a mark of deep respect to his mum Michelle's grandfather, for whom she was very fond and had a deep respect.

Lauren shares her middle name, Anne, with her mum. Her other middle name, May, is a hat tip to my mum's mum.

And so, with the genes of those fierce and determined women fuelling her veins, there was never a doubt that Lauren Anne May Brewer would leave an indelible mark on anything she set her sights on.

Her courage to pack up and move to the other side of the world in her 20s to start a new life illustrates her adventurous spirit. Her commitment to completing her university degree is a further testament to her tenacity to grow her skills.

One of the many, many things I love about my wonderful daughter is the rock she's been for me when my roads have been bumpy.

I also love her beautiful heart. She's been absolutely committed to supporting and being a bestie for her mum and me, is conscientious enough to look after her personal well-being and isn't afraid of sharing the occasional vegan recipe. She is a generous donor and regular volunteer at Rosie's Youth Mission, a mobile soup kitchen that provides sustenance and support to people living and sleeping rough. To top it off, she is an incredible rescue mum to a gorgeous, gangly greyhound named Tigger.

Lauren has already created a significant mark in the Australian real estate community. She's made a name for herself on her terms and based solely on her ability to build relationships.

It's funny how life progresses; the clock ticks and the wheel of life turns.

There was a time early in my real estate career when people would say, "Oh, you must be Iris Brewer's son."

Several decades later, people would meet Mum at an event and say, "Oh you must be Peter Brewer's mother."

It was the same with Lauren and me. In the early days, I'd introduce Lauren at industry events as my daughter.

Today, I love that Lauren has stamped her authority in our profession across Australia. It's now not uncommon for people to say to me, "Oh, are you Lauren Brewer's dad?"

How good to witness the passing of the baton!

As life has progressed, I've tried hard to be a better dad. I still struggle, though.

Who knows what's right or wrong? How much do you inject into your children's lives? Do they actually want you hanging around? They've got busy lives, families and partners of their own.

Is it enough to be on speed dial?

I have no idea.

I keep searching for that elusive manual on how to be a good dad. No one seems to have a copy. So, in its absence, I'll continue to bumble along and be there for my brood.

I'm very proud of their values, work ethic and depth of passion for social responsibility.

I have 2 wishes:

1. I wish Yusuf Islam had written a closing verse to his classic to tell me how the rest of the story is meant to unfold.
2. Given that I never received a manual to teach me how to master the job of "Dad", I think it'd be unkind for anyone other than me to hold a scorecard and rate my performance in the role when my final bell tolls.

In the meantime, I'll keep doing the same thing I've been doing since they tumbled off their first bike, had their hearts broken for the first time, kicked or threw their first goal, had their heart broken for the second time, drove a car for the first time, got their first pet, said goodbye to their first pet or needed to be flown home from another city or hemisphere.

I'll keep topping up their jars with unconditional love and the occasional fistful of dollars.

Am I doing it right? I really have no idea. But I'll keep fudging my way along at this unique thing called fatherhood.

Just as Yusuf Islam says in his timeless classic:

> "Look at me, I am old, but I'm happy."
>
> Cat Stevens (Yusuf Islam)

She is risen

When I commenced writing this memoir, Mum was in hospital in Brisbane recovering from a series of falls and surgeries and was in a fight for her life. She spent several weeks in the ICU in an unconscious state, her clock counting down quickly.

The prognosis dictated a conversation needed to be had with her doctor about sustaining her life or letting her go to the next place. The doctor, a very direct chap, seemed immune to the enormity of the message he was delivering. It was delivered like his daily coffee order as I stood with Mum's partner Graham at the foot of her bed in the ICU.

In an insensitive, matter-of-fact way, he told us he was very good at sustaining life but that sometimes "life" doesn't carry the word "quality" as its companion.

Mum's late-in-life partner Graham is a truly caring, old-school gentleman. We continued a bedside conversation about what the charismatically-challenged doctor thought Mum would want. By that point, Mum had been in bed, seemingly lifeless with little change and little sign of hope. Machines beeped as they breathed for her. Her nutrition was delivered intravenously, and her eyes only occasionally flickered. She hadn't communicated any emotion or expression for almost a week.

The doctor continued, "I can keep her alive, but she'll be spending the rest of her days in a vegetative state in a nursing facility."

And with those words, it was as if the Lord Jesus Christ had rolled back the rock at Easter.

In a comeback for the ages, Mum sat bolt upright in her bed and shared these immortal words: "I'm *not* going to a nursing home!"

She then returned to her apparently comatose state. Shocked, I could only muster, "She is risen."

Mum was a fighter and was clearly up for the fight at that stage. Having been told she wouldn't be strong enough to come home for 2-3 hours for Christmas lunch, she mustered all her strength to defy the odds, a look of determination shining in her eyes.

Her frail 40-kilo body was hooked up to more drips than a government flat. Her left ankle was in a moon boot after metal plates were inserted after a fall in the hospital, and her back ached from spine surgery 2 weeks prior. Yet, she managed to defy almost every prediction the doctors made.

Fighting the pain crippling her tiny, malnourished body, she repeatedly lifted herself from the bed onto a walking frame, on one leg, and then back to the bed again. All the while, I watched the determination and focus building in what had been her sunken, fading eyes for the last 6 weeks. The lights were coming back on.

Mum's determination was growing. After all, she was a consummate performer, known across Australia for her musical talent. She'd started her illustrious singing career at the age of 14 with Peter's Pals, a live radio program of her time. A lady of the stage, she had entertained countless crowds on radio and theatre stages and in clubs across the country until her dying days. She must have heard the famous rallying call that drove her career a thousand times before: "It's showtime!" Each day, she fought harder than the physiotherapist asked her to, and, like the show lady she always was, she topped it off with a final encore.

(What is it about stage performers and bloody encores?!)

Mum was a fighter with zero interest in closing the final curtain. That time and place would be completely on her terms.

It ain't over 'til the skinny lady sings!

PART 2

PB's Life Lessons

Wait 'til your mother gets home!

It'll come as no surprise to many who know me that I may have been a challenging teenager. Fortunately for me, I was blessed with 2 incredibly loving parents who gave me more licence to be me than most other kids got. Unwittingly risking all kinds of mayhem, they encouraged me to explore my individuality.

As those troublesome teenage years marched on, I started to realise that being a serial pain in the posterior was probably a poor long-term life strategy. Fortunately, the rebellious Peter disappeared. I began to develop some self-awareness and appreciation of the privilege, freedom and latitude I'd been afforded.

Parents influence our formative years, guiding us through life and, at various waypoints, giving us a clip round the ear or kick in the bum to tweak our moral compass back to the North.

The thought of disappointing them would cause fear sweats and an elevated heart rate. *(This may well be the source of my atrial fibrillation, which causes my heart rate to stop and start like a dodgy Leyland P76.)*

My mum and dad weren't the parents who flogged us for our poor life choices. However, the fierce glares of disapproval I'd receive when my "intelligence and actions" became misaligned would melt the hardest of hearts. Those deathly stares of disappointment from Mum and Dad rarely needed any words. You knew when a line had been crossed, and if you valued your survival, it wouldn't happen again.

I clearly recall incurring Dad's wrath after he'd gifted me his typewriter so I could further my early-teens passion for news and politics.

At age 14, despite my lack of interest in the classroom, I was deeply interested in all things relating to current affairs and a functioning society. I'd flick through the morning and afternoon newspapers daily and be glued to the evening news and current affairs TV shows. I'd often sit in my room authoring my own editorial piece on the daily news on Dad's hand-me-down typewriter.

I should also confess to having had a slight preoccupation with other more colourful journals that testosterone-fuelled boys procured in discrete brown paper bags "for the articles". So, for a short period, my typewriting diversified into authoring some more risqué and creative prose.

On one occasion, I made the rookie error of leaving a partly completed "man-uscript" sitting in the locked jaws of the rusty old typewriter. There was no such thing as password-protected docs in those dark ages. The only private folder was in your third drawer, hidden under an untouched copy of the New Testament.

Unfortunately, on this occasion, I'd made a classic *faux pas*. Dad often sat at my typewriter and enjoyed reading my take on the day's news. Finding a handwritten note from him at the bottom of my work wasn't uncommon. It was recognition I really enjoyed. But on this particular Sunday night, I returned home to find Dad's usual "Great work Pete – 9/10" replaced by a two-word signed critique of my X-rated creativity:

Bloody Disgusting
DJB

I struggled with disappointing Dad my entire life. He had high expectations of his family and himself. Needless to say, that was the last saucy story emanating from the trusty old typewriter. The love of writing continued, but the themes changed.

In so many families, the afternoon catch-cry of, "Wait 'til your father gets home!" is one of life's reality checks on decisions made without full committee approval.

In my case, it was, "Wait 'til your mother gets home." That's not to say Dad wasn't a strict parent. In fact, at various stages, his glare was reminiscent of "the Dennis Lillee stare", a much-feared trademark of the great Australian fast bowler coming in off his long run. It was a look that terrified a generation of quivering Pommy batsmen. A pissed off look from Dad could instil terror in my heart.

Dad could certainly be a force of nature. But in my family, Mum was the influencer (yes, we had them back then, too) for whom you'd move heaven and earth to not disappoint. Mum had *chutzpah*; she exuded extreme confidence. She wasn't cocky or arrogant, just focused, unwavering and a force to be reckoned with.

Yep, that was Mum. Strong and forthright. Intent. Fearless. Fair.

Iris and Peter at age 17

Radio is the theatre of the mind

I've always been fascinated by the power of a great radio broadcaster.

Australia has some incredibly talented radio personalities. My top 10 from the modern era of broadcasting include, in no particular order, John Laws, Alan McGilvray, John Miller, Rod Tiley, Peter Dick, Ray Hadley, Spencer Howson, Norman May, Greg Cary and Wayne Roberts.

Each of those icons had a distinctive style. They're all great broadcasters in my eyes, primarily because they excel at storytelling, perfecting the art of well-timed humour, capturing the imagination, digging deeper when the moment requires, exuding passion for a cause and often challenging my own thinking.

I reckon we've all listened to an interview and found ourselves screaming at the radio for the presenter to ask the bleeding obvious question that their guest has just dropped in their lap. A skilled broadcaster knows the immense power of using the right words and, sometimes more powerfully, using no words.

Most importantly, great broadcasters are well-researched, well-versed, respectfully fearless, fair and prepared to do what it takes to extract the gems from their subject. Sadly, many of those skills are disappearing. DJs with deep or giggly voices and shock jocks shrilling fake outrage on almost every topic are sadly taking over the airwaves.

I'm not sure where I first heard the phrase, "Radio is the theatre of the mind." In the hands of a great broadcaster, it's a really apt term. It could have been Richie Benaud, Alan McGilvray or Norman May who once told an emerging commentator that the best way to call the great game of cricket was to imagine you're explaining it to a blind person. Truly gifted radio storytellers really can create theatre for the mind.

From my early days, listening to and studying the power and delivery of words used by talk-back radio legends became an obsession. The greats became my constant companions, from sun-up on my car radio to shut-eye on the pocket transistor under my pillow.

I cared deeply about how the masters deployed their skills. I'd mimic their perfectly-timed pauses, accentuated tone, faster-paced delivery and strategic use of silence.

The master for me was Greg Cary. His longevity and versatility, seamlessly gliding from sport of any discipline to the politics of any country, the delicate topic of climate change, the world economy, great authors and what the Brisbane City Council is doing about Beryl from Balmoral's waste collection bin earns him, in my view, top spot on the winner's podium as Australia's most consistent and prolific broadcaster.

Greg's authority on any topic seemingly knew no bounds. Unlike many of his contemporaries, he took his craft seriously, deeply researching his interviewees. Greg's *modus operandi* proves that brilliant background research, knowledge of your subject and well-prepared questioning can lull even the most seasoned interviewee into a level of complacency a great interviewer can drive a truck through. No shock-jock fake outrage – just fair, insightful broadcasting.

Greg never sought to trap or humiliate his subjects to score a headlining "Gotcha!" moment. Instead, he used well-researched, respectful questions to allow his guests to speak their truth while allowing his audience to make their own conclusions.

Greg's early radio days brought a fresh perspective listeners loved. His popularity gave station management little choice but to elevate the young bull to co-host. He went on to host several of Brisbane's most respected radio programs over several decades, covering the most important stories of my life.

It's a testament to his balance that after 30 years, I still wouldn't hazard a guess at his personal politics. That's a tribute in itself. Greg's impact on my life is difficult to articulate.

Sadly, my 60-year, deep, passionate love affair with the radio dial is starting to tune out.

Peter Brewer, Peter Cupples, Greg Cary

The personalities with the depth and balanced interviewing style that made radio what it was for so much of my life are in decline. A hat tip to Hadley, Howson, McDonald and Formica, Mark Levy and the evergreen professional, Peter Psaltis, who continue to fly a fledgling flag for their craft.

I'm forever thankful for the gift of radio and how it shaped my mind and life.

> "I prefer radio to TV because the pictures are better."
>
> Alistair Cooke

I'd rather die than speak in public!

Firstly, let me say, be careful what you wish for!

There's no doubt that the nerves, cold sweats and rush of debilitating fear that goes hand-in-glove with speaking in public can be a terrifying thing for many. I'm with Mark Twain when he said: "There are only two types of speakers in the world. 1. The nervous, and 2. Liars". Those almost crippling fears of facing an audience certainly found a comfortable home inside me for the first two thirds of my life.

In my experience, we've all been there – gripped by a fear so strong it can send even the most confident, capable experts into the foetal position under a desk.

I've tried most of the suggested remedies to defeat the beast on my shoulders. But given that my audiences have, in the main, been middle-aged real estate people, the thought of imagining them all sitting naked in front of me is equally, if not more, horrendous than the phobia of speaking in public.

It's kinda crazy that we can be well-credentialed industry experts on our topic, presenting to a group who are clueless about what we have to share, and yet we can still be intimidated.

The brain is a powerful thing! It can convince us that the one or 1,000 people sitting in front of us with arms folded have the words "go on, impress me, fat man" etched on their foreheads. The reality is that there is no such thing etched on their foreheads, but that pesky inner voice keeps fuelling the fear.

I do need to make one qualification. Occasionally, you come across audience members with blank stares and deathly looks who you're pretty sure would benefit from an internal pep talk from their brains to remind their faces that they're not dead yet!

In my very early days, the very thought of having to stand in front of an audience, with or without a microphone, was enough to have me searching for the exit sign at the back of the room and planning my prompt escape. It became a crazy conundrum for me, and to a much lesser degree, it still is today.

To make matters worse, I've continued to offer myself for industry leadership roles. Talk about taunting myself! I knew I had a deep passion for particular issues or organisations, and I could elicit my thoughts well in writing. But when the need to stand and speak my piece in public came, I became almost crippled with fear.

The final straw came at my son Sam's 18th birthday party. We'd assembled around 30 of his mates to celebrate his coming of age at a local hotel. Lots of mirth and frivolity abounded.

As the evening marched on, we cracked the cork on a bottle of "Samuel" port that had been safely stowed since Sam's birth. Much merriment ensued, and then, in an unscripted and totally unanticipated moment, someone looked at me and shouted the words that still throw my heart into palpitations, "Speech, PB!"

Suddenly, 30 sets of eyes were on me with longing looks of anticipation at what pearls of infinite wisdom I'd prepared for this momentous evening of celebration.

The call of "Speech" echoed further across the room. It gathered momentum from Sam's mates. My heart raced faster. The beads of sweat formed on my brow and made their way down my cheeks.

Instinctively, my highly trained eyes performed their now habitual and laser-like sweep of the room, searching for that exit sign. Fight or flight kicked in. It was my beautiful son's 18th birthday, so "flight" was immediately removed as an option.

Silence fell across the room as I got up and took to the floor. Somehow, I managed to mumble some words of love and support for Sam and called on all present to raise a glass to our wonderful young man.

In retrospect, it probably wasn't a bad speech, but it most certainly wasn't my best. And in my view, it certainly wasn't fitting for the occasion.

I left the party that night with a fierce commitment to eliminate the butterflies that had plagued me for so long and beat my paralysing fear of public speaking once and for all. I was determined that I would be able to approach any stage or gathering in future with confidence and command.

Years on, I was chatting to a speaking friend, and a person of great inspiration in my life, Winston Marsh, about whether he still experienced butterflies when he spoke in public after a 50-year speaking career.

"Brewer, I absolutely still get butterflies in my stomach every time I speak on a stage. But these days, I've taught the little bastards to fly in formation."

Winno's wise words still carry me through today when I start to glance around the room for that bloody exit sign.

Each time I walk onto a stage these days, I'm armed with a couple of light-hearted remarks that have become my trademark. My opening almost always begins with, "Thank you for that wonderful introduction, and may I take this opportunity to say that your very kind and warm introduction is, without question, the most recent." It's a gag that usually gets a few chuckles and smiles from the audience. More often than not, I'll also add, "I can't wait to hear what I've got to say today! It could be fascinating."

Neither of those gags is about getting the audience onside. They're 100% about me trying to create an ice-breaker and flush out some friendly faces to connect with. Once I've secured those first few smiling faces, I work hard to build the number of smiles across the room. Getting a smile on the dial of the hardest nut to crack in the room becomes a personal challenge.

My job is to share valuable information and the occasional snippet of wisdom. It's what the client has paid me to do. I owe it to them, and I 100% owe it to myself to fight those debilitating inner voices that taunt me. When it comes down to it, I remind myself that I'm a well-researched subject matter expert on the topic I'm presenting. I'm providing valuable information that will help them, and most will walk away with copious notes and ideas. I also remind myself that most of the people in that room would apparently rather die than swap places with me at that moment.

Now, please excuse me. I've got an exit sign to find.

> "A wise man speaks because he has something to say; a fool speaks because he has to say something."
>
> Plato

A fabulous head for radio!

Even before my time chatting about real estate on Brisbane's airwaves, people would often ask if I was on the radio. Many said I had a fabulous head for it. I certainly had a passion for it, and I'd studied hard to craft some of the skills of the great radio voices. The pause, pitch, accentuation, calculated silence and varying speed of delivery became skills I worked into my living room presentations and negotiations in real estate and later in my life when speaking on stages. The power of voice isn't properly appreciated.

One of the greatest opportunities I received came from Ross Davie, a radio icon in Brisbane in the 80s-00s. Ross and I had built a good friendship through real estate transactions and fundraising work we did for the National Breast Cancer Foundation. He was the comedy component of the 4BC breakfast show, partnering with now sadly deceased Brisbane journalist and documentary maker John Miller.

Ross asked me to comment on the state of the property market on that breakfast show. The topic was right in my wheelhouse and allowed me to experience firsthand the adrenaline rush of live radio that I craved. I promptly accepted the opportunity and decided to deal with my fear of public speaking later.

Ross and John nurtured me through what was meant to be a one-off interview beautifully by asking simple questions to boost my authority with the audience, adding lots of oohs and aahs at my apparent pearls of wisdom and giving me reassuring nods and smiles that boosted my confidence as we chatted.

I recall walking out of the studio that morning thinking it was quite possible, bordering on probable, that I would receive a call from 4BC management offering me my very own show! In my ears, a star was born. *(Yes, I was a dreamer then, too.)*

Radio Days with John Miller and Ross Davie – 4BC

The phone call from management never happened, but Ross did call me again, asking me to present a weekly slot in the John and Ross breakfast show, chatting about the weekend's real estate market. I grabbed the opportunity.

The duo were easy to chat with, and our chemistry was exceptional. We laughed often and raucously. Good chemistry in radio lifts people. It energises both those delivering and those receiving.

We certainly knew how to take the proverbial out of each other.

For instance, live on air, John would refer to my regular fishing trips to Fraser Island with a dozen drunken hooligan mates as community work mentoring troubled young men.

"Good morning, Peter. Firstly, congratulations on what you're doing up there with those troubled young men. Tell us, what's happening in the real estate market this week?"

I'd then attempt to answer from a phone booth without snorting or spilling my beer while those "troubled youths", aka my mates, waved various parts of their anatomy at me.

John was an excitable and exuberant chap with an impressive little black book compiled from years of making exceptional TV documentaries, working as a career journalist and presenting TV current affairs.

He often used his vast connections to assist people in need. On one occasion, he convinced our then-Premier, Peter Beattie, to donate 30 minutes of a one-to-one chat in his Ministerial suite for an auction. No aides or other advisers were allowed. Just Premier Pete and the highest bidder.

John opened the bidding on day one of the 5-day auction at $5,000, apparently with a bid he had received from an unnamed businessperson. That bid sat unmoved for the next 4 days.

Two weeks after John's auction, I was summoned to the station manager's office. I wondered if this was the lucky break I'd hoped for. Was radio veteran John Laws retiring? Did they need a fresh-faced, under-50 expert to attract a younger demographic?

The station manager entered the room. Known for his directness, he simply said, "Peter, is there any reason why you haven't honoured your $5,000 bid for the chat with Premier Beattie?"

After I regained my breath, I replied, "I haven't paid $5,000 because I hadn't actually bid $5,000. That'd be why. Is this a gee-up?" I searched the room for hidden cameras.

It turns out that John's opening bid was a dummy starting bid, offered in the hope that bidding would reach $10,000 or more for his charity. However, it was to be the one and only bid. No such bidder actually existed. When John was put under the pump on who the unpaid bid was from, he offered one name: mine.

That afternoon, I delivered $3,000 in cash to the radio station and left with John's left testicle in a pickle jar. John had been a good friend, and his intentions to help a charity were honourable. I figured I could use the tax deduction. Plus, John's pickled left nut made a wonderful talking point sitting on my office desk!

My "prize" of a 30-minute one-to-one with Premier Peter Beattie blew out to 2 hours of conversation, which reached into the early evening with our feet up on teak desks, sipping several of Milton's finest while watching the sunset on our beautiful river city. Premier Pete went on air the following week and glowingly praised me as a great bloke and a wonderful Queensland businessman. That I continue to dine out on that story today makes that $3,000 the best tax-deductible personal marketing I could ever imagine.

Ross and John's confidence in me instilled a belief that I had something valuable to say and a voice that could deliver that value well. I became a regular on the 4BC breakfast show, and then a dedicated Friday spot was added. Over the months ahead, the station also added me to weekend programming across the network.

That "one-off" interview with Ross and John grew to 3 hours a week of live radio on Brisbane's top-rated talkback station for 6 years.

I never asked for or received a cent for the time I gave. Frankly, I often contemplated how I wasn't paying 4BC for the opportunity to craft some skills I was passionate about. I gained massive exposure to an incredibly loyal listener base, generating a valuable volume of business and helping me build relationships in media, sports and politics that I still hold today.

Over those 6 years, we helped hundreds of people "off-air" with their real estate challenges. We righted many wrongs and saved good people hundreds of thousands of dollars from scams and swindles by just giving good, honest advice. Those are the best rewards of that fun but fleeting chapter of my life.

Do I miss the rush of live radio? Absolutely! But I'm forever thankful for 6 of the most entertaining and rewarding years of my life.

Peter with 4BC Drive Host Chris Adams

Stay with me, caller!

People buy people

I've always prided myself on my passion for various causes, organisations and people. And at the risk of pumping my own tyres up, I've enjoyed some wonderful feedback from business colleagues, friends, clients and event organisers about the passion my presentations exude.

When I convey my passion, you can be assured it's 100% real, born of a genuine conviction and delivered with the absolute best intentions from my heart. Over time, it's become a trademark of my business and personal brand that I'm very proud of. It's a quality that makes me a horrible poker player.

It may be a value I inherited from my mum as a stage performer and community worker. It may stem from a strong desire to help people be the best version of themselves that they can be. It's probably a hybrid of a few things.

During my career, from the moment I walked on stage or into a client meeting or a boardroom and saw people's eyes light up, my blood would start to pump a little faster, my energy would lift, and my passion would kick in. I'd become even more intent on delivering a powerful message and sending at least one participant home with renewed enthusiasm, embracing a new concept or positively contemplating their business or life direction.

I once received a brief from a client who wanted my annoying enthusiasm to help encourage 150 staid and conservative 55+-year-old real estate agents at a conference in Rotorua, New Zealand, to embrace the new opportunities of the digital world. At the time, the adoption of technology in real estate in NZ was minimal.

Challenge accepted!

After a generous introduction, I was fairy-clapped onto the stage to be welcomed by a sea of unimpressed conservative faces. It seemed most had already formed a cynical view that no 60-year-old smart-arse Aussie was going to teach them about marketing in the new world. In fact, I think they'd have been much happier to have had someone on stage talking about letterbox drops, door-knocking scripts and "the good old days".

On the rare occasion I've experienced that body language from audiences, I've faced it with an even stronger conviction to make a difference. I decided that I hadn't travelled all this way for a fucking fairy clap. Game on!

I launched into overdrive, drawing on everything I'd learned in radio, negotiations and working a room. Their apparent ambivalence had fuelled a fierce determination that I was gonna uncross some folded arms and wake them from their 1980s comfort zone by putting on a performance that would leave them wanting more.

Peter at home on a stage

I gave it my absolute all: effective use of voice, tone, modulation, pause to elicit a point, strategic use of awkward silence, high animation, bold hand and body gestures, warm smiling with my eyes and enquiring head tilts at some of the more interesting responses to the challenges I posed. All humility aside, it was an impressive stage show, and I was proud to have delivered it.

I received a standing ovation at the end of my presentation that day – a rare accomplishment for a speaker at a real estate conference, particularly to an audience of 55+ men more attuned to fairy-clapping!

I levitated from the room, proud that I'd delivered on the client's brief and confident that I'd converted a healthy percentage of the participants to adopt some of the opportunities in the brave new digital world.

On the long drive back to Auckland Airport, I received a phone call from the organisation's chairman.

The call went a little like this:

Chairman: "Brewer, that was fucking magnificent! We couldn't have asked for any better! You absolutely fucking nailed it, bro!"

Me: "Wow, thanks, AJ! I really appreciate the feedback! Do you think the message hit home? Do you think that helped challenge their thinking on the new world?"

Chairman: "Nope, they have no fucking idea what you were talking about, but they fucking loved your energy and passion. It was amazing! Thanks, bro!"

<click>

The lesson? People won't always buy what you're selling, but they will always appreciate what's in your heart!

People buy people. Let your passion shine.

What's your definition of average?

In one of my favourite real estate workshop presentations, I invite participants to share their last "WOW" experience as a consumer. It could be anything – the last time they ordered a cup of coffee, bought a TV or just a random moment in their day when a person made them go "WOW".

I'm usually met with a long silence and a lack of inspiring customer service tales.

When I share my frustration with this apparent lack of stand-out customer service experiences, a room full of heads nod in exasperated agreement.

But here's where things get awkward.

I then flip the question to my audience: "When was the last time YOU made someone go 'WOW'?"

I challenge them to share their magnificent point of difference. I'm digging to understand why I should choose them over a bazillion other people in their field. In a real estate transaction, that could mean $50,000 in commission.

In sales, customer service or marketing, where people are paid for their ability to sell something, market a product or service or solve a problem, you'd think this should be a pretty simple question. Sadly, I've continually found it to be the reverse.

Have we been conditioned into swimming in a vast, unimaginative sea of blandness? Or are we just afraid to poke our heads out of the trench and proudly share that unique WOW factor that makes us special?

I've never understood why people and businesses settle for providing "average" service. It's not rocket science. Find out what your customers want and deliver significantly above it.

If the goal is to separate someone from their hard-earned money, why not make that experience memorable and give them a reason to enjoy it, rave about it to others and return? Wash, rinse, repeat.

Sadly, the concept of delivering a genuinely good experience seems to have gone out of vogue. Nowadays, even just extracting a friendly smile from a retail worker can be cause for celebration as an above-average experience.

My good mate Winno, who also happens to be a marketing genius and one of the best public speakers and podcasters I know, perfectly defines the word "average".

He says average is "the best of the worst, or the cream of the crap".

It's a definition that's worthy of self-reflection by us all. Ask yourself: Do I make people go "WOW"? Or is my offering average? Am I just the best of the worst?

Businesses spend millions on advertising to bring customers through their physical or virtual doors, only to meet them with below-average service. It baffles me!

If only they embraced just how simple and cost-effective it is to create amazing experiences that naturally foster loyalty and a bottomless cup of repeat and referral business.

Delivering WOW experience creates "sneezers". Sneezers are people who can't help but spread positive word-of-mouth about your business, product or service. And here's the best part: sneezers are free. And as an added bonus, their word is 1,000% more believable than any boring press ad or flyer that boasts, "We're not as crap as the other guy."

Follow these 7 simple steps:

- Consider what actions would genuinely delight your customers.
- Set minimum acceptable service standards based on them.
- Set an expectation across the entire team that they are non-negotiable.
- Adopt a fi-fo* position with any team member who doesn't align with your business value of making people go "WOW".
- See your marketing expenses drop.
- Watch your business fly.
- Thank me.

*What's *fi-fo? (You'll work it out.)*

Average or awful? Woeful or wonderful? You get to choose!

Vices

One of my proudest achievements to date has been quitting smoking. I had a hateful relationship with the filthy darts from 18 to 35. I hated the way they made me lightheaded. I hated that my clothes and breath smelled like an ashtray. I despised that, against all logic, I still lined up at the newsagent each day to pay $15 of my hard-earned money to ensure I had a packet on hand. *(If you're a smoker reading this and rolling your eyes, that was a shit-load of money back then.)*

My stupidity, like the cigarettes, left me breathless at times. *(I just had to re-read that paragraph to remind myself that I really was that stupid.)*

My old mate Winston Marsh's words of wisdom would constantly ring in my ears: "It's impossible to smoke and look intelligent at the same time".

With full knowledge, I still shoved the filthy things into the hole in my face.

Today it seems unfathomable that, as a child who grew up with asthma and chronic bronchitis, I'd sometimes find myself sitting in the waiting room of the local doctor's surgery while sucking the life out of a "bunger" in the belief that the doctor would prescribe me a pill or some magic medicine to take the wheezing away.

(*Hey, I told you I was stupid.*)

Then one day, stupid became lucky. In 1993, we were pregnant with Lauren. Her impending arrival made me determined to be a responsible father. I'd started the nicotine patches and was avoiding social situations where others would be on the bungers.

Whenever I felt a craving, I'd poke myself in the eye with a fork. Okay, that part might not be entirely accurate. But I would refuse to dwell on that craving and went about immediately changing my environment.

I'd previously lacked the discipline to go cold turkey, but my desire to quit was stronger than ever this time. It's fair to say that the turkey had been slaughtered, plucked and was ready for stuffing. Fortunately, life threw that increased desire a much-needed turbo boost in the shape of a dreadful flu that belted me flat in bed for 4 weeks.

After those 4 weeks of bed-bound misery and total withdrawal of nicotine, the cycle had finally been broken. The cravings were gone, Lauren was a month closer, and for me, there was no turning back.

Through good luck and a touch of good management, I miraculously kicked the horrendous habit. My former friends Benson and Hedges would have to make their millions without my daily donation. Another 30 years on and I still haven't touched one.

I'm fortunate they have been my only real addiction.

When it comes to gambling, I'm too miserable and sceptical to wager on a dodgy pony or two flies crawling up a wall. Aside from winning $50 after sticking a quarter in a slot machine in Las Vegas, I've mixed in enough circles to know that punting is a mug's game. Your average punter rarely stands a chance.

Caffeine had me in its grip, but only for a short stint. I enjoyed the social component of sitting in a cafe with a friend or client over a coffee or 2. It made for a relaxed social setting. But in time, I was to discover that, for me, there was a fine line between usual me and the amped up me buzzing from the artificial highs from a second or third cup of coffee.

The realisation first came in the form of a listing presentation I'd been invited to give to a family selling a property in Lota. The family's decision-makers had gathered to judge the marketing prowess of the area's best real estate agents. I'd been referred to as the best in the area, and the odds of winning the listing were stacked in my favour.

I'd invited Kris, my "mini me" PA, to join me in the presentation. Kris was a smart young man. Seven years at McDonald's had made him more capable and confident than the average 22-year-old male.

I completed my presentation, confirmed the family had no questions, thanked them for their time and very confidently strutted my way to the car, self-assessing my presentation as a solid 15/10 and determining that every other agent would be wasting their time that day.

Back in the car, Kris – never backwards in giving me feedback – looked at me and said, "I've got some feedback I'd like to share."

I've always said that feedback is a gift, so I welcomed Kris's insights. What I got was a little different to what I'd expected from my number one supporter.

In an exasperated tone, Kris exclaimed, "What the fuck are you on?"

My enthusiastic response clearly demonstrated that I wasn't quick in picking up social signals that morning: "I'm on fire. I was brilliant, wasn't I!"

Quickly bringing my feet back to earth, Kris shared that he thought my presentation was horrible, that I was rambling and illegible, and that my self-confidence bordered on arrogance. He then respectfully suggested I retrace my steps this morning.

"What have you done that's different from your normal morning routine?" he asked.

I recounted that I'd met with 3 different clients in quick succession over coffee before 9.

It goes without saying that Ronald McDonald's smart-arsed love child was right. My presentation had been a caffeine-fuelled embarrassment.

Needless to say, I didn't get that listing. But I quickly (and expensively) learned that caffeine and I are not friends. I'm now an unashamed coffee snob, allowing myself one cappuccino per day before 11:00 am. And, given I'm restricted to one, it better be a good one!

And then there's that other vice – booze. Despite my long-standing reputation as the guy with a Corona in hand, I can take or leave a drink as the years march on. The recovery time from a night on the sauce has moved from hours to days, and sometimes sparkling water refreshes the temple just fine. I'd be telling porkies, however, if I didn't accept that there was a time when the demon drink could have taken me in a different direction.

I recall a conversation with my mum while "trapped" in the car with her when I was about 23. Out of the blue, Mum would sometimes suggest, "Let's go for a drive."

It took a few of these "drives" for me to realise that when Mum suggested we go for a drive, you were about to be quietly but firmly schooled inside the privacy of 4 car doors on your most recent *faux pas*.

I vividly remember one occasion being held captive in Mum's car while heading along Tingal Road at Wynnum past the ambulance station.

She subtly queried in a firm but fair tone, "Pete, do you think you might have a problem with alcohol?"

Always a skilled negotiator, Mum posed the question for my pondering instead of telling me she'd determined I had a problem with the bottle. Mum was a wicked wordsmith.

I acknowledged that while I would spend most nights and Sundays at the local RSL Club, it was to play snooker and soak up wisdom from the most delightful old gentlemen you could meet. I enjoyed their company, and they enjoyed hearing my tales. We'd drink and laugh, and as the evenings wore on, we'd embellish our achievements and glory days of wars long past. What could the harm be in that? I gained more wisdom and life lessons from those wonderful men than any university degree could ever give me.

Although it was easy for me to justify those times at the RSL to myself, Mum's words of wisdom made me realise how easy it would be for this vice to become a full-blown addiction. I became vigilant that I would never fall into the trap of becoming a barfly who saddled up to the same stool at the same time every day to talk the same crap on repeat.

These days, I still love a drink on a hot day – quite often on a cold day, too. But the days of endless Coronas and 2 am tequila shots are, for the most part, over. *(I'm sure my liver is eternally grateful.)*

In an interesting twist of fate and completing the never-ending circle of life, 40 years on, I found myself needing to have my own conversation with Mum.

Although Mum had been a proud, card-carrying member of the Temperance League for 8 decades, she had ventured into a late-in-life 180-degree turnaround. To put it as elegantly as I can, Mum wasn't spending the afternoons of her senior years "unrefreshed".

So, I had the unenviable duty of sitting with her to "have a chat". Mum was a wily beast and, despite her age and battles with small strokes, had a killer memory of people, places and events. Thankfully so! Because as I worked through how I'd have *that* conversation, I fumbled these words, "Mum, when I was about 23, you took me for a drive down Tingal Road…"

She stopped me in my tracks: "I remember it like it was yesterday, Pete." She looked at me and, in an almost apologetic tone, proffered, "Do you think I have a problem with alcohol?"

I only had to nod. Her next, seemingly nervous and bordering on remorseful words were, "I think you're right."

Just as Mum had done with me 40 years prior, I decided it wasn't my place to judge her for her late-in-life love for liquor. My role was to let her know that I knew that all was not well for her and that I was unconditionally there for her, whatever the cause of this newfound grip of the grape. Because, as many of us have come to know (often the hard way), the problem is rarely ever the problem.

I've learned – sadly a little too late – that it's not my right to judge people for their vices or addictions. We all face enormous challenges on our life journey, and each of us has a different coping mechanism. Too often, we internalise our challenges, grief and frustrations, and the channel used to deal with whatever crappy card life has dealt us is to bury ourselves deep into an addiction.

(Even work can become an addiction. At times, I buried myself in my work in a bid to escape whatever was going badly in my life and in search of validation.)

So, before you take a position of judgement on someone, think about what challenges they might be facing today. Think about what news they might have received and what might be happening in their life. And then consider how much their world might be brightened in that moment, not by indulging in another vice, but by a warm smile, words of encouragement, the warmth of a handshake or a comforting hug.

A simple act of empathy or providing a "no judgement" ear could be just what they need. As one of my favourite idioms notes, "A problem shared is a problem halved".

Pride is both wonderful and awful. Too often, we internalise our challenges instead of finding a safe space to confront our demons and deal with our vices. Often, our battles are fought solo due to our fear of being judged by others for having a weakness. Here's the thing, though: battles are fought best by armies. Who's in *your* army? Whose army can you join to help someone else win *their* battle?

Whatever your battle and whatever it is you're trying to beat, remember... you're not alone.

Put me in a cage and I'm probably gonna rattle it

It's still difficult for some people to fathom how a minimally educated kid from the burbs of Brissie found himself as Executive Chairman of one of Queensland's largest real estate marketing groups for 10 of its highest growth years, and later as Chair of that Australian business still befuddles some of my harshest critics. I certainly didn't ever have it on my bingo card waiting to be called out. But I've found that life is forever full of twists and turns if you have a mindset for helping people. Putting my apparent lack of modesty and trademark self-deprecating humour aside for a minute, in both cases, I was the right person for those jobs at those times. Right place. Right time. Right bloke.

Now, I'm the first to put my hand up to say I'm not the right person for all occasions. But if things need some shaking up, the odds are pretty strong that I'm your man. I bear no resemblance to Elon Musk in either style or values system. When Musk walks in the front door of a business, there's about to be ruthless, rampant slicing and dicing. That's not my jam. I like to think that when I'm invited in to rescue a business, I'm about 50% Gordon Ramsay and 50% me.

Sometimes, a business or organisation needs a "no BS" style of person to rock their boat. And despite my lack of a university degree or any formally recognised tertiary qualifications, I do proudly possess a diploma with high distinctions in the art of bullshit detection gained from the school of life. There's truth to the saying: "You can't out-bullshit a bullshitter".

When I'm invited into a business, it's often to help them chart a new course. Sometimes, it's just to reassure the passengers that the boat isn't sinking; other times it's to help the captain understand that he or she needs to walk the plank or to let people know that, despite some weather changes and rocky seas, which might see them knee-deep in the bilge, with a few course adjustments, everything will be okay.

That, my Friend, has become the stock-in-trade for Peter Brewer 2.0 since around 2014. Through that time, I've absolutely loved helping rescue some business owners from tough times and sometimes from themselves. It's been personally rewarding and results-focused, and it's been easy to demonstrate tangible results.

The results have often been life-changing for the organisations and businesses I've been engaged to help. I've proudly assisted good people to save their businesses, protected their family homes from needing to be sold and supported people unsuited to business to transition to another career with a fistful of cash and, most importantly, their dignity.

While on the topic of highly rewarding roles, being Chair of the peak body for my profession in the great State of Queensland, the Real Institute of Queensland (REIQ), and being continually re-elected to that Board for the maximum 9-year term and elected unopposed as Chair 7 times has been up there with my proudest life achievements.

I'm more than aware that my ongoing appointment has caused some of the staunch traditionalists to look over their horn-rimmed glasses with disdain at my agenda for modernisation. Successfully prosecuting a case for diversity, implementing significant constitutional reform and driving a digital transformation of the business has become a source of incredible personal satisfaction. It's driven an even stronger desire in me to close the book on archaic business practices and principles that should have been buried in 1985.

For too long, too many membership organisations were administered by a protected species of hierarchy that can only be characterised as male, pale and stale. Fortunately, time has moved on, and organisations are now embracing proper corporate governance principles.

I'm left with some wonderful reminders of how far we've come during my time as Chair of the REIQ.

After winning my initial election by the membership to the Board, I was ushered aside and "instructed" (threatened) that I ran a very real risk of being the subject of a "No Confidence" motion at my first meeting if I didn't wear a suit and tie. That probably should have been the first red flag that this "independent type of lad who has potential" might have a few tigers to tame.

The attempt to intimidate me and have me quietly sit in the corner was precisely the additional motivation I needed to expedite an agenda for modernisation that the membership had endorsed me to deliver on. Cages were about to be rattled. And a little louder and faster than I'd first planned.

Change isn't something a particular vintage and type of people cope well with. They're often the people who sit in exactly the same chair at every meeting. They use buzz phrases like "the need to be nimble" while turning almost apoplectic if sausage rolls are omitted from the Board's morning tea. They're the breed who express an opinion that a business needs to be modern and appealing to females and younger people, but God forbid giving our sisters a voice! They're often in their position based on outdated bylaws that made them "koalas" – a protected species – rather than on their boardroom performance.

Well-managed diversity in a boardroom is life-changing for businesses and those with open, free-thinking minds. It's one of the most rewarding experiences to witness a traditionally marginalised gender, age or interest person or group being afforded the respect to share their views and beliefs without fear of repercussions or ridicule.

Several times in 2019, when I was supporting Rob Honeycombe, a good and decent man, to prosecute a Board diversity campaign, I used the example of what the answer might be if a question about the future needs of the profession was asked of 6 conservative, aging white men. The obvious answer is pretty self-evident.

Now, would the same answer be arrived at if the same question were asked of a regionally-based female, a person under the age of 35, a city-based female, a regionally-based male and 3 others of any gender from across the state?

I'd wager that the second conversation would be much more thought-provoking and the answer way more colourful, better informed and properly representative of the entire profession.

And so, here I find myself, 9 years on, having rattled some cages, chairing a boardroom with not a single suit or tie to be seen. I celebrate that times have changed, the world has caught up, and the old guard has moved on. As a business, we've embraced diversity to ensure our conversations and strategies appropriately reflect the needs and future of our profession and digitally transformed a 107-year-old organisation.

I initially pursued a position on that Board because I held a deep belief that I could do several things:

- I could help make a difference,
- I could ensure our focus was on our relevance to our members' current and future needs, and
- Regardless of whether you're a commercial salesperson in Cairns, a property manager in Biloela, a residential salesperson on any of our coasts or a buyer's agent in Brisbane, you could truly believe that the REIQ has your back.

Finally, I wanted to ensure that others with short-sighted agendas didn't jeopardise the investment and faith we'd placed in a dynamic and passionate CEO. We found a gem with the drive, vision, passion and energy to transform the place, and I didn't want us to lose that opportunity. My job was to ensure she had clear air to drive a much-needed agenda of modernisation.

REIQ CEO Antonia Mercorella with Peter

40 years into my business career, I'm incredibly proud of what we've achieved, the changes we've driven in big and small businesses, and the cages I've rattled along the way.

If there's a fool born every minute, then I'm the man of the hour.

Never eat Nanna's famous home-grown mushrooms

I'm often asked where my love of cooking comes from. If I'm completely honest, it's something I had to learn quickly as a survival skill.

I'm not saying my mum was a bad cook. It's a lot nicer to say that, as a child of the depression, she had a penchant for maximising value from every last scrap left on a plate, several times over, if required. She also had scant regard for pesky things like use-by dates.

Mum learned her cooking skills from her mum, my nanna.

I have fond memories of Nanna. A strong country woman with a great sense of humour. When I was a young child, she once told me that she had married 4 times in her life and that all 4 husbands passed away prematurely.

Curiosity ultimately got the better of me, so I asked her the circumstances behind their untimely demise. She responded that life on the farm meant they had to make use of anything that grew in the garden. She shared that creativity was king and that sometimes she had to take risks with various plant matter to feed a big family.

Nanna continued with a gleam in her eyes. Her first 3 husbands had apparently all died as a result of eating poisonous mushrooms. A massive coincidence, I thought. Naturally inquisitive, I asked how the fourth had passed.

Nanna maintained a stoic poker face and delivered the punch line: husband number 4 died from a hammer blow to the back of the head.

Aghast, I dug further into how that tragedy came to pass. Her reply came with a wry smile. "He wouldn't eat the mushrooms," she quipped.

It was with the fear of Nanna and her mushroom story ringing in my ears, coupled with experiencing Mum's regularly served "soup" – concocted from the week's leftovers mixed in a blender with 2 spoons of Gravox (a powdered gravy base) and a cup of water – that made me determined to become self-sufficient if I wanted to live a long and happy life free from an addiction to Gaviscon and excessive sick days.

Mum could turn almost anything into a meal by adding 2 spoons of Gravox and a cup of water. Amongst her repertoire were "delicacies" such as steak and kidney, tripe with onions in white sauce, boiled chicken giblets, and Dad's favourite, liver and bacon.

I once took the family on a bonding tour of New Zealand. Mum had been through a difficult time, and we all needed some pleasant experiences after a couple of years of hell. The final day dawned. Knowing we had to drive from Queenstown to Christchurch to fly home pre-dawn the following morning, I treated everyone to a massive all-you-can-eat breakfast buffet. I'd figured that if I filled everyone's belly, we could avoid stopping for a roadhouse lunch on our 6-hour drive to Christchurch.

The buffet boasted an impressive array of foods, including some sausages that had enough spice in them to blow your head off. Everyone in our crew elected to push them aside on their respective plates in favour of something less volatile.

The drive to Christchurch was comfortable. We arrived at our motel around 5:00 pm. Once settled in, I told the crew that I was heading out to get us some fish and chips for dinner so we could get an early night to be fresh and ready for our 5:00 am flight.

"Hang on, Pete," came the call from Mum. "Don't get fish and chips. Just get a packet of Gravox."

Confused, I looked back at Mum as she was slowly retrieving 6 cold, spicy sausages wrapped in greasy red napkins from the pockets of her trench coat. Never one to waste a scrap, she'd cleaned up our morning's breakfast plates and invited them along on the drive to Christchurch!

So there you have it. My love of all things culinary comes purely as a result of seeking a long life and a fear of needing to undergo a stomach pump procedure.

I'm super proud that Sam and Lauren are excellent and creative in the kitchen. Both can confidently whip up a snack or a feast in a blink. They're critical life skills and wonderful parenting skills to share with your children. They might also be skills that save you from an early demise from a hammer blow to the back of the head!

"Part of the secret of success in life is to eat what you like and let the food fight it out inside."

Mark Twain

The bionic man

"Gentlemen, we can rebuild him. We have the technology. We have the capability to make the world's first bionic man. Steve Austin will be that man. Better than he was before. Better—stronger—faster."

In the 1970s TV series "The Six Million Dollar Man", they rebuilt a NASA astronaut who had all but expired by using a suite of bionic parts that gave him superhuman strength. Now, the rebuilds that I've encountered thus far haven't exactly made me superhuman, but taking inflation into account, I reckon the good people at Bupa Health Insurance are haunted daily by the chance that the ultimate price tag to rebuild various parts of me to keep me functioning could hit 6 million dollars too!

Mid-Covid, I, like many people, found myself with not a lot to do. Business had ground to a halt, and I had a lot of spare time on my hands. I pondered doing some renovations to my apartment, but that idea was short-lived. My family has forbidden me from ever using anything that mildly resembles a power tool again after some unfortunate incidents that might someday be revealed in a sequel to this first confessional.

I pondered other things I could do rather than twiddling my thumbs each day. Suddenly, a brainwave hit me. As history would prove, if it wasn't my dumbest idea, it certainly would earn a place on the podium.

Instead of renovating the apartment, maybe I should renovate myself!

It was no secret that many surgeons had been forced to hang up their scalpels while the spicy flu was doing its seemingly endless laps of honour around Oz.

So, I started searching for surgeons in Brisbane who hadn't bought a kombucha franchise or weren't stacking shelves at Woolies.

To my surprise, I discovered that I could book a boob job or a facelift really easily. But neither of those options would help me solve 60 years of abuse that had rendered my arthritic knees virtually useless and constantly painful.

Finally, I stumbled upon a knee surgeon who was happy to give me 2 new knees in the one theatre procedure.

The doctor described the procedure. He'd break each leg in 2 places, saw out the old joints and then superglue 2 new joints back in. What could possibly go wrong?!

As luck would have it, the operation went perfectly to plan, and 4 years later, I can attest that I'd do it all again in a heartbeat.

But there are 6 things I learned about myself, life and, surprisingly, real estate from enduring bilateral knee replacements.

I've even built an entertaining sales meeting presentation around those 6 key learnings, should you ever need a fun, high-energy presentation to give your team some perspective. Keep me on your speed dial. I'm not cheap, but I'm definitely fun.

1. Expectations

I'd been told many things in the lead-up to getting the double knee op. One thing that surprised me – but that I was fiercely holding onto – was that I'd be home 4 days after the procedure. That news came from my physio, who also assured me that there would be no need for any modifications to my apartment or chairs or shower or toilet.

And so, 4 days after the procedure, and after strictly following a rigorous, gut-busting hourly exercise routine, I was shocked and more than a little dismayed to find myself still being winched in and out of bed, bath and toilet in excruciating pain. I also struggled to put one foot in front of the other for more than a dozen steps, despite being supported by a walking frame.

That I'd failed the 4-day expectation set by my physio lapsed me into a deep depression. I lay in my bed, sobbing in pain and personal disappointment at letting myself and my team down, not even noticing the doctor entering the room.

Approaching the bed and observing my tear-stained face, he asked why I was so distraught. I explained that, in my view, there was no chance of me going home that day. I could barely lift my left cheek to fart, let alone lift my legs to walk.

The doctor looked at me quizzically and asked, "Who told you that you'd be going home after just 4 days?"

I replied that his very healthy, young, touch-footy-playing physio had set that expectation.

"Peter, I'm gonna be frank with you. You're an unfit, overweight 60-year-old, not a 20-year-old Brisbane Bronco. Mate, the only place that you're going to is St Vincent's Private Hospital rehab unit for at least the next 2, maybe 3 weeks. There was never any chance of you going home in 4 days!"

A parallel happens daily in the real estate profession, with ridiculously high and unachievable expectations put on new entrants who are none the wiser. Many career dreams have been smashed to smithereens by expectations that couldn't be lived up to. It needs to stop.

For the record, I spent just over 3 weeks domiciled in rehab, undergoing twice daily intensive physio and occupational therapy learning to walk again and significantly improving my fitness and mobility. It was never gonna turn me into the Six Million Dollar Man. But I'd never asked for that in the first place!

The lesson? Let you be the only person to set expectations. Tell everyone else to butt out.

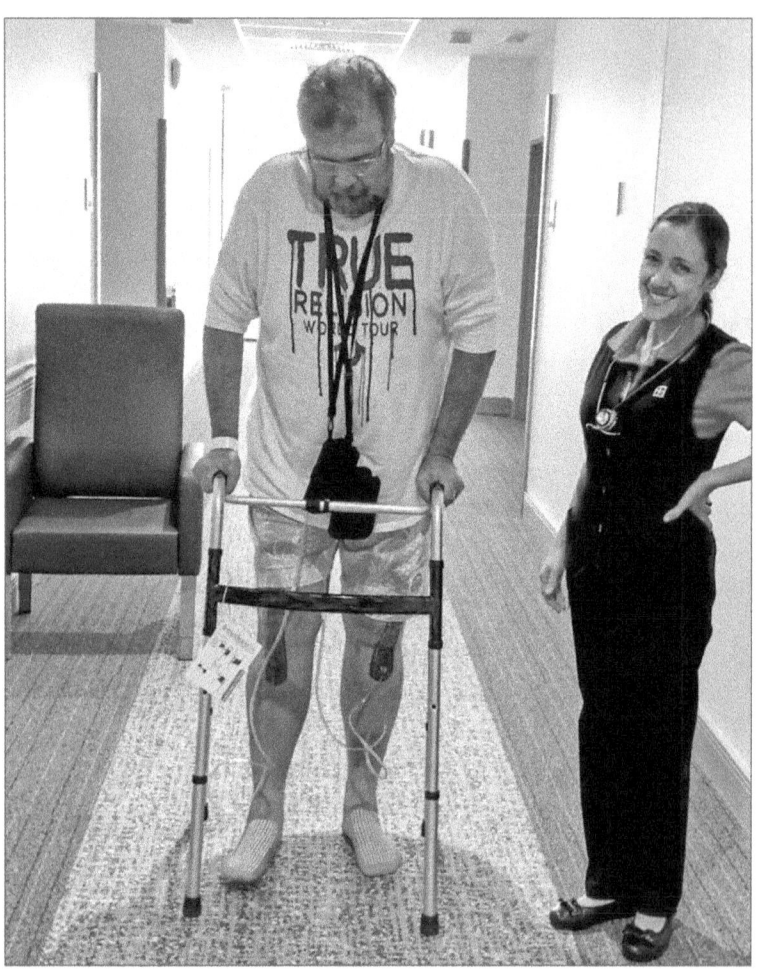

The long road to recovery.
(I'm not sure Vivianna was ever going to catch me.)

2. Pushing the Help button

Lesson 2 for me came on my second day in rehab. The hospital's evangelical support person paid me a visit to see how I was settling in. She sought my feedback, and I somewhat foolishly chose to share my frustration that ice wasn't being packed around my wounds on the hour and a couple of other things that, in retrospect, should have stayed behind my lips rather than blurted out in a moment of misguided self-importance.

Elizabeth was her name. Empathic but also forthright. She looked at me, and in a mild Scottish accent, asked me whether I'd thought to press the "Help" button when I was in pain and needed assistance.

Sheepishly, I told her I hadn't.

Her response contained much-needed perspective. "Peter, this is a busy hospital. We have people dying here every hour. You have 2 sore knees. Can I suggest that if you really need help, that you take the time to push the Help button? I assure you, someone *will* come and help you."

As I tucked my tail back in, it dawned on me how many real estate careers are crushed because someone failed to push the Help button. Forty years have taught me that there is a legion of people who would shift heaven and earth to help if they knew that a colleague, particularly a newcomer, was in need of assistance.

So, my Friend, never be afraid to push the Help button. And for those of you with a few more summers up your sleeve, make it your contribution to the betterment of your profession to let others know that you're there to help.

3. Celebrate the true heroes

Recovering in various hospitals, I had time to watch nursing, cleaning and catering staff go about their day with precision, and never in pursuit of fanfare.

These dedicated people get on with the job of comforting people in pain. There are no ticker tape parades of streamers and balloons as they enter the building. No media seeking their comment, or paparazzi snapping a pic of them emptying a bedpan. They're just doing what has to be done.

I remember one young lady who delivered my breakfast and lunch each day at North West Hospital. Her name was Susan. Every time she came, it was a contest to see whose eyes would light up the most.

Susan shared that she'd been in that role for around 12 years and that she aspired to move into hospitality one day, where she felt she could "make a difference".

I was stunned and told her how she made a difference every time she walked into a room with that beaming smile of hers. It occurred to me that she didn't realise just how much of a difference she made to people's worlds because no one had ever shared their genuine appreciation of her work.

Our society needs to be championing the unsung heroes like Susan and let them know they're making a difference. Ever since I left hospital, I have made it my mission to celebrate those real heroes, not the pretend ones served up to me by the media. Come join me. I dare you to drop a dozen doughnuts, a bunch of flowers or even just a nice, handwritten card to your local hospital, ambulance station, doctor's surgery or nursing home acknowledging their contribution. I know it'll fill their hearts, and it just might fill yours, too.

4. You're stronger than you think

I'd shared with some mates that I would be spending 3–4 hours a day in a hospital gym under the guidance of a physio and fitness team after my surgery. I told them I'd be doing a range of strength building exercises that would allow me to re-enter the real world stronger and fitter than when I entered hospital.

Their first reaction was that of laughter and sniggers. Obviously, they knew me and my lack of love for exercise well. And if I'm honest, I've only typed 56 words of this book this morning and I find myself looking for the drinks cart. But onwards I press for your literary enjoyment, dear Reader.

One of the things I learned quickly in the hospital rehab gym was that I wasn't the sickest person in the place. It really is home to the walking wounded – people coping with twisted or missing limbs and chronic pain and once fit people, brains now destroyed, trying to fight past the frustrations of their inability to communicate. It doesn't take long to gather a humbling perspective.

I had absolutely nothing to moan about. Whenever I was asked to do 25 minutes on the treadmill and started to host my own private pity party, all I needed to do was glance left or right at someone who'd give me everything they owned just to have both legs to allow them to stand on a treadmill. Every time I complained about pain in my shoulder from lifting some weights, I only had to see the patients beside me permanently hooked up to a drip that was feeding a ketamine cocktail into their veins.

Those moments of perspective inspired me to walk a little faster, stay on the treadmill 10 minutes longer, lift weights 20 minutes more and get to the gym 20 minutes earlier.

My rehabilitation team kept me honest

I met some courageous people in that rehab ward. I entered thinking I might be able to motivate them. But I soon learned that it was them and their stories and courage that motivated me. Their courage, humour, tenacity, commitment and drive to get themselves closer to the hospital's front door was inspiring.

Ultimately, we're all stronger than we think we are. I just needed to be tested. It's a lesson I am forever grateful for.

From a real estate perspective, I ponder how often we catastrophise what might go wrong in that next listing presentation, whether the reserve price might be too high, or whether a buyer might get knocked back on finance. I sometimes see people too scared to pick up the phone to call a client and give them some hard feedback on their price.

Real estate is a lonely business. You can think you're in your own battle. At times, you can think it's all too hard. But taking a look around you at others who have fought or are fighting massive mental and physical battles can give much-needed perspective. Find those people. Learn how they beat their challenges. I know you're way stronger than you think you are. Like me, maybe you just need to be tested.

5. Find your tribe

Spending over a month in hospital is sometimes a bigger test on those around us than it is on us. For my Tara, there was the daily decision of whether to visit. Does he need anything? Would he appreciate some company during his nightly pity party? Who's gonna rub his feet and tell him he's got dreamy eyes? Will he survive the night if I don't sneak in his 4 nightly shots of tequila?

Y'know, all the important stuff.

Being in hospital is really challenging in more ways than one. There should be some clear guidelines around hospital visits. Perhaps they could be as simple as: "If you do something stupid enough to land yourself here, then you're on your own 'til you can get yourself out of here." As Seinfeld's famous soup seller would say: "No visits for you!"

Seriously, the lengths some visitors go to each day to "demonstrate" their love is staggering. All the visitee has to do is sit there and be fed and medicated. Meanwhile, the poor old visitor gets lumbered with the guilt of whether or not to venture in each day. They have to navigate peak hour traffic, miss their own dinner or lunch, make small talk and sneakily glance at their watch, mindful that their week's salary is being swallowed up outside by a parking meter with a thirst greater than Bob Hawke.

My 4 weeks in hospital and rehab helped to crystallise who my tribe was. Their support in person or by way of email, text message, friendly phone call, inspirational card, flowers and thoughtful gifts of fudge and beer or tequila (the latter for medicinal purposes only, of course) gave me strength and filled me with warmth. I am forever thankful for that tribe.

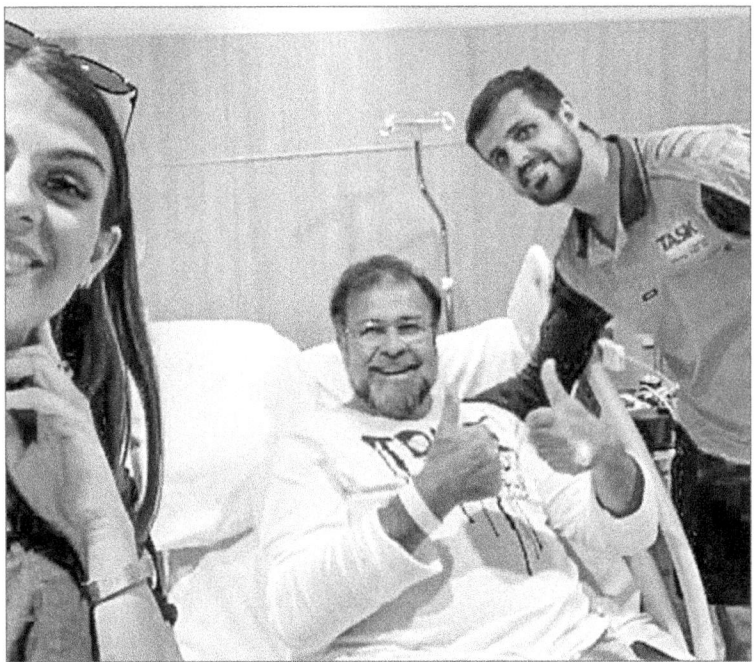

My tribe

Who's your home tribe? Who's your business tribe? Maybe they're the same? Whatever. Whoever. Wherever. Foster them. Fuel them. Love them. Tell them you appreciate them. If they're truly your tribe, they will appreciate you. And if you have no tribe, take it as an opportunity for some self-reflection and personal growth.

6. Home sweet home

In the hospital, I was provided everything I needed to function: a warm bed, 9 uncomfortable pillows and fresh linen, 3 warm meals every day – and yes, even the salads and ice cream were warm! The tea lady would bring me what seemed like 18 cups of tea and 36 Jatz crackers each day. I always had ample painkillers and, as is always the case in hospitals, you have to invert your entire body and crane your neck to be able to enjoy the flowers, gifts and cards strategically placed behind you. I'm sure that particular torment is part of every nurse's induction training!

As much as I jest about hospitals, they do an exceptional job of caring for their patients and sustaining life. But as the song goes, "Be it ever so humble, there's no place like home!"

Walking through the front door of our home after a month away was euphoric. In a touching and much-appreciated gesture, Tara had strategically placed 3 passionfruit cupcakes decorated with the words "Welcome Home Boo" on the kitchen bench.

Tara's perfect welcome home gifts

Aah, the familiar scent of home! That comfortable familiarity of knowing where the tea bags are, which drawer the sticky tape is in, and in which cupboard you've hidden the emergency tequila. In the words of the great Australian philosopher Darryl Kerrigan, "Money can't buy that".

The same goes in business. Often, I'll meet salespeople or property managers who've hung their hat at a business. And just like me in hospital, they get the basics to keep them alive. Metaphorically, there's fresh linen and a cup of tea available. But time and time again, I see that there's not much else going on for them. There are no cupcakes. No handwritten notes. No sign of appreciation. And definitely no tequila!

They've found somewhere to wait each day, but they haven't really found "home". It begs the question to business owners: are you providing a home for your people? Is it a warm, nurturing, supportive and inviting environment? Or are you just churning and burning?

I recently heard about a department manager who told the CEO she would need to let a particular property manager go because she wanted more money than they could afford to pay her. The CEO immediately replied, "Just pay her the money! If we can't afford to pay her the money she's worth, we sure as eggs can't afford the time and money to have her leave, experience the downtime, recruit her replacement at a higher salary, induct them into our business and train them how we want them."

So many times, I see businesses cutting costs on people and culture. But in reality, the most successful businesses do the opposite. They deeply appreciate and reward their people in order to build an amazing workplace culture. Recruit, reward and retain good people, and you'll never have a people problem again.

I once attended an Inman conference in New York City and Simon Sinek was on stage to speak about people and culture. After his presentation, he agreed to take some questions from the floor. A mature-aged woman addressed the microphone and said, "That's all very good in theory, Mr Sinek, but what if you've got an idiot working for you?"

Sinek's response was a moment of magic. He looked straight back at the well-intentioned woman and pointedly asked, "Who employed them?"

The bionic man is still a work in progress.

A reminder – You're selling houses, not curing cancer!

I love watching a sports winner celebrate. Warnie cracking 700 test wickets. Kieren Perkins winning Gold at Atlanta. Allan Border raising the Ashes urn in 1982. Me smacking a hole-in-one on the 9th at Wynnum. All were amazing international triumphs of incredible humans at their peak.

Don't get me wrong, I'm also a big fan of modesty and humility. I have a strong belief that most don't think people in my profession are wankers because of a bad service experience. They think we're wankers because, frankly, a really high percentage of people in my profession carry on, well, like wankers.

Sometimes, it's not that difficult to connect the dots. I mean, whoever in their right mind thinks that an almost daily Instagram happy snap that includes a $30,000 watch, the steering wheel of a leased BMW and 3 contract forms with the hashtags: #Humblebrag #StreetRecord #LivingMyBestLife #RockstarAgent #HustleandGrind #H8tersGonnaH8 #BazillionDollarAgent is a good idea? Seriously, we must do better. Consumers see those posts and shake their heads in fear of encountering one of these beasts in the wild.

#BreakingNewsPeople! No one apart from you gives a rat's arse about your watch collection, your overcommitted car lease, and your cupboard of plastic trophies. As the great Australian auctioneer Justin Nickerson once said, "Let's try a little humility."

You'll never see the Sandgate Fish and Chip shop post: "Another flathead and chips out the door!" #Boom #Crash #Kapow. And I'm yet to see a Dentist post: "Another Molar Record Today – 25 Wisdom Teeth Removed and 12 Fillings" #LocalAnasthetic #HereComesMyNewPorsche.

Look, I'm all about celebrating wins and enjoying success. And I get it. Real estate can be a tough gig. You gotta give yourself a pat on the back at times. But where's the modesty and humility?

Now, before you label me a #H8er or #Ungr8ful, let me share how I used to celebrate every single sale I made from the privacy and comfort of my own, fully-owned Holden Commodore with dark tinted glass. I'll start by painting the picture.

Kamarin, Rickston and Greta Streets at Manly West are exactly 4 minutes and one second long when navigated safely at 55 km per hour. Coincidentally, the Van Halen song "Jump" is also 4 minutes and one second long.

The song is bright, has some killer 1980s synthesiser riffs and builds to an almighty crescendo and finale. "Jump" became my victory song. Every time I sold a property, I would venture over to Manly West, put on my Top Gun hat, adjust my Aviators and crank the song to full volume on my car's CD player. Then I'd fire up the afterburners and launch my trusty Commodore into a series of celebratory barrel rolls for 4 minutes and one second along my well-worn trail up and down Kamarin, Rickston and Greta Streets.

No one got hurt. And no one thought I was a tosspot, apart from the confused man at 86 Greta Street when I wound the window down and raised a salute as I buzzed the "tower".

Sure, get out there and have fun like I did in my prime. Celebrate the wins. Knock yourself out with your street and suburb records. Just remember—the consumer you're trying to impress with your braggadocious #Wanker post could have been your next seller and celebration-worthy sale had you been more humble and less of a tosspot!

> "Self-confidence is very important.
> But without compassion and humility, it's just arrogance."
>
> Steven Furtick

People who need people are the luckiest people in the world

I don't believe any midwife on earth has ever delivered a baby, slapped it on the bum and handed it to its mother, proclaiming, "Congratulations, Beryl, it's a boy, and he's going to be a real estate agent when he grows up."

I'm no genetics expert, but I don't believe we are born with a chip that has our destined career pre-programmed into it. And I don't buy into the theory that some people are naturally gifted. Sure, we might be in awe of a magnificent sportsperson or a brilliant entrepreneur. But we rarely see the years of unwavering commitment, training and dedication that elevated those "naturally gifted" people to stardom. Ultimately, each of us is a product of our environment, the people around us and our efforts. Some of us embrace opportunities while, sadly, others ignore or waste them.

I've had a fortunate life and wonderful parents who encouraged me to aim high. Their nurturing introduced me to many kind and generous people who created opportunities for me. But, as my friend Jeff Turner says, "Life can open doors for you, but you still have to get off your arse and walk through them". *(I may have embellished Jeff's original words for effect.)*

On the other side of almost every one of those doors I walked through was someone who gifted me life skills or knowledge. Their collective wisdom has had a profound impact on shaping my business and personal values. It taught me to develop and maintain relationships with people who share the common ethos I call "give to get". It's a formula that's kept me fuelled, fed and focused for 6 decades. You've gotta be prepared to give something with no expectation of receiving. My experience is that the universe sorts the rest.

Unfortunately, not everyone aligns with the "give to get" ethos. Early in my business life, I invested heavily in attending events fronted by some "smart" people. I quickly learned how to differentiate the genuine entrepreneurs from the "contrepreneurs" who peddle their wares to an ever-changing audience of gullible people in search of the elusive silver bullet.

I've witnessed too many contrepreneurs separate good people from their assets, leaving their lives and dreams in tatters. On stage, they peddle and co-promote each other's "million-dollar success systems" while shamelessly exchanging brown paper bags filled with the hard-earned dollars of their adoring fans backstage. I once rejected an invitation to speak at one of their cult-like events when one of the leaders proudly smirked that "the punters don't even realise they're being sold to".

Hint: if the cost to attend a course on how to achieve a maximum fee for your service is either free or heavily discounted, then running a mile in the other direction should be your first move.

There was a time when I was ridiculed by a partner who saw my investments in attending great events as a weakness. They couldn't comprehend my desire to nurture and expand my mind.

News flash: just as no mother has ever given birth to a bouncing baby Gold Medal Olympic swimmer, no successful business leader has ever jumped out of a womb and chaired BHP's AGM. All have sought opportunities, stepped through open doors and committed to putting in the hard yards and investing in themselves to develop their knowledge and skills.

It's pretty simple. If you don't nurture and expand your knowledge, then the one guarantee you'll have in life is a career or business limited to your own insular thoughts.

Throughout my career, I've built a network of amazing people who appreciate that I put their wisdom into practice. The more

I invested in myself with the help of others, the more the tables started to turn where others would seek my views on business or life. It's even more fulfilling to see people acting on my humbly provided thoughts.

There's a world of knowledge waiting for you to tap into. Whether your preferred learning is via book, podcast, networking and learning events or reaching out to business leaders, find what works best for you and commit to nurturing your mind.

Despite my disparaging former partner suggesting I was weak for reaching out to good people to nurture my mind, I'll forever argue that not developing knowledge and not expanding your brain is the real weakness. There are people who'd happily swap their positions in life for the opportunities sitting at the feet of most of us.

Each of us arrived in that birthing suite with nothing but a heartbeat and access to a world of opportunities. I encourage you to take the steps to identify and reach out to people who are happy to help you learn. Explain what you're seeking, how it'll help you and what it would mean to you. Most importantly, respect their time and wisdom and act on their advice.

"People who need people are the luckiest people in the world."

Barbara Streisand

Make your own kind of music

Growing up and living in a conservative community as part of a high-profile family from the 60s to the 90s, I had a large target on my back. Swerving more than 5 degrees off-centre was brave.

I was a bit of a rebel back then. Flared pants, hair that hid my collar, a sea of colourful shirts and, God forbid, the audacity to challenge mindless bureaucracy. I was quickly labelled a rebellious troublemaker – a label with potentially terminal consequences in a small town.

Still, I wasn't prepared to "sit in the corner and shut up" like good little boys should. Ultimately, ignoring that advice proved to be one of life's greatest gifts. It gave me the confidence to be me.

The 1950s cult figure James Dean was labelled a "rebel without a cause". If that's a true description of a talented and passionate young man frustrated by society and family, then to brand me a "rebel without a clue" would be a fitting and appropriate assessment of a young Peter Brewer.

Decades of data show that vanilla is far and away people's favourite ice cream flavour. In comparison, sales of Neapolitan and Rainbow Swirl pale into insignificance. But being true to my rebellious ways, I've always respectfully questioned and challenged what's deemed "normal". I've chosen to live a life influenced by bright colours but with just a touch of vanilla to remain grounded. In the absence of receiving any sensible answers to my challenges, I became more confident and comfortable that I had things to say that might be worth listening to.

Life blossomed as my confidence grew. The more I made my own kind of music, the better I felt about being in my own skin.

In this chapter's title song, Mama Cass sings, "They'll try to tell you there's only one song worth singing."

Yeah-Nah. Not for me.

Whether fuelled by my mother's vast cabaret repertoire or my own love of music, I became determined that my life wasn't going to be the same song on an endless loop.

I figured out early in life that I marched to the beat of a different drum than the other kids. The way I dressed, the long hair, even the Datsun 240Z sports car I drove in my late teens. And while that was initially a very lonely place that messed with my head for not being "normal", I eventually found my tribe. One by one, I started to gain the friendship and respect of people who mattered. And over time, those friendships came from the most unexpected people and places.

As a contemptuous 15-year-old, I idolised Australian cricket royalty Jeff Thomson and Dennis Lillee, who were both rebels. *(What a coincidence!)* I emulated their cocky attitudes and had the long, flowing locks to match. Sadly, I was unable to match their abilities on the cricket field, but that didn't stop me from donning my red-striped Adidas cricket boots while others opted for plain white Dunlop Volleys.

Was I a poser? Probably. Did it build my confidence and make me feel like a better cricketer? Absolutely! *(That might just be an early hint as to my future dress sense – or lack thereof!)*

One memory that still brings a smile stems from the father of one very unappreciated girlfriend. I was 17 and the classic, clumsy, selfish boyfriend. Kelly (name changed) was a delightful young lady who deserved much better.

Her dad, Rusty (name also changed), and I became besties. Like me, he was the rebellious type. He loved a drink and a game of snooker. So did I! And so, in the most bizarre of love triangles, I would visit Kelly and her dad 3 nights a week. Kelly and I would snuggle on the couch watching movies until 9:30, when she would be sent to bed. Rusty would then summon me downstairs to his bar where, for the next 3 hours, he and I would play snooker, drink booze and share stories like "besties".

After 3 years, it was pretty obvious that Kelly deserved a better partner than me, and we sadly parted ways. But, in a plot twist, Kelly wasn't the one who was devastated by the breakup. Rusty, my 55-year-old mate, was absolutely gutted.

About a week after the breakup, a very sad Rusty called me at home and almost pleaded with me, "Just because you two have broken up doesn't mean we have to!" And so, Rusty and I continued our friendship, our snooker nights, our fishing trips, and our boozy ways.

It was that friendship – and the respect that came with it from a highly successful local businessman – that gave me the confidence I needed to push through the loneliness of being left of centre and back myself.

As an aspiring 21-year-old real estate agent, I know I raised more than a few eyebrows and heard the word "wanker" muttered more than once when I had the letters PB subtly monogrammed in silver on the doors of my burgundy, gangster-style Commodore with blacked-out electric windows.

Remember, this was mid-80s conservative Australia! For context, pizza was still an exotic dish only offered by Pizza Hut, The Proclaimers were topping the charts with their classic hit, "I'm Gonna Be", featuring the iconic verse: "And I would walk 500 miles …". And if your sex position of choice was anything other than missionary, it was an offence punishable by law. *(Only joking, but you were considered a bit weird.)*

In 1994, the REIQ's AGM minutes reflected that I was in attendance as a member. What they didn't reflect was that – much to the chagrin of the assembled establishment of the day – I was wearing shorts, a T-shirt and deck shoes and was accompanied by my 4-year-old son.

I could feel their "how dare he" looks of disdain piercing my bare legs and lack of collar. If only I could bring them forward to the 2020s when shorts, T-shirts and deck shoes are a common business attire at the REIQ and children are welcome.

In my 40s, my relatively strong media profile saw me strike up respectful and valuable friendships with former Queensland State Premiers Campbell Newman and Peter Beattie. Having their ears and respect – and both their numbers on my speed dial – gave my strongly harboured feelings of imposter syndrome a much-needed boost that maybe, just maybe, the boy from the bayside might actually have a voice worth listening to.

My 50s and 60s have afforded me positions of power, great responsibility and platforms from which I have been able to share my sometimes unique perspectives. I've relished the opportunity to speak freely and unmuzzled, unlike those who aren't so lucky due to their corporate obligations, pay cheques or personal political agendas.

The fact that many of the wannabes who've played on for a few seasons too long continue to treat me with contempt is a badge of honour I wear with pride.

Queensland State Premier Campbell Newman and Peter

I urge you to be inquisitive of industry organisations and their true effectiveness. Scrutinise who is in charge, why and for how long? Dig deep into what you're actually paying for. Question the need for expensive 5-star travel and meals in a digital world when Zoom is just a click away. The lure of titles, fine wines, room upgrades and wider plane seats can be enticing to someone at the senior end of their career. You may be surprised by what you're receiving for your investment!

As I sit at the magnificent Beach Hotel in Byron Bay, typing this chapter late on a Friday afternoon, I'm surrounded by music, incredible scenery, cold beer and people living their lives to the full. At the same time, there are people in offices back in the cities in suits and uniforms chasing their dreams and their own version of success and happiness.

Peter and Queensland State Premier Peter Beattie

What drives them to do that is none of my business. Perhaps it's a mortgage. Maybe it's personal ambition or to ensure they're not endlessly locked onto a hamster wheel to fit societal expectations. If my stories prompt one person to stop and reflect on how they're living their lives and appreciate that the number of Saturdays they have left is diminishing quickly, then my job is done. Life is short. Each of us is literally running out of Saturdays.

In April of 2023, I returned to my hometown and stood before a gathering of local folk to deliver my mother's eulogy. At 64, I proudly shared stories of her beautiful life of service. Mum's incredible, unwavering support of me from the day I was born made it 100% okay for me to be uniquely me throughout my life. Her blessing has been priceless in my personal growth, from being an unsure, lonely kid to being completely confident in my own very stretchy skin.

The toughest speech of my life

As I delivered the words that acknowledged some of Mum's contributions to the world, I scanned the crowd and saw the faces of a few people who had labelled me a rebel 5 decades ago. I felt strong, in command, empowered and filled with a need to demonstrate to them that the little boy they'd tried to crush was now a strong, independent man who'd created a successful life despite their judgements and my failure to fit their cookie-cutter mould. I also saw an overwhelming number of people who had been in my cheer squad for years, some for decades. It was a great reminder that one vote against you and 94 in favour is a resounding win that should be celebrated with pride and to find the tribe that celebrates you for you.

Standing before that sea of people was also an opportunity to remind myself that I'd come a long way since the days of ducking blackboard dusters hurled at me at school. The kid who cowered at his desk, was abused by teachers and cried at home for not comprehending the difference between nouns, pronouns, adjectives, verbs and adverbs was now writing a memoir unaided by AI, unphased by the intricacies of grammar and deliriously happy with the 3,328 Saturdays he'd carved out so far!

As I type this, I hear Mum's angelic voice singing the song that inspired the title of this chapter. I love how she continues to inspire me.

Throughout my life, I've always wanted to be a shepherd rather than a sheep. My heart told me to lead rather than be herded into conformity. I wanted to make my own kind of music. What I've learned is that when you follow your heart, there is an amazing and incredibly supportive choir waiting to sing harmonies with you.

"They'll try to tell you there's only one song worth singing, but you've gotta make your own kind of music"

Mama Cass Elliot

I moustache you a question

By the age of 25, my confidence and real estate career were blossoming. I was building an identity and reputation as a high-performing agent. I drove a nice car and dressed well. I had also grown a pretty impressive moustache that was quickly becoming my personal and professional trademark. It wasn't just your everyday garden variety face fungus. My tash was flash! My trademark bro-merang put the biggest and best Mexican lip mop to shame.

I've been asked many times what inspired me to cultivate such an impressive soup strainer.

Now, I could repeat what I've told people for decades – that my 1980s cricketing heroes Dennis Lillee and Max Walker inspired it. I could bluff that one of my musical heroes, Glenn Frey from The Eagles, birthed the beginning of my bushy lip bristles. All 3 boasted facial fur that would be the envy of Melbourne's trendiest hipster barista.

Pancho Pete was born!

But the time has finally come for me to fess up about my famous lip toupee.

Truth be told, the real reason I grew the much-heralded face fluff is that I'd invested pretty heavily in a marketing campaign to adorn the bayside with 20 bus stop seats boasting my real estate success and including a photo of my smiling, then fresh-faced melon.

Now, in the 1980s, our local graffiti artists lacked creativity. I also don't think spray cans of paint had been invented. So, the best work any aspiring graffiti artist could muster was to use a big black Nikko marker pen to draw an oversized Mexican style moustache on every one of my fresh baby-faced photo signboards.

Whether I liked it or not, overnight, Pancho Pete was born!

My original plan to make me look professional was backfiring. The graffiti-ridden photos were having the opposite effect. I had some quick decisions to make. Removing them wasn't an option as I was contracted to keep them for a year, and I soon discovered that replacing them would cost me an arm and a leg. So, I decided to apply a theory I'd learned from a friend that had served me well thus far – WWATAD, which is short for What Would A Tight Arse Do?

A man of many hats

Turns out it was much more economical to grow a big bushy mo that would match me to the lacklustre efforts of the local graffiti gangs. In any case, I figured the guys who'd added the hairy handlebars to 20 of my bus stop seats were no doubt a tenacious lot. There was a fair chance they'd be back if I restored the face to *au naturel*. So, as they say, "If you can't beat 'em, join 'em!"

And so, the now trademark mo was born. For reasons I'll never fully understand, though, it further helped stamp my authority on the suburb as an agent with personality who was clearly a little bit different.

Forty years on, my moustache retains its pride of place. It's now a little more wiry and has a whole lot more grey in it. My top lip has only ever seen daylight for one week over those 40 years. And that was for a bet. In fact, I'm not sure my kids, now in their 30s, have ever seen me without it.

I conclude this whiskery confession by extending my heartfelt thanks to Wynnum Manly's unimaginative graffiti artists of the 1980s. I'm particularly thankful that, of all the body appendages you could have drawn over my face on 20 bus stop seats, you lamely chose a moustache. I've much preferred being remembered for my moustache than being known as a dickhead!

Where there's a will, there's a relative

A former lawyer friend often joked, "Where there's a will, there's a relative."

As the Executor of Mum's estate, I was about to discover how right he was.

Imagine the following scenario. You've been knocked out on the canvas from managing the stresses of illness and profound loss. Hope and mood have been at an all-time low. You're black and blue. Almost punch-drunk. You've sought counselling, and you're finally fighting your way back up. You look down a pitch-black tunnel and see a pinprick of light in the distance. I saw it as hope! Suddenly, you realise that pinprick of light in the distance is the blinding high beam of a train about to smack you to the ground and derail whatever small amount of sanity you thought you'd started to reclaim. Metaphorically, of course.

I'm one of two sons. Mum had appointed me the sole Executor of her estate. My brother, a lifelong non-conformist, relocated to the Philippines around a decade ago with no intent of returning for fear of legal repercussions. We are 2 very different people.

His decision to abscond caused Mum overwhelming grief in her later years. Mothers have a deep love for their children. His severing of that physical tie caused her incalculable sadness and I believe did nothing to help her late-in-life depression and battles with alcohol.

My brother made a conscious adult decision to not be around to support her during her final time of need. I will never forgive him.

What can also never be forgiven is that, while continuing his Philippines beach lifestyle, he continued to "borrow" from Mum's purse.

And to top it all off, he engaged a law firm to challenge Mum's will on the basis of insufficiency of the inheritance she'd provided for him. Apparently, a million dollars doesn't buy you much these days. Who knew?

Sadly, my brother's actions not only caused me further pain but also considerable legal expense and a significant delay in allowing me to satisfy Mum's final wishes. His legal challenge of Mum's clearly documented instructions was a final betrayal of trust that left me devastated. I'm pretty sure Mum would have felt the same way.

In August 2024, I received a late-night call advising that my brother had been found unresponsive in his beachside hideout in the Philippines.

I will never rationalise his actions.

A word of counsel for you, dear Reader, to conclude this life lesson:

> Plan your estate wisely. Because where there's a will, there's a relative ready to draw pistols at dawn over the good china.

PART 3

Lessons in Leadership

Ricky Gervais once famously said, "When you are dead, you do not know you are dead. It's only painful and difficult for others. The same applies when you are stupid." I love that quote.

I've worked with some inspiring leaders and others who couldn't lead a dog on a chain. The character traits that make some leaders stand out are rarely singular. Excellent leaders exude a combination of many life and leadership qualities that inspire seemingly ordinary people to achieve extraordinary results.

It's also important to be cognizant that being a leader and a manager differs markedly. Great leaders have the rare ability to bring out the best in their people without micromanaging them. After all, no one ever jumps out of bed in the morning, exclaiming, "I can't wait to get to work today so I can be managed!"

My profession has never been short of here today and gone tomorrow charlatans with promises of becoming a million dollar agent by attending their dodgy $47 courses. The real leaders I'm inspired by are genuine leaders who've demonstrated style and substance over a sustained period.

Great leaders inspire.

Having worked with many leaders with contrasting skills, I thought I'd share some of the lessons I've learned from the very best I've encountered.

Leadership Lesson 1: Charisma

Who isn't charmed by a charismatic leader? We all know people who grace a sport or profession and only require a single name to identify them. Mention "Wally" or "Alfie"; everyone knows who you're referring to – at least if you're a Queenslander. Drop the names Farnsey or Barnsey; you know we're talking Australian music royalty. Utter the name "Richie" and the masses will shout "2 for 22". I'm talking about icons.

In Australian real estate circles, if you've been around for more than a few property peaks and troughs, you'll recognise a widely-celebrated icon who is known simply as "Camfo".

Charisma is a key leadership trait that industry veteran Peter "Camfo" Camphin delivers in spades. In case you don't know, Camfo was CEO of the Ray White Group in Queensland from December 1996 until August 2014 and an advisor for the group for more than 10 years after that. Then, and in the years since, Camfo's charisma has had an incredible impact on the careers of many of Australia's highest-performing real estate professionals, including mine.

Camfo is a non-assuming guy who lights up a room with his aura and magic smile from the moment he enters. I first met him in 2005 at an event sponsored by *The Courier-Mail* – the *King Kong* movie launch at a Gold Class Cinema. I was the bushy-faced Executive Chair of a competing real estate brand dressed in joggers, jeans and a T-shirt.

There I was, swilling the free Coronas and chomping down sausage rolls like there was no tomorrow, while Camfo – immaculate in a suit and tie – networked the room like a boss. He greeted all present by name and engaged with them while slowly savouring a glass of champagne, napkin in hand, and politely declining the buffet of free snacks and booze to which I was intently glued.

Fast-forward 20 years, and little between us has changed other than my enormous respect for him, which increases daily. He's still style and substance and I'm still at the buffet.

Along with Camfo, I was recently booked to speak at an event in Mackay. One of the event staff, a young lady named Alex, warmly welcomed us both to the club. She showed us the facilities, confirmed our food and beverage requirements, assured us our AV was under control and said she would be on hand during the event should we need anything during our brief 3-hour parachute drop into Mackay and the venue, of which she was clearly very proud.

Camfo deliberately tailors each presentation to suit the differing audiences and locations. Walking on stage that morning, he scanned the audience, ensuring Alex was in the room. Over the next hour, he referred to her warm welcome, attention to detail, pride for her club and genuine care for her customers as outstanding guiding principles to replicate for business and personal success.

Alex later said Camfo made her feel like she was the most important person in the room. But so did everyone else in the room that day. Camfo is a master of the art of charisma. It's not staged. It's deeply ingrained in his DNA.

That morning – like in every other interaction of his I've witnessed – Camfo engaged with every member of the audience, acknowledging people by name, warmly shaking hands, referencing past interactions and gracefully working his charismatic smile through the entire crowd. No wonder he's been revered for so long and is regarded as an icon of our profession.

Great leaders exude charisma. They know how to build an army to march behind them. Now free from the shackles of corporate responsibilities, Camfo is openly consulting and sharing his charisma and wisdom across the entire real estate profession in Australia.

Leadership Lesson 2: Never shy away

Let's not confuse "never shy away" with "never back down". They may sound similar, but they lead to very different kinds of meetings and interactions. One invites open discussion; the other risks becoming a cage fight.

To never shy away means having the courage to face tough conversations head-on, even when they're uncomfortable. It's about stepping up, not stepping on. Never backing down, on the other hand, can veer into stubbornness. It's the "I'm right even if I'm wrong" mindset that rarely ends well – unless your goal is a stand-off.

Australian Band Savage Garden's iconic song "Affirmations" shares a lyric: "I believe the sun should never set upon an argument". I wholeheartedly agree. Letting upsets or disagreements fester almost always amplifies the original issue, usually blowing it out of proportion. A spotfire can quickly turn into a raging inferno without a prompt and appropriate response.

Antonia Mercorella – aka "The Chief" – a dear friend and "work wife" for 8 magnificent years, is a brilliant exponent of never shying away. If there were a gold medal in that craft, Antonia would be the reigning Olympic champion.

For Antonia, a qualified lawyer, nothing gets in the way of her prioritising a quick resolution to an issue that's gone or could go pear-shaped. In situations where others might fear confrontation and allow things to fester in the hope they'll go away, Antonia skilfully gets all stakeholders to put their views on the table and work together to find a resolution.

If there's any confusion, miscommunication or misinterpretation on an issue with a policy maker, institute member, staff member or a consumer, Antonia seeks to resolve it promptly. A master of seeking to immediately understand why someone is aggrieved, she is relentless at ferreting out the facts, putting them on the table and using her powers of communication and rational conversation to find a mutually agreeable outcome.

Nothing ever gets put off in the hope that it'll go away. Because, guess what? It won't. You don't need to be a lawyer like Antonia to take this leadership quality on board. Deal with the dilemma on the day and move on.

Leadership Lesson 3: No surprises

I'm a fan of the ethos of "no surprises". It comes when leaders and managers have earned an unequivocal level of mutual trust to feel safe and confident enough to fess up when they flock up.

I was first exposed to the "no surprises" rule by Clubs Queensland's former CEO Doug Flockhart. It began as a shared value between Doug and his Chairman of the day and quickly evolved across his team.

In its simplest form, Doug and his Chair had a clear understanding that there needed to be complete transparency between them. No surprises in the balance sheet or P&L and no hidden agendas in the meeting notes. Pure. Simple. Trust. The permission to speak freely. No surprises.

Fostering an environment where your team has the confidence to be open and honest about their *faux pas* creates a unique culture. Great leaders empower their people to give new things a crack. In this context, "no surprises" doesn't mean no mistakes; it means no *hidden* ones. It means your team feels safe enough to say, "Hey, I stuffed this up", *before* it hits the fan. That way, you can course-correct together – no finger-pointing, just forward motion.

Leadership Lesson 4: It's about the customer

My trusted friend and US real estate events and publishing royalty, Brad Inman, always focused on ensuring every customer experience was exceptional. For example, he insisted that every presenter run their presentation in front of him on the day preceding an event. Brad had high standards. To quote his words, "I have no room for chuckleheads in front of my customers."

Brad was 100% focused on the content and the finer details that ensured his customers' experience was second to none. In the USA's busy conference and events space, mediocrity was not an option for Brad over his 20 years of convening flagship events.

Brad is uncompromising that things need to be simple on the surface. Any cumbersome process that might have been designed to make life "nicer" for "Susan from Accounts" in preference to making the experience better for his valued customer was short-lived.

I once watched him "democratise" 40 vacant "Reserved for Media" chairs in the front rows at one of his marquis events after spotting paying customers standing at the back of the 4,000-seat auditorium. He simply consigned the "Reserved" signs to the rubbish bin.

For Brad, it's all about delighting every customer with an unforgettable experience. He has a keen eye for detail and a high expectation that his events team members embrace the same ethos. My friend Sean Carpenter writes of an event staffer at one of Brad's events in San Francisco who, at each refreshment break during the 3-day event, would meticulously straighten the 4,500 chairs shuffled around by the real estate agent attendees so that the room would look as if it were morning one on their return.

I'm not suggesting you go to the lengths Brad and his team went to, but it's a great example of putting the customer first. Details matter. Standards matter. But what matters most is the person you're doing it all for: the customer.

After all, if you're not here to serve every customer, what *are* you here for?

Leadership Lesson 5: Will it make the boat go faster?

Folklore has it that in the early 2000s, the Kiwi America's Cup team was raising funds to emulate what the Australian team had done in 1983 when wresting the Cup from Team America for the first time in 132 years.

For America, it was a difficult pill to swallow. The only people more aggrieved by the fact that Australia held the coveted America's Cup were our cuzzies from across the ditch.

It quickly became apparent that the Kiwis desperately wanted to get their fingers on that second-hand piece of rusty tin.

A fundraising campaign was run to get a few Kiwi dollars together to enable them to update the motor on their national dinghy, which I'm told bore the name K1W1.

Kiwis are pretty passionate about sport, even more so if it means beating us Aussies.

The fundraising campaign was an enormous success, with some of NZ's biggest businesses spilling support overboard for their tilt at relocating the old tin cup to their then-empty trophy case.

The campaign was literally a-splash with cash. Word has it that a spending spree rivalling Amazon Black Friday sales ensued by team management.

The first million Dunedin dollars got burned up quickly on a range of trinkets and beads deemed "necessary" by the terra-firma-based corporate team. The suggestion is that the team that actually sailed the boat held a vastly differing view on the wisest way to apply those funds.

It's reported that an intervention of epic proportions took place led by the K1W1 team leader, Sir Peter Blake.

Sir Peter reportedly entered the room where the spending spree spoils from the sponsors' donations were housed, pointed to each of the feel-good trinkets laid out for all to see, and repeatedly enquired, "Will that make the boat go faster?"

The questioning continued, item by item: "Will that make the boat go faster?"

Sir Peter was making his point abundantly clear.

I've read various iterations and origins of this lesson. But regardless of its origin, there is such a great lesson in this tale.

Will it make the boat go faster?

It's easy to spend a small fortune of hard-earned cash on "stuff" that'll make us feel warm and fuzzy. Instead, Sir Peter insisted that every dollar be spent on achieving the objective of making the boat go faster.

It's a lesson that applies equally in our personal lives. As I edge closer to the ship docking on my own 3 score and 10 years, I reflect on a lifetime of purchases and indulgences and ponder how many actually made my boat go faster.

My infatuation with all things "shiny" definitely saw me make many other people's boats go faster! And that's okay. My journey has been amazing! But I can't help but reflect on what might be different if I'd been armed with Sir Peter Blake's wisdom.

I'm not suggesting we shouldn't enjoy our own boat race of life with a nice bottle of Piper from a comfy chair at a lovely beach house. But asking whether your next purchase will make the boat go faster – whether in your personal life or at work – is a wise life and leadership lesson to adopt.

Leadership Lesson 6: Empowerment

Throughout my career, I've encountered various leadership styles – autocratic, democratic, the people-pleaser, bureaucratic, transactional and transformational. Each brought its own insights, especially as I worked on developing my own approach.

Leaders who knew how to empower their teams were the ones I enjoyed working for the most. Unlike the chaotic or disconnected leaders, these empowered leaders focused on trust, respect and shared vision. They didn't just dictate a destination; they painted a clear picture of it, encouraging everyone to co-own the journey. They clearly outlined each step and were open to input, even crowdsourcing better ways to reach goals when appropriate. With their teams, they celebrated each milestone along the way, making the journey as rewarding as the destination itself.

An example of empowerment in action was Alan Bond. Despite his later controversies, Bond understood the power of delegation. He knew he couldn't do everything alone and valued the insights of others. Unlike many leaders with large egos, Bond realised he didn't have a monopoly on good ideas. Understanding that his own time and energy were limited, he scaled his impact by empowering those around him.

Bond's approach was straightforward: when a team member presented a well-thought-out idea, he didn't just add it to his own to-do list. Instead, he'd hand it back with a simple mandate: "Great idea; make it happen." By trusting and empowering others to own projects, he created an environment where his investments could multiply at scale. His team felt valued and empowered to contribute meaningfully.

While Bond's life may not have been a perfect business model, there's a powerful lesson in his approach to empowerment. "Great idea; make it happen."

Leadership Lesson 7: Looking for weather shifts

In business, I made a point of budgeting time to visit real estate offices across the globe. I found it suited my hands-on learning style. One of my many study tours took me across the ditch to Paul Lochore's office in Birkenhead, Auckland, to learn more about his leadership style.

Paul enjoyed a great reputation as a fearless leader and was a confident and clearly successful Kiwi. His brother Brian played for the All Blacks. Leadership ran in the family.

While touring Paul's office, I noticed an interesting, framed piece of art opposite his impressively tidy desk – a painting of a grand old tall ship sailing on a calm sea. I thought it an unusual choice of art for someone who wasn't a sailor.

As I studied it closer, Paul joined me and pointed out a lone figure standing atop the mast, scanning the horizon.

"That's my job," he said. "My job is to stand on that mast and look for changes on the horizon."

Curious, I asked him to explain.

With the passion of a true leader, Paul shared his perspective. As the captain of Lochore's Real Estate in Auckland, he said he saw his role as more than just navigating calm waters. His job, he explained, was to be vigilant – always scanning for changes in the "weather" that could affect the business.

Metaphorically speaking, whether it was shifts in wind patterns, changes in the tides, increasing swells on the horizon, new ships or shipping hazards, Paul made it clear that he stayed alert to any subtle shifts that might pose risks to the SS Lochore.

I learned a critical lesson from Paul that day: a good leader is never complacent. They keep a close watch on the seas ahead, constantly adjusting and anticipating shifts that could impact the safety and survival of their crew.

The painting sitting opposite Paul's desk kept him focused on his key role of remaining vigilant and being proactive as captain of the ship.

There's always a storm brewing somewhere on the horizon. Knowing when to tack, when to trim, and when to set the spinnaker can save you and your team from a disaster of Titanic proportions.

Leadership Lesson 8: Take people on the journey with you

I've seen too many leaders with great vision frustrated that no one was following their lead. The reason? They either hadn't earned buy-in for their vision or had failed to share it.

Imagine a world where our nation's leaders laid out their leadership roadmap live on TV or online once a week. No edited sound bites, no zingers, no catchy campaign slogans – just an honest weekly update. *(If only!)*

I could be wrong (except I'm not), but most people appreciate a good leader. It baffles me that our political leaders don't see the potential goldmine waiting for them if they bothered to take all Australians on the journey with them. Not every decision they make will be popular, but most Aussies are willing to back an idea if it's explained honestly and thoughtfully.

Failing to clearly share a vision leaves people rudderless and confused. Whether you lead a nation or a business, you gotta paint a picture and take the team on the journey with you.

Two leaders from my time, Premier Peter Beattie and Sir Joh Bjelke-Petersen, each had traits I respected.

Beattie, in particular, was a master of owning up. He understood that Australians have a willingness to forgive mistakes – as long as there's no cover-up. If he or someone on his team messed up, Beattie would get in front of a camera with an apologetic, earnest look on his face, take responsibility and promise to do better. No dodging or blaming. He'd take people on the journey by owning the mistake, facing the music and moving on. It was a smart and rare leadership strategy that kept him in office for a record term.

Sir Joh gained my respect for doing what he believed in. You may not have liked his policies, but he had the courage of his convictions to follow them through. Never one to mince his words, Sir Joh would address the media – or "feed the chooks", as he called it – to announce his plans, and then he'd get on with it. He wasn't one for backflips or vague positions. Whether he prioritised Queensland's interests over his own is for others to debate. I just appreciate that he was a leader who said what he intended to do and then did it.

The lesson here? A strong leader shares their vision, enlists their people and, importantly, stays accountable and takes them along for the journey. They're also honest about the progress and the challenges. A leader brave enough to offer that kind of transparency and accountability would see their approval ratings reach new heights. Even better, they could unite us instead of driving the wedges deeper.

Leadership Lesson 9: Don't be a dick

This one might be blunt, but it's a golden rule that's crucial in every leadership scenario: don't be a dick. Too often, people in positions of power forget the basics of decency and respect. They think authority gives them free rein to act however they want, often treating people as disposable. Nothing tanks a team faster than a leader who is rude, self-centred or dismissive.

I've worked with all kinds of personalities, and the ones who genuinely made an impact weren't necessarily the smartest or most experienced. They were the ones who treated others with respect, listened and led with humility.

Good leaders can walk into a room, make decisions and drive success without ever needing to put someone down or act superior. Those are leaders people actually want to follow.

I've been known to change the title on my business cards to Janitor, Receptionist, Cleaner, Assistant or Tea Lady from time to time. Then, I'd perform those roles alongside the people who actually held those roles. I found that spending time in their shoes to understand their role and challenges earned me more credit with them as their leader than any gold-embossed business card ever could.

Being a good leader doesn't mean being a pushover, and it doesn't mean avoiding hard decisions or critical feedback. It means delivering those tough calls without arrogance or unnecessary harshness. People will accept tough truths and even painful feedback when they know it's coming from a place of respect.

At the end of the day, "don't be a dick" is a simple but essential reminder to treat everyone with respect, keep your ego in check, and remember that you're there to guide, not intimidate. Leadership isn't about proving you're better than everyone else; it's about lifting the whole team.

Leadership Lesson 10: Don't tolerate the 9,000-pound gorillas

Most people want to be led by passionate, enthusiastic leaders who inspire and motivate.

If you walk into a workplace where 90% of the team seems

disengaged, miserable and uninterested in their work, you're looking at a leader who's accepted mediocrity as the standard. Whether in families, teams, schools, communities or nations, we need leaders with 4 key qualities: firmness, courage, passion and empathy.

I'm not sure I was ever a great leader, but I know I brought enthusiasm and energy. I'd like to think my passion rubbed off on the people around me. But, like many people who progress from being a successful salesperson to a business leader, I didn't initially have the skills or the appreciation of how important they were.

There were two areas where I fell short as a leader. Firstly, I initially struggled with sharing a clear vision for our business. I didn't always paint a picture of where we were going or why it mattered. I imagined everyone would love my business as much as I did. Realising that wasn't the case was a fast, rude and expensive awakening. I learned that the right people will get behind a vision if it's clear and consistent and if they feel supported along the way.

The second shortfall resulted in a tougher lesson. For way too long, I tolerated the 9,000-pound gorillas. These were the team members who threw their weight around, causing disruption and friction with behaviour that was frankly toxic. Whether it was tantrums rivalling a toddler or bullying that should never have been tolerated, I let it slide too often. And that was on me.

Nine-thousand-pound gorillas are everywhere. We all know one (or several). On the surface, they might perform well. They may even be the life of the party and often contribute strongly to cash flow. But beneath the surface, they're manipulative, eroding team morale and undermining trust. Their behaviour can also dissuade talented people from joining or staying with the business.

Getting rid of a toxic presence can be difficult financially, but it's nearly always the right move. Removing a bully from the team lifts morale, reduces stress and often allows fresh talent, enthusiasm and new ideas to take root. It's not always easy, but the results are almost always worth it.

There's genuine substance in the saying, "Be slow to hire and fast to fire". Sometimes, letting go of the 9,000-pound gorillas is exactly what a leader must do for the company to move forward. It takes courage, but once done, there is no looking back.

Leadership Lesson 11: Ditch the rope and let people breathe

I once worked under a manager who proudly boasted, "Everyone who works with me starts with a length of rope around their neck. And the longer they work with me, the shorter the rope becomes until they eventually hang themselves." Quite the morale booster, right? It was their way of saying, "I'm watching your every move".

From day one, we all worked under the threat of that "rope", which seemed to tighten around someone's neck each week for the slightest misdemeanour, like daring to breathe too loudly!

Here's the problem with management by fear: it paralyses productivity. In our case, instead of being super productive, the team was busy tiptoeing around, afraid to make a single move that might tighten that heavy rope. Creativity? Gone. Innovation? Not a chance. Risk-taking? Are you kidding?

The first thing to go in a fear-based workplace is confidence. No one wants to be the person who admits, "Hey, I need help with this," when asking for help might mean getting one step closer to "death by hanging". As a result, collaboration plummets, and people do the absolute minimum to stay out of the spotlight.

Eventually, this approach takes a toll on everyone's sanity. Stress levels hit new heights, morale nosedives, and people start running like it's Black Friday at a department store. Pretty soon, you're left with an office of people constantly searching employment websites or biding their time until they're shown the door.

Ironically, fear-based management is self-defeating. The "rope" strategy doesn't lead to higher performance; it leads to bare-minimum work, creativity on life support, and everyone's dreams of innovation tucked away, with updated resumes being their most sent items.

It came as no surprise to see the board of that business ultimately tighten the length of rope around the neck of that particular CEO to an inescapable noose. However, unfortunately, the damage created during their reign of terror was irreparable.

Lesson learned? Fear gets you nowhere. Great leaders don't intimidate; they inspire. A team that feels safe to take risks, make mistakes and actually enjoy their work will always outperform a team trying to dodge the boss's imaginary noose. So, ditch the rope and let people breathe – you'll be amazed at what they can do.

Leadership Quality 12: Diversity and inclusion (aka "No one likes burned sausages")

In these modern times, being open to embracing diversity is not just a choice; it's a necessity. The positive impact of diversity and inclusion in professional settings has been undeniable, and it's time for our political, business, religious and community leaders to recognise this.

The exclusion zones established by "male, pale and stale" leaders that have either deliberately or unconsciously not fostered inclusion and diversity on their executive teams and conference stages must be abolished. The world has changed and will continue to change. Businesses that insist on ignoring the incredible talent pool available based on gender or sexuality will sound the death knell for those who continue to have their heads stuck up their own fundamental orifices.

Take a moment to view the speaker lineup at many real estate conferences, including those here in Australia. Historically, it's not been uncommon to see a speaker lineup boasting gender ratios of 10 males to one female.

Today, over 50% of real estate practitioners are female. And, unless you live under a rock, you'd have to agree that, generally speaking, the business and home lives of most females are quite different from those of their male counterparts.

Frankly, the only sausage fest that interests *me* is at Bunnings on a Saturday. *(Onions on last with BBQ sauce, please.)*

I'm not sure why so many outdated, rusty corporate executives feel threatened by anyone who might identify as "other". Perhaps it stems from something my mum shared with me as a youngster – the things we dislike in others are the things we fear most in ourselves.

Let me share 2 examples of real estate industry leaders who I believe have shown immense courage in their advocacy for diversity and inclusion.

Brad Inman, a male in his 60s who deserves a second mention in this leadership lesson section, has applied a simple rule of diversity to his events of up to 5,000 attendees. For Brad, it's simple: for every man on stage, there must also be a woman on stage. Brad takes his commitment to diversity even further, breaking new ground with several keynote presentations delivered by subject matter experts who identify as homosexual or transgender. Brad's decision to embrace diversity and inclusion has since been endorsed by a profession not historically known for acceptance.

Honourable mention also goes to Antonia Mercorella, whose push for boardroom diversity has reshaped conversations and, in turn, the direction of the REIQ, a 100+ year-old, historically conservative organisation.

Against significant odds, Antonia, a resilient leader fuelled by a board-driven policy for diversity, successfully and resoundingly prosecuted a case to embrace change to its own historically conservative male-dominated boardroom. The success of this seemingly simple single act has forever positively impacted the future of this grand institution, which now celebrates diversity at its board table and across its management team.

I'm happy to say the traditional corporate "sausage fests" are rapidly coming to an end. As a father and grandfather to 3 amazing young women, I'm excited by the opportunities that are opening up for them.

Each of us, especially those in leadership, has a role to play in living that value, calling out inequality when we see it and championing change so our children and grandchildren can all enjoy a better world.

Vale the sausage fest.

PART 4

People Make the World Go Round

The mix of personalities that make up a community these days is increasingly diverse. And, at times, scary. For many moons, a village was made up of a dozen or more streets, typically bordered on one side by a highway, on another by a bay or a creek, on another by a farm. I grew up in one – the once quiet little village of Manly in Queensland. A long, winding road meandered past rows of modest homes and lush green farms as it took you through the heart of the village. You knew the locals by name or reputation and would commonly say g'day as you passed by. There were always a few village idiots; you mostly knew who they were and wisely chose to avoid that pub, street corner or park bench and any chance of connecting with them. The village was a safe, comfortable place where you felt at home with people you trusted and who inspired, entertained or cared for you.

Most villages had people who, through their actions, had earned positions of trust and respect. They were the inspirational village leaders. Often, they included the local lawyer in his brown knit cardigan, the local priest, who imbibed in a tipple or two, the local publican with the almost mandatory rosy-red cheeks, and a man called David, who had deep passion and vision for the village and valiantly spent half his time trying to herd local businesspeople to see into the future.

There was usually a Mrs Jones who had somehow managed to coach her children's sports teams, run the school tuckshop and the fete, mentor the school choir and spend her afternoons and weekends endlessly transporting her own brood and their mates back and forth across the village in her white Tarago. Her hubby, Baz, a local tradie, was capable of fixing almost anything with a bent coat hanger and a roll of gaffer tape.

In my formative years, the people in our village moulded and shaped who you were. Sadly, though, the world of social media has expanded the village boundaries wider, longer and crazier. It's also become harder to avoid the myriad of characters who now have a stronger voice and access to a wider audience. The village's crazy lady now has 3 even crazier sons and daughters, all armed with channels like X, Reddit, Instagram and Facebook. I don't need to tell you that they're now broadcasting their craziness way beyond the traditional boundaries of the once-cocooned village.

For this and other reasons, I've consciously worked hard to cultivate my own village. Not in a physical sense but more in a tribal sense. I've done this not for fear of hearing other opinions. But as time has marched on, I've become increasingly clear on distinguishing right from wrong, and I have no interest in polluting my one shot at life with negativity or toxic people.

In the following reflections, anecdotes and musings, I acknowledge some of the people in my personal village who've kept me sane, been my rock, my cheer squad, and inspired me to pursue my own path. It's certainly not an exhaustive list. If we're already friends, you'll be under no illusion that I appreciate our friendship. I don't plan to leave this world with anyone wondering.

My life has gifted me the honour of meeting some incredible people. It's impossible to name all of them here, so if you've missed an honourable mention, please accept my editor's apology for the oversight. She's obviously clumsily deleted the deeply passionate piece I'd written about you!

Legendary musician James Taylor has been a constant companion at almost every intersection in my life. His music has lifted me, and his lyrics have provided great counsel when I've been up on the roof or down and troubled.

One of James' many masterly pieces of wisdom etched into my DNA is: "Shower the people you love with love. Show them the way that you feel. Things are gonna be much better, if you only will."

And if I have any particular wisdom to share from these pages, it's exactly that: shower the people you love with love. You'll be amazed how good it'll be for you.

It takes all kinds to make a village.

Bye Bye Blackbird

My dad's kindness, generosity and love for me and my children was undeniable. As life unfolded, he learned not to sweat the small stuff, including what others thought of him and the decisions he made. Things that once needled him would gradually wash over his Teflon coating as the years marched on.

I'm proud to have played a part in that change. I remember sitting in the lounge room of a house we'd just bought, talking about life and its complexities, and repeating the words I'd recently said to my accountant, who'd been agonising about what his clients would think of him if he bought a luxury car: "Who'll give a stuff in a hundred years?"

My accountant latched onto those words of wisdom as he ordered his shiny new Merc. And those same words helped shape a more relaxed Dad. I love that we'd be somewhere together contemplating a business deal, and he'd turn to me with a wink and a warm smile and say, "Who'll give a stuff in a hundred years? Let's do it!"

My dear old dad left this earth on June 14, 2013. He wasn't overly keen on the idea. Dad kept a disciplined calendar, and this particular event wasn't scheduled in his diary. The only notation he'd made for that day was Sam and Lauren's mum Michelle's birthday. So, to say he was just a little pissed that he'd received no advance notice of his sudden demise would be an understatement. It's a lesson we should all be aware of. Live your life to the full before it's unceremoniously over.

When he passed, Dad and my relationship had endured all of the crap most father/son relationships are challenged with. Fortunately, over time, we were able to bust down the walls and banish the macho, archaic BS from our family. The respect, freedom to openly say "I love you" to one another and unconditional love that flowed in both directions made for a beautiful, loving relationship and family life. (*Yes, "I love you's" were finally exchanged with zero avians harmed.*)

Our relationship went from strength to strength, and in his later years, Dad was generous in helping shape my family's future. It was an honour to be his son. So, while the sadness at his unplanned passing was immense, I knew Dad was aware of my absolute appreciation of his unconditional love for me. He was, and we were, completely at peace.

Funerals are usually sombre affairs where no one knows what to say and family members who only manage to tolerate each other are forced to shake hands and feign condolences.

Traditionally, someone – often the eldest son or daughter – has to get up on stage, fight back the tears and recite a long history lesson of the deceased's life before the church keyboardist plays "The Lord's Prayer" closely followed by "Nearer My God to Thee". Psalm 23 may get a run, too.

Don't get me wrong. They're decent songs and passages, but let's be honest – they're not the most uplifting, particularly at a time when everyone's spirits are low. They're even less uplifting when only a tiny percentage of those assembled know the words and mumble along out of tune.

In our particular flock, the "heathen"-to-Christian ratio is significantly weighted in the "heathen" column. So, I figured listening to a priest and singing hymns at my Dad's life celebration would leave our crew befuddled and thinking they'd shown up for the wrong send-off. That's why we chose a non-denominational service in a chapel.

As luck would have it, the daughter of Dad's late-in-life partner Judy was a civil celebrant. She gave us a framework of the legal requirements and free rein to fill the rest of our allocated time at the chapel. One problem though – I had no idea how we should celebrate Dad's wonderful life. All I knew was that he wanted a poem called "Mates" recited, which honoured the contribution of National Servicemen, and an Australian flag draped over his coffin. But I ignored his suggestion to "Save yourself a few bucks and throw me in a pine or cardboard box"!

Other than Dad's few simple requests, I was at a loss as to how the order of service should flow. I'd been elected unopposed to the privilege of honouring Dad's life and that responsibility weighed heavily on me. My only dad. My first funeral. No manual. What could possibly go wrong?

After much deliberation, I came up with a plan. Despite Dad's usual adherence to formality, I hoped he'd approve of my decision to do a 180-degree flip from your common everyday garden variety send-off. I decided we should have a singalong interspersed with impromptu yarns with people he'd met in his well-lived life.

Decision made, I hired some roving microphones and engaged the services of a musician friend, Peter Cupples, to sing a few numbers to keep toes tapping as people entered the chapel and provide melodic support for the singalong to a few of Dad's favourite tunes.

There's a great (and true) saying that "the number of people at your funeral will be in direct proportion to the weather of the day". Fortunately for Dad, it was a stunning winter's day. Blue skies. Perfect sunshine. A light breeze. He would have loved it.

Would he have loved the service we sent him off with? Well, I'd like to think so.

During the proceedings, my brother and I, both seasoned adlib performers, handed microphones around and encouraged key figures in Dad's life to share their fondest and most irreverent or inspirational stories of their time with him. It worked a treat. It was a casual chat full of fun stories, reminiscing, tears of happiness and joy, but still a deeply respectful celebration of a life well lived.

Family members – mostly consisting of my wonderful nephews – also played tunes that I'm sure their Poppa Don would have loved.

I loved that we celebrated Dad's life to the sounds of live music and a group of people reflecting on who he was and the lives he touched in his 74 years.

It must have been an okay send-off because several friends have subsequently asked me to arrange their farewells when their bells toll for the final time. And our musical maestro said it was the best funeral he'd ever attended. More than a dozen people slapped me on the back, congratulating me on turning a usually dour event into magical moments of love, music and happiness.

Did my slightly left-of-field celebration of Dad's life leave the staunch traditionalists doing backflips of disapproval? Probably not. However, no doubt some would have been aghast at the informality of the event. No long-winded, teary eulogy; no sombre music.

That was never going to happen on my watch. He was my dad.

We sent him to that great Masonic temple in the sky with fun stories of admiration and respect. He was serenaded along the way with the sounds of his grandkids' voices and music, his business and long-time mates joining his sons in belting out the "Hits of the Blitz" by one of his true loves, Dame Vera Lynn. Then, as the curtain finally closed on his magnificent life, his swan song was an upbeat guitar solo of his favourite "happy place" tune, "Bye Bye Blackbird".

I reckon Dad's only disappointments would have been not being able to join in on the singalong and not having a right of reply to some of the stories we shared.

As always with the Brewers, though, there was a plot twist. Dad was a stickler for detail. The i's had to be dotted and t's had to be crossed. In life and business, everything had to be measured twice and cut once. He had little time for ill discipline and was quick to let me know if I'd missed something important. It was a rare day that Dad didn't have the last say on everything.

After Dad's farewell, we were having a few beers and congratulating ourselves on giving the old fella a 10/10 send-off when a loud knock rattled the front door. The unexpected visitor was a very proper-looking woman from the funeral directors, carrying 2 small, mysterious velvet pouches, each tied with a purple ribbon.

A tad confused, I tentatively accepted them as she explained, in a hushed, almost reverent tone, that one pouch contained a locket of Dad's hair. And the other? Well, let's just say it was a final pinch of Poppa Don, apparently as per my request.

Now, I was 100% certain that neither I nor any of the family had made any requests for burnt offerings or a locket of Dad's hair. In fact, in his latter years, Dad was pretty follically challenged.

I asked our guest to have a seat while I explained that my dad was all about details and would be asking who on her team hadn't dotted their i's, crossed their t's or measured twice before they'd cut. He'd also be inquiring which family was anxiously awaiting a special home delivery and who the hell was now sitting on his kitchen table. I couldn't help but add that I hoped we'd just farewelled the right coffin and urged her to triple-check that the old fella was interred into the right memorial garden.

I chose to see the lighter side of life that day. I could almost hear Dad saying, "10 out of 10, eh? I think I'll knock that down to a 7!" I figured that my dear old dad managed to find a way of having the last word right to the very end.

"So, make my bed and light the light,
I'll arrive late tonight, Blackbird, Bye Bye."

Donald James Brewer
20/9/1933–14/6/2013
Beloved husband, father, grandfather and great-grandfather.
In our hearts forever.

Quiet please, there's a lady on stage

What do you do when the person who gave you life and stood by you through every self-inflicted disaster every day of your life without a moment of judgement finds themselves on the receiving end of a terminal diagnosis?

My biggest supporter from day 1

In January of 2023, I was to find out.

Initially, there was sobbing and overwhelming sadness, helplessness and a sense of hopelessness I'd never felt before.

To be told that your greatest ally in life has been given the news that their magnificent life of service to their family and community is drawing to a premature close is devastating.

I was taught early that you only learn true perspective when you spend two moons in the other person's moccasins. So, if I was feeling devastated, how must my beautiful mother be processing this gut-wrenching diagnosis?

All my life, my mum has been the one person who'd shared

consoling words of comfort from my very first tear. She'd provided words of wisdom and reassured me that all would be okay when I lost my first dog. She was the loving human who put my broken heart back together from the pains of first love. She was that reassuring voice that whispered, "Everything will be okay," and it was. It was her warm, loving strength and perfectly tuned heartbeat that gently rocked me to sleep when all hope in life and love seemed lost.

At 86, Mum still had bold plans to spend more time exploring the world with her "First Mate", Graham. Unfortunately, that was not to be. But even after the devastation of her terminal diagnosis, Mum did what she has always done – she thought of everyone else first. She cared more about easing her family's pain and ensuring Graham's ongoing care than preparing for her own challenges.

Beyond the sadness, Mum was at peace with her world and intent on ensuring the comfort of others, showing courage and retaining dignity until the end. She calmly, bravely and lovingly shared that while she felt sadness that her time on earth was coming to an end, she was at peace and had faith in her Lord.

Mum shared that she was proud to have reigned as the grand matriarch to her close and extended family. She was thankful for her incredible life and the opportunity to serve her Lord and community.

That is courage at its finest. Those are the words, actions and key character traits of one of the most outstanding leaders I've ever had the honour to work alongside.

Mum had lived a life filled with incredible optimism. She weathered storms that would leave others marooned. She had blazed a trail for her sisters, her community, her Lord and for social justice.

I'll confess that, for a short time, I held my own pity party trying to imagine a life without my greatest supporter. After all, how does a son deal with the impending loss of his amazing mum?

Well, in my crazy world, and having been inspired by Mum's love of all things music, parties and community, the idea of throwing a party seemed like a perfectly appropriate "Brewer" thing to do.

Doctors couldn't predict if Mum had 3 weeks or 3 months. Just that her clock was ticking. Time was of the essence. So, with my partner Tara on the team, we set about putting together a shindig that would call on Mum's community, church, friends and family to gather for a day of music and accolades to celebrate and honour her.

Armed with a clear mission to give Mum's tribe a chance to shower her with much-deserved love, we set about putting together a day that would be the biggest group hug ever seen. We all needed some reasons to smile.

Mum had taught us early in life that, "If you don't ask, you don't get." And so, with those words of wisdom ringing in my ears, I set about doing some asking.

My first task was to find a place to party. In Mum's case, there was nowhere better than the Old Shire Clerks Cottage, of which she had chaired the restoration. Tick!

Next up, we needed some entertainment to honour Mum's love of music that had seen her travel far and wide as an accomplished cabaret singer. A few phone calls later and we'd acquired the services of an 18-piece showband, my wonderful nephew Mikey and his melodic mate Seamus on guitar, and the angelic voice of the amazing Laura Doolan.

We also acquired the services of Mum's extraordinary lifelong friend Don Lewers to do a couple of cameos on his banjo.

Musical talent acquired. Tick!

When it came to community service, Mum was a quiet achiever of extraordinary things. I could fill an entire book with all the good she did for her community, her church and people in times of personal crisis. I'm pleased to say her achievements did not go unnoticed. She was awarded a Silver Jubilee Medal by HRH Queen Elizabeth II and she was recognised by Quota as their Woman of the Year. And to receive a call from the Member for Lytton, Joan Pease MLA, advising that she wanted to induct my mum into the Hall of Fame as a Bayside Great was beyond special.

I was reduced to ugly tears when retiring Anglican Archbishop of Brisbane, Phillip Aspinall arranged for one of his Bishops to personally deliver and read a letter of appreciation, love and a blessing to Mum at our event. Tick!

Mum inducted as a Bayside Great by Joan Pease MLA

Our soiree to celebrate Mum was coming together.

My children, Sam and Lauren, agreed to honour their nanna by MCing the afternoon's festivities. A joyful character-building experience for them both, and a display of love and appreciation for their nanna that warmed her heart. Tick!

According to Tara's meticulous event planning spreadsheet, all that was left to do was find someone to capture people's reflections on video for Mum (and family) to enjoy at the event. Done and tick!

What ensued was a day of love, reminiscence and celebration that I know warmed my mum's heart.

It was another lesson for me on what's important in life. In just 2 weeks, we had managed to arrange a powerful and mighty celebration. It led me to try and rationalise the times when a younger me had brushed Mum's kind dinner invitations aside because I was too tired, too busy, or too lazy to savour more magical moments with my mum while I could.

Right up until the day she passed, Mum taught me to be a better human.

Mum passed away on the morning of Sunday, April 24, 2023, just 3 months after her diagnosis. After a blessing with oil on her forehead and a reading, she made her final departure from her home of 40 years – flanked by a guard of honour consisting of her partner Graham, Father Sam (her parish priest), Joy Kruger (her closest friend) and me – via the front stairs to an awaiting ambulance. Her pain was managed, she was dignified, and she was ready to meet her Lord.

At Mum's funeral service, I delivered the toughest speech of my life. Mum would have expected me to orchestrate an upbeat celebration, and letting her down on her swan song wasn't an option. Holding it all together in her honour was mission-critical. She'd dedicated her entire life to keeping it together for us. The least I could do for her was hold it together for 45 minutes.

I went to great lengths to make Mum's farewell just as she would have wanted it. I chose music for the service that reflected her life of performing on stages, including a 1980 recording of a Radio ABC concert recording of Mum singing the Judy Garland classic, "Somewhere over the rainbow". And I ensured that the scones served at the wake were adorned with Mum's own home-made strawberry jam. The fact that she got to feed her guests and sing at her own funeral would have met with her approval.

I also thought it appropriate to call the congregation to order with the captivating Peter Alan song, "Quiet please, there's a lady on stage".

Quiet please, there's a lady on stage
She may not be the latest rage
But she's singing and she means it
And she deserves a little silence
Quiet please, there's a woman up there
And she's been honest through her songs
Long before your consciousness was raised
Now doesn't that deserve a little praise
So put your hands together and help her along
All that's left of the singer's all that's left of the song
Stand for the ovation
And give her one last celebration
Quiet please, there's a lady on stage
Conductor, turn the final page
When it's over we can all go home
She lives on, on the stage alone
So put your hands together, help her along
All that's left of the singer's all that's left of the song
Stand for the ovation
And give her one last celebration

"Stand for the ovation and give her one last celebration."

Iris Ena Brewer
13/9/1935–24/4/2023
She had hope in her voice,
Joy in her songs
Grace in her steps
And love in heart

The Pink Lady

Reflections on loss

I'm writing this on a day when I'm struggling to find positives. I know I will, eventually. I always do. I was taught to look for the silver lining in everything. I know that elusive rainbow is there. Somewhere.

It's been 14 days since my beautiful mum passed away and 6 days since I gave the toughest speech of my life. It's also 6 days until Mother's Day. It'll be the first one without my mum in 64 years.

I've never before noticed how many advertisements there are for Mother's Day. I wish I could turn that daily taunting off! Only 6 days to go.

It's a cold May morning. Fittingly, it's the first of a handful of chilly days we call autumn in Brisbane. The wind is up. The sun is rising into a deep blue sky.

On a table outside sit the last of the flowers from Mum's funeral service. Tara, so thoughtfully, removed the sad and jaded bunches yesterday – I'd have struggled to do that. She gently moved the remaining beautiful ones outside, still within my view. Fittingly, they're the ones that adorned Mum's coffin. They're still colouring the world like a paint bomb of amazing purples and pinks – Mum's favourites – and, right on cue, they're sharing their pollen to keep my already watery eyes red.

Will these tears ever stop?

Nothing can prepare you for the range of emotions you experience when you lose a parent. I'd said goodbye to Dad 9 years ago, and that was really tough. But this was different, and I can't tell you why. Perhaps it's because Mum's death marked the end of an era. Or maybe it's that inextricable maternal link that we have to our mums. I just know it's cold, surreal and it hurts. A lot.

I recently met a delightful young lady by the name of Julia Hearn who works with an organisation that assists people with their mental health. Instead of asking clients to share how they're feeling and them ambiguously replying, "I'm fine", Julia asks them to express how they're feeling as a number out of 10. A 7 is pretty good; a 2 means you're doing it tough.

I can't tell you how helpful that's been to me. Tara and some of my friends now know to simply ask me for my number when they sense I'm feeling low. It helps me explain my mood without going into detail and gives them a guide as to whether to press for more information, strike up a different conversation, give me a hug, a kick or offer me some space.

This last weekend, I've been fluctuating between a 5 and a 7. My goal is to get to 9.5. I don't expect I'll ever be a 10 again. I've lost my mum.

I've read about how little things can trigger strong emotional responses. I've never considered myself someone with a great eye for detail – well, at least not until this past week. It's been a real education in how much we unconsciously filter out from our surroundings until something suddenly becomes relevant.

It's like that old chestnut about blue cars. You never notice them until you decide to buy one. Then suddenly, it feels like everyone on the planet is driving a blue car – usually the exact model you've just picked out.

Funny how the smallest things can set you off.

I was watching a TV show last night with my mood score hovering around 5.5. It was just TV noise. I wasn't engrossed in it. My mind was elsewhere. Then a country singer walked on set and started singing. Nice voice. A good melody. Happy lyrics were lifting my mood and I could feel myself going from 5.5 to 8. Suddenly, I noticed a blue cameo jewel featured on his guitar strap. It was an almost exact replica of a thousand cameo brooches that I'd sat assembling at the kitchen table as a 12-year-old with Mum as she and Dad made jewellery to create other income streams to help feed their young family. I plummeted to a 3 in a heartbeat.

Based on the energetic and diverse life that Mum lived, I have a feeling that those triggers are probably gonna keep sneaking up on me for a little while to come.

Mum and I would chat on the phone often. More often than not, she'd cut me off mid-sentence, hurrying to get off the phone. I finally figured out that she didn't find our conversations boring; it's just that she was a child of the Depression era. Her mind still lived in a time when phone calls were ridiculously expensive. Every penny was important.

A sinking feeling comes over me when I instinctively reach for my phone to call her about small life events. I'm met with the sobering realisation that if I dialled her number, I'd hear my voice recording telling people of her passing. I've promised myself that I'll cancel her phone plan soon. Much easier said than done. For now, her phone and her scent sit on my bedside table.

It's always been my thing to write Mum a Mother's Day card, detailing just how appreciative I've been of the wonderful mother she's been. The handwriting may have gotten worse over the years, but the depth of gratitude in the words has only grown stronger.

I'll still write and post her a card this year. I know she'll be expecting it, and I figure she'll have sorted out a mail service up there. It'll be addressed:

Mum
c/Heaven

Just as some of the smallest, seemingly insignificant things can cause my mood to plummet down the emotional scale, music often has the opposite effect. One song immediately springs to mind: Paul Kelly's "My Mother's Voice". The words and music in this song bring me enormous happiness, warmth and reassurance in my darkest hours and can lift my mood from a 3 to a 9.5 in a heartbeat.

Every day the sun comes up
Like the day before
Every day I fill my cup
Stand up straight and walk through the door
Every day my mother's voice
Talks to me
Every day I make my choice
What to do and how to be
And every day I build my life
On her sacrifice
And every day I face my strife
But I know where to go for advice
Ooh, many roads I could have gone down
Many, many ways to disappear
And every day I hear the sound
Of her voice right by my ear
So clear, so clear
She taught me to be strong
I guess I got lucky

Postscript: Last night, I felt emotionally strong enough to resume the task of sorting through reams and reams of Mum's writings, press clippings and 80 years of photographs. I'm trying to approach it as a respectful, honourable cull – one not clouded by too much emotion. It's a challenge.

But my heart melted as I opened a red folder. Inside, in neat chronological order, were the last 35 years of Mother's Day cards I'd sent her. That teary moment reminded me that Mum valued words over "stuff". In a world quick to throw things away, she'd saved my words of love and appreciation.

I got to read back over 35+ years of Mother's Day cards and know, without a doubt, that Mum never questioned how deeply I loved and appreciated her and the upbringing and opportunities she gave me.

I'll remind my own wonderful kids that on those annual days of celebration, I, too, have no need or desire for "stuff". But a homemade, handwritten card? Now, that's priceless.

Letters of love

Is home a place or a feeling?

One of the most significant and daunting responsibilities in administering Mum's estate was managing the process of selling her home of almost 50 years. You'd think it'd be a pedestrian thing for a bloke who had transacted thousands of homes over his life in real estate. But this was different. This home was Mum's sanctuary – her safe haven – an Edwardian era house that started as a blank canvas and a dream. A place she'd woven into a bright and beautiful tapestry over 5 decades and where she enjoyed her colourful life of music, family, friends and community.

If those walls could talk, they'd captivate an audience for days.

How can you put a price on those stories and memories? Would anyone else embrace the great "conversation room", where our families would gather to sing "You Are My Sunshine" and where so many of Mum's famous concerts with her friends were hosted?

Would they appreciate the love-filled "grand room", where every Christmas morning for 40 years, noisy grandkids raced in to find presents sturdily stacked against and around the fireplace and polished timber floors ended up knee-deep in wrapping paper and glitter?

Would any potential purchaser appreciate the solid oak kitchen and granite benchtops where Mum would make her locally-famous strawberry jam using kitchen instruments and scales that were older than me?

Would anyone else be prepared to pay a penny for the commanding Moreton Bay views and cooling breezes that flowed across the shaded outdoor balcony where Tiki umbrellas rustled and beckoned friends and neighbours for lost afternoons and late nights of cold refreshments?

I had to accept that the memories were solely mine. They had no value to anyone else. Like a good book, the roof and walls had played their role in being host to the stories and memories. The time had come to take the memories with me and for someone else to start to weave their own tapestry on this fine canvas.

In December 2023, an auctioneer closed another chapter of

my mum's life. Fittingly, that auctioneer is a good friend and was briefed by my daughter Lauren. Her nanna would have been so proud that her beautiful granddaughter, who had grown up playing in that yard, ripped Christmas presents open by the cosy fireplace and learned to sew in the attic, was actively giving counsel in the sale of the property.

Thankfully, the house is now in the possession of new owners who are adding their own personal touches and creating memories there. And, as fate would have it, they're a real estate family and really wonderful people. I know Mum would approve.

Selling is one thing, though; letting go is another altogether. Memories can fade fast, especially at my age! So, to ensure those fond memories were kept alive for my family and generations to come, I commissioned iconic Australian artist Pro Hart's son, Kym, to capture Mum's house on canvas. I didn't just want a mere replica. I wanted a piece of art that paid homage to some of the special memories the grand old dame had hosted.

The painting I commissioned became more than just a picture; it became a living tribute to Mum's life, legacy and the people she loved. At its heart is Graham, her devoted partner, a quiet constant in her later years. Bright irises bloom in the garden, a nod to Mum's name and favourite flower.

In the yard, my children, Sam and Lauren, are captured mid-play, just as they were over 3 decades of visits. My nephew, Billy, who left us far too soon, is there too – symbolised through a billy cart, joyfully present in spirit. My granddaughter, Sydney Iris – who shares Mum's name and was one of the last little feet to touch those front steps – makes a cameo.

Threaded through the scene are subtle acknowledgements of Mum's extraordinary life. A gavel represents her trailblazing auctioneering career. A crown nods to the Silver Jubilee Medal awarded to her by Queen Elizabeth II. A 1953 signwritten FJ Holden ice cream delivery van – iconic of that era – is a hat tip to her time in the Peter's Pals troupe, which launched her musical career at 14. And, unmistakably, overlooking her home from the heavens is her signature Pink Lady dress and hat – symbols of the charity work that made her legendary in her community.

Never forgotten

At the start of this chapter, I asked whether home is a place or a feeling. Which resonates more with you? Is it a particular house that feels irreplaceable, or is it the presence of certain people or emotions that define "home"? Perhaps, for you, it's both – a symbiotic connection between place and feeling. I'm not sure I have an answer. But what I do have is a beautiful, deeply personal and unique piece of art that Kym Hart delivered in outstanding fashion. It evokes warm, wonderful, loving memories and will be passed on through my family for generations to come.

Bonkers

There are life-impacting people to whom even the most talented wordsmith could never give adequate justice.

Armed with the realisation that no words can adequately describe the miracle of my nephew Billy "Bonkers" Brewer and his impact on his friends and family, I still feel a deep need to try and honour his memory with whatever words and emotions my limited vocabulary can muster.

I suspect we all have suppressed emotions that can be triggered by a specific smell or sound. For me, it's the song "Tennessee Whiskey". With its first note, the waterworks immediately start – tears mixed with sadness and happiness. Its notes cause deep pain in my heart for a family who lost a beautiful, talented and much-loved young man way too soon.

We've all met people we immediately realise are special. We become drawn to them because they make us feel safe and at home. In meeting Billy, you'd have been instantly immersed in his infectious smile, deep and attentive eye contact and lingering handshake. Spending time with him would have had you appreciating his cheeky laugh, musical talent, deep knowledge of world history and ability to easily provoke civil, considered debate through insightful conversation on polarising global issues.

These are rare life skills only special people possess: the ability to transcend generational divides, demonstrate free thinking, respectfully accept a colleague with a strongly opposing view and, when it's all said and done, insist everyone have a hug and a beer before they part.

That was Billy Brewer. He was a beautiful, courageous young man who was stolen from us at age 33 by that evil bastard – bowel cancer.

Rarely did a year pass without us catching up to celebrate our birthdays or special events. It wasn't uncommon for Billy to call to suggest we catch up for a beer or to discuss my thoughts on whatever topic he was researching at the time. Billy had an inquiring mind, and I valued that he cared deeply about the world.

I have a strong bias, but on several occasions, I urged Billy to audition for *The Voice* or *Australian Idol*. His musical talents and voice were that good. Each time an audition was suggested, he'd blush, shrug his shoulders, give an embarrassed smile and warmly say, "Aw, shucks, thanks, Uncle Pete."

Peter - Tara Christianson - Billy Bonkers Brewer

Australia would have loved Billy Brewer. Sadly, his song finished before they got that opportunity.

Held deep in my heart is a night Billy and I shared at a Mexican restaurant in Surfers Paradise before his cancer diagnosis. He had texted me to say he was keen to catch up. I think he was keener for Uncle Pete to buy him a belly full of Mexico's finest export, the Coronarita. I'd previously described this exotic beverage to Bonkers, and he was pretty intent on taste-testing it. (*For the uneducated, a Coronarita is a margarita with a bottle of Corona strategically tipped upside down into a margarita glass. As the drink is sipped, the level inside the glass is equalised by the Corona bottle. Seriously delicious!*)

Whether Billy's enthusiasm was to catch up or because I was footing the bill, the fact that he rode his skateboard 5 km from Southport to Surfers Paradise for our rendezvous made me feel very special. We had a fun night with the usual belly laughs. How he managed to safely steer that skateboard home after a night of tequila-infused Mexican mayhem remains a miracle.

A few weeks later, on a Saturday morning, I received a call from a rambling and agitated Billy asking how he could urgently book a night in a 5-star hotel for him and his girl. I managed to slow his racing words to learn he'd just been given terrible news: his young body was riddled with aggressive cancer, and his time left on earth was being measured in weeks, possibly months, but most definitely not years.

To say my heart sank is an understatement. As gut-wrenching as it might be, take a moment to imagine being 33 years old and being told your hourglass is almost empty.

Billy and I discussed what he wanted to achieve that day. He'd never stayed in a 5-star hotel, and he wanted time alone with his girl, time to come to terms with what he'd just learned, and time to be surrounded by love.

I arranged a suite at one of the Gold Coast's finest hotels and ensured it would include all the bells and whistles. But Billy didn't make it to the hotel check-in counter that Saturday afternoon. Instead, he booked himself into the palliative care unit at Gold Coast Hospital for urgent pain management.

Sadly, Billy left us on June 7th, 2018.

Bonkers was a wag, hence his nickname. He loved challenging authority, and that included cancer's authority over him. One of my favourite videos of him post-diagnosis is him skateboarding full throttle through the streets of the Gold Coast, playing an electric guitar with a battery-operated speaker around his neck, raising two fingers to cancer and singing "Drift Away" by Dobie Gray at the top of his voice.

Lauren Brewer and Billy Brewer

He had built a wide network of people who cared for him deeply. They surrounded him, gave him strength and support and, most importantly, expressed their love and appreciation of each other and Billy through the universal language of music.

Appreciating the importance of music in Billy's life, his close friends sourced an acoustically perfect, graffiti-ridden, disused railway tunnel. Knowing that time was of the essence, they quickly arranged a night of music to celebrate Billy's life. Bonkers was joined in song by his musical mates and family. The event was recorded and made into a beautiful video that is a lasting legacy for his survivors to reflect on and enjoy.

I often take time to enjoy the gift of Billy's music and use it to ground myself and as a reminder of how fortunate I am and how fragile life is.

In the quickly diminishing days he had on this planet, Billy remained optimistic. He married his love, Roxanne, in a private hospital ceremony. On his passing, he gifted his body to science to help others. He was generous and still searching for answers to the very end.

William "Bonkers" Brewer left an indelible mark on me and many others in his 33 years. The world is a lesser place without him.

I'm thankful for the lessons he gave me, his smile that warmed me, his defiance that bolstered me, his laughter that energised me, his music that lifted me, and his courage that made me stronger.

There will be no more tears in heaven.

"Hey, dickhead!"

In most countries, if you were met with the above greeting by someone, it wouldn't be unreasonable to feel threatened or sense some animosity in the air. However, in some Australian friendships, such a greeting is a show of respect, affection and endearment. The Australian film "They're a Weird Mob", directed by Michael Powell, takes aim at the less-than-subtle nuances of Australian culture in the mid-60s.

It's, therefore, no coincidence that one of my longest and most treasured friendships also dates back to the mid-60s, and the common greeting I receive each time I see that friend in the 60 years since has been, "Hey, dickhead!" I won't share my response to that greeting. I'll leave that to your imagination, which will probably be correct.

Join me on a trip down memory lane. The year is 1965. It's January. I'm 6 and it's my first day of second grade. My teacher, Miss Fields, welcomes a nervous me into her classroom and instructs that I sit beside a shoeless, skinny, part-Chinese guy with a very un-Chinese name, Greg.

Grade 1 hadn't been fun for me. I'd struggled to fit in. So, I was hoping that with the help and friendship from that skinny Chinese kid, grade 2 might be an improvement. Greg was a quiet kid. But what he didn't express with his voice, he more than made up for with his freakish ability to make almost any sporting instrument sing.

Days, weeks, months, years and now decades have passed since Miss Fields' Manly West classroom, and Greg's economic choice of words hasn't changed one iota. He still greets me with "Hey, dickhead!" I still respond appropriately, and our conversation – always entertaining, educational and peppered with laughter – resumes where it left off. Our farewells also conclude with similar terminology: "See ya, dickhead!"

I've now spent 60 years with that now not-so-skinny Chinese kid, experiencing almost all that life has to offer.

Fifty years ago, I had the honour of introducing Greg to his now-incredibly-tolerant bride, Kate, under the goalposts at the Wynnum Manly Football Club. She still hasn't forgiven me.

In the 90s, Greg developed a deep interest in the environment and nature. It earned him the nickname, "Discovery Channel". His knowledge of nature became encyclopaedic. I was astounded. It certainly hadn't been a character trait I'd witnessed in 10 years of school.

I was so impressed with Greg's newfound thirst for knowledge that I rang him one night to chat about something I'd seen on the evening news, figuring he'd be able to enlighten me further on it.

His response? "I don't watch the news."

Astounded, I checked back on his words. "You don't watch the news?"

"No. I know you do. I figure if something important happens, you'll ring me and tell me."

It was my first appreciation for effectively employing the skills of delegation and leverage.

Over time, Greg's nickname has been upgraded to "Captain Camper". It probably comes as no surprise that we share a love of camping, good food and watching the great outdoors from the comfort of a camping chair with an ice-cold beer in hand. We have exactly the same cars and caravans. We both have a lifelong love of the music of the Eagles and, more recently, the joy and fulfilment of helping our children and spoiling our grandchildren rotten.

There's something magical about the friendships you make early in life. They're very special. These people are your tribe.

As a side note, I was standing in line waiting for a beer at the Gabba a few summers ago and heard 2 blokes chatting. One mentioned that he'd been to his high school reunion the previous night. His mate asked how it went.

The eloquently delivered reply was gold.

"Nothing much has changed. The good blokes are still good blokes, and the dickheads are still dickheads!"

Finding your tribe and cherishing those friendships can be life-defining. It has been for me. Whether they're friends from a book club or a marauding gang of absolute larrikins who love going fishing, enjoying too many cold beers and seeing who can tell the biggest lies, they'll be the people who will lift you up and dust you off when life offers you its inevitable speed bumps.

Sixty years on since Miss Fields sat me next to that skinny part-Chinese kid called Greg, I am forever grateful for that friendship and all that stemmed from it. It's been the ride of a lifetime.

"A friend is someone who knows all about you and still loves you."

Elbert Hubbard

Dooley

If you were alive in Brisbane in the mid-1970s to 2000s, you'd have seen – or at least heard of – the Wickety Wak® Showband. "The Wak" was an eclectic mix of incredibly versatile performers whose combination of musical magic and vocal versatility created entertaining parodies of some of the world's greatest performers. Their melodic maestro and comedic genius, Greg Doolan, led the Boys – Tony, Robbie, Pete and Pahnie – all equally talented and brilliant.

I first met Greg in 1979 when I was 20. The band was in its infancy doing small pub and club work. From recollection, they pretended to be fly-ins from Perth to charge venues more as an interstate act. In reality, they'd mostly come on a bus from Logan City in Brisbane's south! They were always creative.

Greg was a larger-than-life, fun-loving guy with a constant smile and a genuine will to help people. I caught up with him at a gig he and the Boys were doing in the city, and we discussed The Wak performing a show at the Wynnum RSL in our 500-seat auditorium. Despite my young age, I'd become actively involved at the Wynnum RSL in an effort to modernise the tired, dated club. (*Modernising tired old businesses seems to be a common theme in my life.*)

We agreed on a price of $600. The band was quickly gaining notoriety, and crowds were flocking to their shows across southeast Queensland.

At that stage, the Wynnum RSL auditorium had a permanent booking every Saturday night for 21 people from 7 'til 9:30 for an "Old Time Dance" group. You could set your watch to those 21 oldies turning up with their own bottles of lemonade, a thermos of hot water or coffee, 11 tea bags and a plate of dry biscuits at 6:59 on the dot. They were creatures of seemingly immovable habit.

I still recall approaching RSL club management to explain I'd managed a coup to get The Wak to Wynnum for $600 for a prime Saturday night gig. I was so excited at the prospect of exposing Greg and the Boys to our club.

My excitement was about to be tested by a somewhat archaic club manager. His view was that if they proceeded with booking Wickety Wak, they'd lose the (almost zero) income they received from those old-time dancers. At the same time, I could see the income and exposure the club would receive as an entertainment venue, generating huge liquor sales and member satisfaction from the other 479 seats. Basically, the manager was worried about losing a $25 weekly booking fee from a dance group whose members did not spend a brass razoo.

When club management finally agreed to take the risk of booking The Wak, it was on the basis that I personally underwrote any losses incurred. I agreed to that commitment. Deep in my heart, I knew that Greg's trademark passion, natural exuberance and enthusiasm to entertain would ensure a special sell-out event.

For the record, 500 tickets sold out in under 48 hours. The night was a smash hit. Bar takings set a new club record, and The Wak became a regular feature act at Wynnum RSL.

From memory, the boys carried and set up their own gear that night at the Wynnum. Since then, they've become Australia's number-one showband with their own team of roadies. The last time I booked them, their fee was $10,000 – a far cry from the few hundred bucks they earned all those years ago.

After the band members went their separate ways years later, Greg went on to have a highly successful career. He was named Australian Entertainer of the Year more times than I can recall. He had an incredible following, and his humility was such that he was always around to meet and greet his adoring fans pre and post-show.

His duet shows with his equally talented wife, Laura, were iconic and brought happiness to thousands across the Queensland Clubs network. Regardless of whether they were on stage in front of 50 people at Goodna RSL or 2,000 in the auditorium at Twin Towns, they delivered their music and love of entertainment with the same energy and passion.

Greg greatly appreciated me for going to bat for him and the band in 1979 at Wynnum. I was honoured that he was the guest act at my 21st birthday party and even more flattered that he and Laura were the guest acts and MC 29 years later at my 50th.

Whenever I saw Greg's name (now affectionately known to me as "Dooley") pop up on my mobile phone, I instantly knew it would be a fun call filled with stories and laughs.

At Christmas in 2016, I booked a group of seats at Greg and Laura's Christmas show at Twin Towns Services Club. Mum, her partner Graham and my Tara said g'day to the dynamic duo before we enjoyed the show. As is the case with many singers, I noticed Greg had a nasty rasp in his voice as we chatted that night, and I quietly hoped he'd be able to get through the show. I figured it was the year's end, and I guessed he'd overworked the vocal cords.

We had a magnificent night, with lots of laughs and loud singing. Afterwards, we thanked them for their music and the much-needed injection of Christmas spirit and bid them both a fond farewell.

The following morning, we sat at Currumbin, having a family brekky and discussing our personal highlights of last night's show. The phone rang. It was an unexpected surprise call from Greg thanking me for coming and bringing a gang along. As always, we laughed and reminisced. I had a feeling he had something else to share, but the connection was patchy and we cut the call short, agreeing to catch up sometime soon. I remember feeling honoured that he'd called but also a little curious.

Fast forward 2 months, and after a short battle with cancer, Greg was gone.

Greg was a warm, empathic man who actually gave a stuff about people, no matter what side of the track you came from. He was a man for all seasons and all people. He selflessly provided happiness and joy to several generations and is sadly missed, not just as a musical and comedic master but as a magnificent human.

Dooley's trademark hat was his 21st birthday gift to me. I feel a deep loss that I misplaced it over the years. Now, more than ever, it would have been a symbolic reminder of a brilliantly talented but incredibly modest man who lived every waking moment with a warm, energetic smile.

Love ya, Dooley. Thanks for the lessons!

I learned many things from the great Greg Doolan. Much of which can never be published. However, the most important lessons he taught me include:

- Smiles are infectious. Keep smiling.
- Never take life too seriously.
- Always appreciate those who helped you on the way up. You might need them on the way down.
- Humility is one of life's most important but underutilised qualities.

- Never burn bridges.
- Look for the best in people. It's there. Help to bring it out.
- Live large and laugh loudly and often.
- Leave an indelible mark of goodness on this earth as your legacy.
- A good dose of live music will fix most things. (*Except cancer. Fuck cancer!*)

Getting the band back together

I've had a life enriched by wonderful relationships. I've engaged with some of the most amazing people at home and across the globe – as far as the United States, Europe, the United Kingdom, and, in this case, just across the ditch in the Land of the Long White Cloud, where the men are men, and the sheep are scared.

There's something unique about the Kiwis. They're a resilient but quirky bunch of bros. Maybe it's the distance from anywhere and anything fun; it could be their apparent deep affection for sheep; or perhaps it's their lack of a sense of humour when it comes to combining cricket and lawn bowls. Remember, the Kiwis are a race that kills possums so they can use their fur to manufacture nipple warmers. They're a strange breed. Who knows what motivates their weird ways. In fact, who really cares? The Kiwis have a deep affection for Australia to the extent that there's growing validity to the rumour that Bondi Beach will soon be renamed South Auckland when the last remaining Kiwi finally leaves NZ and heads to Oz.

There's an unwritten understanding between the Cuzzy Bros that bridges Australia and the home of fush and chups, chully bins (eskies), and their weird affection for using the word sex instead of six. We love taking the piss out of them, and they love taking the puss out of us.

The roles of captain, coach, sole selector and man of the match for the K1W1's puss-taking team roles have been well-earned by the inimitable Andrew James Mark.

Andrew prefers to be called AJ. I assume that's because it's simpler for him to spell. I'm not suggesting that AJ is as thick as two planks. I'll leave it up to you to work out if I'm taking the piss here, dear Reader.

AJ, the crazy Kiwi, has been a good and loyal friend for 30 years. It wouldn't be right if I wrote this book without making some highly edited G-rated reference to the fun we've had and the mutual "puss-taking" we've partaken in during our wonderful, warm friendship. He's one of those colourful characters who lights up every room he enters. There is colour in everything he does – not just in his vibrant, charismatic personality, but in his trademark crazy socks, endless supply of crazy ties and very dapper suits. Being a landscaper from Upper Hutt outside Wellington, he's the most unlikely style icon. However, he is the King of Cool.

I met this terrible troublemaker through a real estate organisation I was involved with. AJ was the Chair of that organisation in "Un-Zud", while I was the Chair in Queensland. We'd meet at various events when our organisations got together.

One thing you could always count on when the band got back together is that AJ would be self-elected as leader of the pack in charge of the shenanigans. And, as much as night follows day, there was an ironclad guarantee that there would be much frivolity, sore ribs from laughter, a trail of confused and amused hospitality staff, and a high likelihood that someone from the band would be found comatose in the corner of a house of some form of ill repute.

You could also guarantee you'd spend the day after a night out with the lunatic landscaper randomly chuckling at the various antics he'd orchestrated the night prior.

As luck or misfortune would have it, we found ourselves in Las Vegas doing a study tour of the National Association of Realtors (NAR) Conference in 2007. Joining us were John Ross and Brian "Ron" Brady, whose respective reputations for the risque almost guaranteed that our US study tour would include an up-close and personal tour of the LVPD watchhouse.

The ultimate boy band of AJ, JR, BB and PB had hit Las Vegas, and our travel insurer was nervous.

True to form, AJ was already plotting and scheming on our 15-hour flight into the Northern Hemisphere. We made the flight with the assistance of a significant amount of refreshments in a very comfortable section of Air New Zealand Flight 1 to LA. My apologies to anyone else on that flight. My only excuses are that we were young and stupid, off our leashes and on a mission!

During the flight, the band of brothers and I discussed that being 10,000 miles from home isn't a bad thing – not for any nefarious reasons or activities, of course. But when you're well-known in your local community, you're always on show. You must be mindful of who's watching, taking notes and judging your alcohol intake.

After finally jetting into McCarran Airport, our first port of call was Jimmy Buffet's Margaritaville on Las Vegas Boulevard. It's a lively bar right on the Strip with aeroplanes hanging from the roof and boat flybridges as dinner cubicles. And on the hour, every hour, a massive volcano "erupts" inside the bar and one of the waitresses slides down the side of the volcano while the Jimmy Buffet song "It's Five O'Clock Somewhere" strikes up, causing the crowd to go into a frenzy. It's quite an experience that unites the assembled masses, regardless of age, gender, religion or nationality. It's always made me think it'd be a great bar for our warring world leaders to conduct peace talks. I'm sure they'd find common ground.

Being in another hemisphere, I quietly enjoyed my newfound anonymity. But it seems it was to be short-lived.

As the night wore on, I found myself 10 Landshark beers and 4 Jägerbombs in. Even if I say so myself, I was carving up some pretty impressive dance moves on the dance deck overlooking the bright lights of the amazing Las Vegas Strip. All I needed now were some blue suede shoes!

And then, out of nowhere, I was suddenly mobbed by about 20 young women chanting my name and yelling in full voice, "OMG, it's Peter Brewer! I can't believe it's Peter Brewer! Wow, is that really Peter Brewer?!"

I was on the Las Vegas Strip, more than amply liquidly refreshed, being mobbed by around 20 gorgeous and glamorous women surrounding me and chanting my name like a rock star!

Excited and a little confused by my newfound glitter strip fame, I glanced to the side, where a smirking AJ and JR stood laughing, pointing at me and giving me the thumbs up.

I'd been set up. My 20 adoring glamorous fans didn't know me from a bar of soap. AJ had slipped them a few drinks, given them my name and asked them to mob me.

Score: AJ – 1, PB – 0.

Our international escapades also took us to the opulence of Rodeo Drive. You can practically *smell* the wealth from one of my favourite places on that strip, in fact, in all of LA – The Luxe Hotel. It's where all the senses go into overdrive.

On either side of The Luxe's front door sit 2 small tables, dressed in crisp white linen and flanked by a couple of café chairs. They're popular spots to sip a coffee or cocktail and indulge in a bit of star-spotting. Within the first 10 minutes, we watched *Predator*'s Major "Get to the chopper!" Dutch – aka Arnold Schwarzenegger – cruise by in a camouflage green T-shirt and matching Hummer.

The star-spotting from those tables is next-level. Even the beautiful people jockey for a seat to watch the even more beautiful people.

So, there we were, the ultimate Boy Band on tour in LA, with front row seats on Rodeo Drive.

Through a stroke of good luck and a significant tip to the doorman, we found ourselves sitting pride of place on Rodeo Drive, enjoying an afternoon of refreshments playing "spot the star" or "spot the wanker" as the cavalcade of Rolls, Bentleys, Ferraris and the occasional tourist bus strutted the hallowed bitumen carpet.

AJ, a man in his 60s at the time, has a face that can tell a few stories. Brian "Ron" Brady is always a dapper dresser. On this occasion, both were suitably attired for the luxurious location. They sat comfortably at one table while JR and I took up the other pole position.

We were to find that we weren't the only star spotters savouring the scenery that warm Friday afternoon in LA. Side-splitting hilarity ensued as two Asian tourists walked by our tables, snapping photos of AJ and BB and pointing at the dapper duo while excitedly proclaiming, "Rook, it's Crint Eastwood and Don Johnson."

The spotters had become the spotees!

One look in the mirrored glass doors, and AJ and BB would have quickly come back to reality knowing they look more like Fred and Barney than Clint Eastwood and Don Johnson. But it was their moment in the spotlight, and they lapped it up!

Andrew and Peter back in town

As well as being an accomplished landscaper, AJ is a master real estate businessperson and an accomplished stage speaker. I worked with the larrikin running business management workshops across Australia for a while. The stories attached to those shenanigans will have to wait for my uncensored, non-G-rated memoir.

AJ was on stage during one presentation at a large gathering of around 250 people. I was sitting mid-audience and taking notes from his wisdom-packed presentation. To my left, I noticed a staff member had entered the room with an envelope. The staffer quizzed one of the event staff, who pointed directly at me. With AJ still on stage sharing his stories, the envelope marked "Brewer" was quietly relayed across the room to me. The theatre involved in getting it to me suggested it must be important. Discreetly, I opened the envelope and extracted the card.

It read:

Get Fucked, Brewer
L&K
AJ

With a subtle glance up to the stage, I saw the great man giving me the cheekiest wink while still in full flight of his presentation. Ah, AJ – ever the master of planning!

As AJ would say whenever the band came together:

"The Boys Are Back In Town!"
Thin Lizzy

I've only ever kissed two men in my life

I'm not one to judge who you plant your laughing gear on. That's entirely up to you. I'm never gonna judge you based on which team – or teams – you bat for. Love is love. As my good friend from Boston, Joe Schutt, says, "The difference between a straight man and a gay man can sometimes be just a six-pack."

For clarity, Joe and I have never shared a six-pack. And despite my love for the saucy Bostonian, I have a preference for the opposite team.

But as the title of this chapter alludes, I may have strayed.

Now, before you think I've gone all Liberace, settle, petals. It doesn't require a Diana Ross fanfare of, "I'm coming out!"

Seriously, I've only ever crossed the line and puckered up for the same team twice. And yes, I actually did like it!

The year was 1984. The city was Perth. The occasion was the national convention for the Professionals Real Estate Group.

A gang of about 40 of us had flown over from Queensland for a few days of networking and learning. If the opportunity arose – and if only to be hospitable – we might partake in a Swan Lager or 70 with our newfound friends from WA. And let me tell you, those Sandgropers from the West know how to run a good convention! I reckon I put 20 litres on that week.

I learned a few really important things on that trip. Sandgropers and Cane Toads have a lot in common. We both seem to take life and, more importantly, ourselves way less seriously than people from other states. Our shared need for elevated self-importance or being back-slapped and adored is low on our list of priorities. It's a first impression I noted in 1984, and it's an instinct that's proven true for the 40+ years since.

That trip also taught me to listen more than I spoke – just as nature intended, given I was born with 2 ears and one mouth. Essentially, shut up and listen. You'll learn much more from absorbing incoming messages than delivering outgoing dribble and edicts. *(If only some of my business colleagues heeded the same advice.)*

By enacting my love of learning through listening and putting it into practice, I continued to amass an encyclopaedic knowledge of my profession over time and still do today. Learning to #stfu is an important skill. I've also become a student of human behaviour, learning from a cavalcade of some of the smartest and most perceptive business minds on the planet.

I believe you'll learn more about humans through witnessing and interacting in person than you could from any textbook or almost any university professor in the world.

One of the wisest and most perceptive people I've met in my life is Keith John Brady. I first met KB at that conference in WA. He was "KB" to his friends and "Mr Brady" to his staff.

Keith was originally a Rockhampton lad and a "Bank Johnny" (a regular guy who worked in a bank). He was also one of the 3 founding fathers of the Professionals Real Estate Group in Brisbane, a group that, at its peak, boasted 505 offices in Australia, NZ, PNG and Asia.

KB, as he eventually allowed me to address him, ran a highly successful real estate office in Everton Park in Brisbane. He may have been born on April 1, but Keith John Brady was no fool. Still today, he is rightfully celebrated as the Father of the Professionals.

Even though we were both proud Queenslanders, it took a conference and a beer (or 30) to get us together, ultimately birthing a business bromance that would last 20 years. The myriad of life experiences from Keith's banking and real estate careers gave him wisdom. He became a career-long mentor of mine, always on hand to lend advice, even when I thought I didn't need it.

Keith was a very measured man. He didn't suffer fools and could sniff a dickhead out from 100 paces. You'd be left in no confusion about his assessment of you if you'd been judged by KB as a dickhead. The corridors of his South Pine Road office were littered with the corpses of clowns who tried to pull the wool over the legend's eyes. Keith didn't need textbooks to understand people. He was a man of the people and a genius at detecting shonks.

He was also ruthless with the red pen. I pity anyone who sent KB a document that hadn't been properly proofed. Feeling the wrath of his mightily wielded red pen tearing metaphorical strips off one of your manuscripts provided a life lesson you'd pick up quickly if you value your life. Keith had high expectations of the little things. He'd declare, "Pay attention to the small details. It'll make you look less of a dickhead." KB had a unique way with words.

KB loved his Saturday afternoons at the Everton Park Bowls Club where he was amongst his people. There he'd sit, quietly studying the form guide, sinking a few frosties and sneaking a few bungers while sharing his wisdom with the local characters who sought his counsel on topics ranging from how to invest in property to which horse to put $50 on in the last race of the day. As was his way, he'd also be keeping an eye out for dickheads. Have you caught on that he had no time for dickheads?

I'm never really sure what KB thought of this long-haired larrikin with the bushy moustache from the Bayside sitting in the driver's seat of the organisation he proudly founded. I'd like to think he was happy with where I took the business. I always feel like he treated me like his own son. By that, I mean he yelled at me twice most days and 3 times on Saturday!

At one point during my corporate leadership, I proposed a change to our "Top Office of the Year" award. Keith's office had won the title more than 10 years in a row. They were seemingly insurmountable. He'd created a business platform and band of high-performing people who had been incredibly consistent over a decade.

Keith and I were very much the Old Bull and the Young Bull when we worked together in the corporate boardroom. In a moment of delirium, and one that could have seen me forever banished to the dickhead category, I suggested to Keith that we might consider inducting his office into a specially minted Hall of Fame. The intent was twofold: firstly, they'd be immortalised for their consistency, and secondly, they'd be ineligible for the award for the next 10 years, opening it up for others to vie for.

It was that one momentary lapse of sanity that almost saw me lose part of my anatomy. A furious Keith shared his disagreement using some of Central Queensland's most colourful vernacular. He told me in no uncertain terms that if I made his business ineligible for the top award, he'd leave the group he'd founded and take my right testicle in a jar with him as a desk ornament.

KB passionately extolled that even though he'd won the award 10+ times, he used the visual of his team standing on the stage to continually drive their performance.

I'm not suggesting Keith was highly competitive, but I'm pretty sure he thought silver medalists were losers. Some might say that Keith didn't think winning was everything; it was the *only* thing.

Once I had my own business, KB was someone I could call for advice, and I did that regularly. He'd solve everything from simple staffing issues to complex business puzzles for me. He'd offer me guidance, and I'd take it. I think the fact that I readily adopted his wisdom made him more comfortable about sharing more of it with me. (*Another important lesson I learned.*)

Today, real estate practitioners and the occasional start-up ask me for my thoughts on business. The number one rule I've adopted is that if you seek my wisdom or direction and don't follow through on it, there's a fair chance I will probably pull the shutters down for you at the shop. Time is too valuable to spend on people who can't or won't be helped – another lesson I learned from KB. He taught me to spend my time wisely and where it'll make the most impact.

In KB's early days working in the bank in Central Queensland, he'd spend hours and days driving between regional towns. No tinted glass, no air conditioning, no sunscreen and sun burning the side of his fair-skinned face. Over time, that relentless exposure to the sun would ultimately contribute to the loss of his life. During his battle with skin cancers that continually invaded his extremities, Keith continued to fight stoically and fearlessly. Each time I'd see the legend, another chunk of his face or arm would be removed or repaired, but he valiantly fought on. His humility and strength as he faced his battle was inspiring.

I was blessed to sit beside the great man in 2006 at a 30th-anniversary lunch celebrating his founding of Professionals at the Breakfast Creek Hotel. I was honoured to stand on stage at the Brisbane Convention Centre in 2005 when we immortalised his memory through the creation of the Keith Brady Medal for contributions to Professionals. And I was humbled to be the recipient of that medal in 2007.

KB was a fair critic and a source of inspiration, and he handed me some pretty humbling accolades during our friendship. Most of all, from the outset of meeting KB at that conference in Perth in 1984, he treated this petulant Young Bull with respect I had yet to properly earn. He always had something to share that would make me a better person, real estate agent and leader.

I visited Keith at St Andrews Hospital through his health battles. I don't know what moved me to do it, but the mood seemed right. I felt that, until then, I hadn't appropriately expressed my appreciation for what he'd done for me, and sadly Keith was nearing his maker.

Inducting Keith John Brady into Professionals Hall of Fame

It was now or never. I held the great man's hand, leaned over and lightly kissed his right cheek. I shed a tear, and through a broken voice, I told him I was forever grateful to him.

His reaction? A firm return squeeze of my hand and a kind, warm smile. There was no need for words. He knew me well. (*I'm also thankful he didn't call me a dickhead. It would have really spoilt the magic of the moment!*)

KB went to that big real estate office in the sky on February 17, 2008. Saint Peter would have warmly and appropriately greeted him at the Pearly Gates with "Welcome, Mr Brady".

So, there's my confession about kissing a man.

And yes, I hear you asking, who was the second man I kissed? I'm gonna leave that to you to work out. It's rude to kiss and tell!

I kissed a man and I liked it!

(My sincere apologies to Katy Perry)

The Jovial Giant

I'm sure each of us can reflect on specific people to whom we can attribute some really important life-changing lessons. This reflection is about the man who inspired creativity and a competitive spirit in me that supercharged my success in real estate.

My parents had instilled in me the finer skills of attention to detail, the need for excellent communication and a good work ethic, but neither were fiercely competitive. In my first 7 days working with the family real estate business, I'd stumbled on 5 property sales. The sales price of each of those homes was around $50,000 with an average commission of $750 per property – a giant leap from the $96 a week I'd previously been surviving on. I remember standing in front of Dad at the time, excitedly extolling, "How long has this been going on?!" In that first year, I earned around $80,000. That was a big income in 1985. I felt invincible. The thought of needing to be competitive or creative to make a living in real estate never even crossed my mind back then.

Enter Neville "Yogi" Brewer. Dad's younger brother.

I need to set the stage here. I come from a family on Dad's side that's good on the tooth. While some people have a penchant for sweets, our crew have never been overly fussed about whether our fare is sweet or savoury. But if you were to ask me who the leader of the pack is when it comes to our lifelong love affair with a good feed, I'd tell you that honour rests with my uncle, Neville Charles Brewer.

While Neville was the name handed to the lovable larrikin at birth, he'd met a cartoonist at his beloved Wynnum Manly Leagues Club who had drawn a caricature of him as a bear on the back of a beer coaster and titled it "Yogi". At that stage, he was a rather large character, both in personality and stature. The big fella's love affair with food, including a couple of pies and a chocolate thick shake for breakfast and a works burger with chips and a Coke for lunch kept the Manly Bakery in business for many years. From that day forward, Neville became "Yogi, the Jovial Giant" and a legend was born.

Yogi had enjoyed a highly successful real estate career in his own right for a couple of decades before he joined our family business. He was quick-witted and a creative thinker. I have fond recollections of enjoying a beer with him one afternoon at Fishers Hotel and being approached by a very thankful guy carrying a bag of mud crabs who handed Yogi an unsolicited beer. The best type of beer there is!

Evidently, the cause for the free beer thrust into Yogi's paws was that the giver of said beer – a young butcher who had been knocked back for finance to buy a home for 2 years – had finally become the proud owner of his very first home, thanks to the creativity of his much-revered agent, the big fella himself.

Later, Yogi shared the full story with me. For around the same 2 years that the young butcher had been looking, Yogi had been attempting to sell a house on Whites Road, Lota – a basic spec home on a small block opposite a mangrove creek. The reason it was so hard to sell was that swarms of mosquitoes and sandflies would do an impressive aerobatic display in and around the property at dawn and dusk each day. They say you should sniff out a property with location, location, location. Well, this property's location had an earthy odour that didn't require a lot of sniffing. To say it hadn't been a popular listing is a significant understatement, and its 2 birthdays on the market attested to that.

Yogi had shown the mangrove "McMansion" to the young butcher, who, by that stage, had virtually lost all hope of ever being a homeowner. While he didn't love the idea of the twice-daily aerobatic displays, he was open to making an offer under the proviso that Yogi could convince someone to lend him the money to buy it *and* find him a way to earn some extra income to help make the repayments.

With the door slightly ajar to create a sale and rid himself of the Whites Road listing before it celebrated its third birthday on the market, Yogi's brain went into overdrive.

Standing on the front porch, he said to the young butcher, "See across the road there in those mangroves? What do you think is in there?"

"Mud?" queried the butcher.

"Sure, but you're missing the point. Those mangroves are also filled with gold – gold in the shape of an unlimited supply of mud crabs, my friend."

Yogi's creativity in the art of doing a deal continued. He masterfully painted the picture.

"If you throw some mud crab pots into that mozzie-infested creek every morning and night, I reckon you'll catch about 20 crabs a week."

Watching the young butcher's eyes light up, Yogi continued, "Cook those 20 crabs up and take them to Fishers Hotel on a Friday and you'll get $10 each for them. That's a tidy $200 of extra income a week."

Coincidentally, $200 was the equivalent of the butcher's mortgage repayments if he were to purchase the property.

The young fella was as happy as Larry. Home ownership had finally become his reality, and Yogi had managed to rid himself of that Whites Road property at long last.

During our time together in the family real estate business, Yogi demonstrated the importance of healthy competition. Before he joined the team, I'd been pretty satisfied with my earnings and success. I was also happy with my weight. All that was about to change.

Seated at adjoining desks, it didn't take long for me to learn 2 things from the big fella – jam doughnuts are addictive when consumed daily for breakfast, and when 2 people work as a team, you can do much more than just double your income.

From 8:00 am on day one of working together, the master motivator would pull his trusty red ledger book out from under his desk blotter and make copious notes. In handwriting that only a doctor could decipher, his notes mapped out the number of listings and sales we'd each need to make for the coming days, weeks and months in order to achieve our commission goals. We'd then agree on our activities and stretch targets for the day. More often than not, I'd suggest a number, and more often than not, Yogi would retort in his deep, gravelly voice, "I didn't realise you'd be satisfied with mediocrity, Pedro?"

In our first year together, I tripled my income. I attribute that success and my added confidence to Yogi. He was a warm, easy-going guy to work with, and his clients loved him, not only for his creative sales techniques but equally for his fun, witty personality.

Sadly, Yogi's passion for pies and junk food led him to an early meeting with his maker. Yogi, the Jovial Giant – my Uncle Nev – was a lovable, competitive rogue who didn't mind stretching the rules to see where the real boundaries were. On his instruction, I made it my business to never upset him. From time to time, he'd remind me that he was compiling a list of people who had mistreated him in life. His rationale for the list? In the words of the Jovial Giant himself, "Pedro, my final act of revenge will be to nominate them as my pallbearers."

I miss the big guy.

"Creativity is seeing what everyone else has seen, and thinking what no one else has thought."

Albert Einstein

The elder statesman

You know those people whose wisely chosen words and actions have maximum impact, not for a fleeting moment but for decades? I refer to them as elder statesmen and women. They're the ones whose generosity of heart and spirit are constant companions and a driving force. They're icons in their business and local communities. They give for no reasons other than having warm hearts and because they can.

They're often great deflectors and are as modest as the day is long. They'll avoid the limelight and refuse to accept credit for their good deeds. These true statespeople spend zero time plucking fluff from their own navels. Their focus is on helping others.

At one point during my Board obligations for Professionals, I'd identified that we needed a change at the top. We needed wisdom and inspiration to help us break the shackles with a turbo boost to supercharge the brand. There was one obvious candidate for the role in my eyes: Gold Coast real estate legend David Bonifant.

I called ahead and asked David if he'd agree to meet with me so I could propose my vision for the future, which, unbeknown to him at that stage, revolved entirely around him as the central player.

We met over a delicious bowl of pasta at Nicolinis, an iconic and authentic GC restaurant run by a fun Frenchman named Freddy and perfectly positioned next to David's Surfers Paradise office.

(There's something predictable about real estate agents and the particular businesses that their offices adjoin. In my case, our business was next to the Manly Hotel. David was, of course, next to an Italian Restaurant. I offer no comment on my wonderful friend David Stewart, who, up until recently, ran his business next to a Thai massage place. I'm unsure what happened with David's office, but I'm 100% sure the story finishes with a happy ending. But I digress.)

David heard me out and gave his warm trademark nods at the appropriate times, his index finger poised on his pursed lips. He listened intently, his eyes engaging with the sky or the table but nothing in between. He appeared to ponder the reasons for my road trip and the concept of a fresh start under his leadership. I felt good about my presentation and hoped I'd secured his agreement to be our driving change. His body language was encouraging. David was usually a man of few words. My experience was that when he did speak, however, his words were always carefully considered.

And so, after what seemed like an eternity of silence, it was time for him to savour the last of his creamy pasta, swirl the final drop of his oaked, buttery chardy and deliver his judgement.

"I couldn't agree with you more, young fella. I think we well and truly need a fresh face, new ideas, energy and passion."

He went on to say that choosing the right person for the role of Chair had been on his mind as well, and as a fellow Board Director, he'd wanted to discuss the path forward with me and was appreciative that we could break bread over the topic.

I was thrilled we were both on the same page. I thought my trip to the GC had been worthwhile.

But there's always a plot twist. David completed his assessment of our similarly shared views and summarised his position: "You'll have my full support, young fella. I think you're just what the doctor ordered. I'm looking forward to supporting you as our new Chair and ensuring you secure the required numbers in the Boardroom."

The campaign manager had suddenly somehow become the candidate!

I shared my shock with David. I tried once again to explain that I sought to support *him* rather than the reverse. The Master closed his earmarked diary, gave me a wink, explained he had another meeting to attend, paid the bill, gave Freddy a tip, and was off on his way, leaving me to ponder what had just happened.

I drove home to Brisbane, trying to reconcile whether David had kindly given me some pleasant platitudes in a bid to move me on or if he actually thought I could do the job. The more I thought about his words, energy and passion, the more I realised I probably had all the qualities he mentioned. But could I actually execute on them?

There was only one way to find out! My next stop was the ballot box to lodge my nomination – which, by the way, nobody opposed.

I make it my business to ring David on his birthday each year. It brings us both happiness and moments of reflection. Now in his early 80s, he's still shaping lives with his work in Romac and Rotary, providing medical and humanitarian aid for children living in remote countries. His joy-filled Blenders Choir continues to bring smiles to people's faces, and he's still mentoring the next generation of real estate professionals in our fine country.

Thank you for believing in me, David Bonifant. More importantly, thanks for helping me believe in myself.

A morning drive to the Gold Coast extended to a winding road and a new adventure! Twenty-five years later, I'm delighted to receive the occasional call or email from someone else with a spring in their step and stars in their eyes. I immediately reflect on David's kindness to me and ensure that I give those future leaders the benefit of my experience.

We all need someone to believe in us. I think one of the responsibilities of holding a senior position is to help shape the next generation. My role today is to nurture and encourage. So much talent is waiting to be realised and nurtured in our country. The next Twiggy Forrest and Emma Isaacs are one call or conversation away from being given the confidence to realise their full potential.

David Bonifant's belief in me jet-propelled my confidence and career. I pose one question to you, dear Reader: What are you doing to help drive other people's possibilities into existence? If not, when will you start?

Time to step up!

Baldy

If a skinny, bespectacled Walter White clone from Santa Clarita, California, named Jeff (Baldy) Turner wasn't the architect responsible for the design of Peter Brewer 2.0, then he most certainly is the person most influential in igniting my fascination with the evolution of all things digital in the real estate profession.

Over the last 20 years, Baldy has garnered an encyclopaedic knowledge in proptech. He not only has knowledge of the base tech but, more importantly, gets the profound, human behavioural and ethical impact that new and emerging technology has and will continue to have on our society. During the course of our time together, Baldy has instilled in me the importance of applying a lens of healthy scepticism to whatever "the next big thing" might offer. His more recent writings on the effect of unchecked AI with no guardrails should be setting off alarm bells in every home and business.

Peter watching Jeff Turner on-screen

Baldy's ability to apply critical thinking has indelibly etched his mark as the person I look up to as the most respected and unbiased authority on the good, the bad, and the downright terrifying sides of the rapidly evolving digital landscape of the real estate profession. I'm honoured to count my follically-challenged friend as an immense inspiration in my personal and professional growth.

I sat with Baldy recently to thank him for the opportunities he provided me to meet and work with some incredible people across the industry in the USA. True to his great modesty, Baldy's response was simple: "Peter, I was just the guy who opened the doors for you. You had to walk through them."

Baldy and his wife, Rocky, are great humanitarians. For many years, they funded an orphanage to provide safe haven, education and hope for 32 young ladies escaping torture and a grim future in Kenya. As a father to my own young daughter, Lauren, I shuddered at the persecution those young ladies were exposed to every day of their lives.

I vividly remember a call from Baldy seeking urgent help to provide a fridge for the Kenyan-based orphanage. I was pretty sure that Harvey Norman's delivery service didn't include Kenya on its map, so I quickly set about finding who did. No mean feat from Australia! But, fast forward the clock by 12 hours, and in a time zone on the other side of the planet, I had been able to fund and arrange delivery of a fridge that still bears my name today.

It was a simple gift of appreciation to a man who has significantly shaped the latter part of my 65 years of free trips around the sun.

Time has taught me that there are people we meet on life's journey who unintentionally transform much of who we are and the path down which we're heading.

May you all find your Jeff Turner.

The Master

Some people just ooze wisdom. One of the wisest men I've met on my journey is Les Thornton. I called him "The Master".

Les was a brilliant businessperson. Meeting him in the early days of owning my business was a heaven-sent gift. He saved my bacon many times.

The Master was a man of very few words. But when he spoke, I sat up and listened.

I served on the national board of one organisation for several years with Les. A conservative man, he was always sceptical of most of our southern state counterparts and their motives, and for good reason. In meetings with those contemporaries, ascertaining whether he was intensely serious about a topic or just using his brilliant, dry wit was always challenging. Sometimes, he'd combine both just to keep others confused. He was a master of the poker face. The only way I'd pick which card he was playing was by catching a well-disguised wink or seeing one tiny corner of his mouth ever so gently rise as he delivered his perfectly timed one-liners. His unpredictability left execs from other states totally befuddled.

While giving me a history lesson on the unforgivable past deeds of a few Southerners he'd dubbed "blow-ins", Les turned to me and quipped, deadpan: "Peter, I don't have a good memory, but always remember, I have a *long* one." Spoken like a true master.

Les had a strict policy that we'd never stay in the 5-star hotels our counterparts from other states stayed in when we'd travel to meetings. Instead, we always stayed in 3-star hotels as a sign to our members that we weren't off on a boozy junket. Staying elsewhere also meant we'd avoid being compromised by the boozy dinners and the ego-inflating our colleagues revelled in.

The Master knew how to manage me. He knew I was a passionate young firebrand. I was his heir apparent for the national role representing Queensland, and he believed I was being groomed by other states to take a softer stance than his more conservative views.

To ensure he had me on side, Les had one of two expertly-timed lines that he'd drop on me just as we were ready to enter the doors of those national meetings. In his dry, monotone voice, he would say, "Peter, I heard that those southern blokes have a nickname for you. Apparently, they call you 'Doormat'. Does that mean they think they can walk all over you?"

Never knowing whether he was serious or just trolling me, my blood pressure would rise to boiling point in a heartbeat. I'd walk into those meetings ready to head-butt the lot of them.

On alternate meetings, Les would expertly bait me again just before we'd enter the meeting room. "Peter, why do those Southerners call you 'Pussycat'? Does that mean they can tickle your tummy, and you'll just roll over?" Always quick to take the bait, I'd be enraged as I entered the meeting while he just sat, nodded and said, "I agree with Peter." Again, the work of a master.

The Master pulled me aside once and asked why I wasn't an auctioneer. I explained that I was intimidated by the flamboyance and quick wit of many auctioneers of the day. I didn't have the confidence to put on a show like they did – there was no way I could emulate their jazz hands.

Les shook his head and reached for a stamp album. Then, in his trademark dry monotone, he quietly began auctioning it off. No fanfare. No smart one-liners. Just a subtle, steady quickening of his banter until he brought down the gavel. It was a powerful lesson in not trying to be someone you're not.

The Master also kept me honest whenever I'd get distracted by something new and exciting emerging in our industry. Fixed in my memory is the time we had lunch at his beloved Ipswich Club. A grand institution. Arriving back at his office, he drove me around the back, where we were greeted by 2 enormous oak barn doors guarding the rear entry of "Fortress Thornton".

"What do you keep in there, Master?" I queried.

"Peter, behind those doors, you'll find all of last year's good ideas," he retorted.

Such a great reminder to not become bedazzled by "the next big thing".

I owe much to Les "the Master" Thornton for teaching me to take my time, dig deeper for the facts, know your numbers in business and not get too distracted by the "shite and briny". And despite his calm and seemingly monotonous approach, the Master taught me that it's possible to auction a bland old stamp album and still make it sexy.

> "A fool and his money are soon parted."
> Thomas Tusser

Dr Tegan: An angel on Earth

I've written previously about Mum's later-in-life health battles, in particular, her courage and never-say-die attitude. Over 2 long, painful months, Mum had been poked and prodded by teams of doctors of various disciplines, seemingly more focused on following procedures than on patient care and communication. My lawyers say it could be deemed libellous or defamatory to write that some of Mum's medical care was performed by rude, obnoxious, self-obsessed, incompetent fools with delusions of grandeur and over-inflated beliefs in their own self-importance. The lawyers said if I waxed lyrical about these doctors' poor communication skills and apparent refusal to listen to their patients, it could result in legal action against me. So, I will observe the lawyers' advice and refrain from making any of those statements and naming doctors or the quasi-protection racket run by those who should know better.

Can you sense that I'm angry at the care my mum was denied? You're 100% right! I felt a powerful sense that Mum's string of medical challenges didn't fit the cookie-cutter mould of plug-and-play solutions contained in the medicos' "wash, rinse, repeat" handbook of 2023. With no solutions easily identified to rid Mum of her pain and suffering and no one truly owning her case and care, she was subsequently moved from the mainstream hospital across the road to the "rehab" hospital.

We were promised that this live-in rehab facility would provide Mum with tailored intensive therapy twice a day to build her strength and get her home.

Within days it became very apparent that those promises were empty. No such rehab was to be forthcoming, and the so-called "rehab unit" was actually their code for "heaven's waiting room".

Now, it'd be unfair to label all of the medicos who looked after Mum during those 2 months as insensitive and disinterested in getting to the root cause of her pain. Some amazing people worked very hard to make her fight easier.

Of particular note was an incredible young lady named Dr Tegan Stewart.

Dr Tegan became Mum's doctor at the rehab facility after it seemed everyone else in the health system had given up. She read Mum's charts and medical history. She took a genuine interest in meeting me. She made herself available for long conversations to discuss Mum's prognosis. More importantly, Dr Tegan took the time to truly get to know Mum and what was important to her.

Where others had given up hope, Dr Tegan went the extra mile in search of answers to Mum's challenges. She studied the charts, dug deeper and resolved to ask Mum to undergo just one more scan. (*Coincidentally, Dr Tegan was Mum's first female doctor since her admission.*)

Twenty-four hours after the scan, Dr Tegan called me in for a chat to discuss the results.

Now, if you ever receive bad news, it's ideal if it's delivered by someone who shows warmth, genuine empathy and the ability to share that news in plain English. Dr Tegan was that human.

Armed with her empathy and pages and pages of big, unpronounceable words, Dr Tegan softly, warmly and caringly sat with us both and proceeded: "Iris, the results of yesterday's scan are back, and I'm sorry to have to tell you, but we've detected several cancerous lesions in your bowel, liver and chest wall, and there's evidence of cancer in some of your lymph nodes as well as a thickening in the main artery in your neck. Would you like me to explain what all of that really means?"

The room fell silent. Dr Tegan warmly held Mum's hand while we absorbed the enormity of what we'd just been told. A rush of emotions swept across my body and brain. Through it all, Dr Tegan was calm. She let the silence rest, and at what seemed like the perfect juncture, she continued: "Iris, there are a range of options available to you, and I'll arrange for the best people in the hospital to have those discussions with you over the next few days. I don't think surgery is a viable option for you, and in your current state of health, you're probably not going to respond well to chemotherapy. What I can promise you, Iris, is that I'll be with you every step of the way in this hospital to ensure that any pain is properly managed, that you'll be comfortable, and that you'll retain your dignity."

Dr Tegan's caring bedside manner gave Mum peace. Importantly, it gave her the answers she'd sought for the last 2 months, answers other medical professionals overlooked in their haste to get from ward to ward and patient to patient.

I mentioned earlier that Dr Tegan took the time to get to know what was important to Mum. She'd learned that Mum had enjoyed a long career as a professional cabaret singer. She'd also taken time to learn that one of Mum's frustrations over those 2 months in the hospital was that, due to feeding and oxygen tubes being shoved down her throat, she'd lost the ability to sing. All she could manage was a gravelly rasp, causing her enormous disappointment.

Singing was the one thing that had given Mum happiness and sunshine during some really tough and unpublished challenges in her life. So, to be unable to call on her love of music to sing her way to peace was devastating for her. While no one, including Mum, expected miracles, Dr Tegan demonstrated her care by listening empathetically.

True to her word, Dr Tegan was there for Mum until she elected to head home, fittingly on Australia Day, 2023. Before Mum could leave that ward, Dr Tegan had a gift for her, a gift that still brings me to tears.

Iris Brewer - Cabaret Singer

To set the scene: I'd brought Mum a Chinese meal for lunch in the hospital library. She loved nothing better than sweet and sour pork and a big bowl of fried rice. Dr Tegan called by the library to say hi. We exchanged pleasantries about the impending weekend's activities and the good doctor headed down the corridor as I wheeled Mum back to her room. However, I had an intuition that Dr Tegan had some unfinished business in her exchange with Mum.

Less than a minute later, Dr Tegan reappeared. With a warm smile, she dropped to one knee, reached for Mum's hand and warmly said "Iris, I know singing has been an important part of your life, and I know you're having trouble with that now. So, I was wondering if it would be okay if I sang for you?"

With a nod of blessing from Mum, Dr Tegan shared a beautiful rendition of Josh Groban's "You Raise Me Up". There we sat: Dr Tegan with an angelic voice singing from the heart, me hanging onto the handles of Mum's wheelchair and sobbing like a schoolkid, and Mum soaking up the joy of her much-loved music.

Suddenly, as if through divine intervention, I felt Mum push back and sit upright in her wheelchair. I saw her head rise up proudly, and I heard her start to sing along with Dr Tegan. Mum's voice was raspy at first, but then, in the magic of one very special moment, she pushed through the rasp and gravel, found her voice and tone, and sang pitch-perfect in harmony with the good doctor. Dr Tegan warmly held Mum's hand and, true to her word, ensured she retained her dignity.

Mum came home from hospital 2 days later. Dr Tegan has since moved on to another health facility. Her impact on Mum and me was profound, and given Mum's love of her Lord, I dare say angelic and heaven-sent. I've not been able to find Dr Tegan to personally thank her for her amazing contributions to Mum's care. Her bedside manner was truly extraordinary, and I hope she continues changing lives with her incredible care and compassion. Dr Tegan is living proof that:

"Not all heroes wear capes."

Dean Cain

Magic moments that mattered

A well-lived life across various careers, industries and professions has afforded me the opportunity to interact with an extensive and diverse range of people. These are just a few short moments that I'll forever treasure.

Hello, Governor!

A fitting magic moment to begin with was the time when this school dropout sat sipping champagne on the shores of Sydney Harbour at the Governor General of Australia, Sir Michael Jeffery, and his wife, Lady Jeffery's residence, Admiralty House, chatting about our shared love of fishing. This by-invitation-only private soiree was an acknowledgment that I'd raised 3 million dollars for the National Breast Cancer Foundation.

For the record, the GG's preferred bait was squid, and his usual catch was blue-eyed trevally. How cool that our nation's ceremonial leader at the time could stand on the rocks dressed in shorts, T-shirt and thongs and throw a line into Sydney Harbour with the iconic Opera House and Harbour Bridge within spitting distance.

I love Australia. A land of endless opportunity.

Seth

I had the honour of sitting on the sidelines while my illustrious "work wife", Antonia Mercorella, and one of the greatest marketing minds in the world, Seth Godin, recorded a relaxed one-on-one chat on a mild Saturday morning to raise funds for a national disaster appeal we were championing.

Fans of Seth's would have paid $50,000 for that opportunity. The master marketer did it for us for free simply because we asked and because he wanted to help us raise money for people in need.

The joy in Antonia's voice and the spring in her step were inspiring. I'm honoured to have played a small part in that meeting of minds. Seth was an absolute gentleman. On top of his kindness with time, he walked the talk, offering USD 10,000 to support our fundraising efforts.

Common ground

I once shared a flight from Adelaide to Brisbane with former Prime Minister Julia Gillard. Despite our opposing views on politics, we shared more in common than differences. Rather than burying her head in a book, the former PM struck up a lively and engaging conversation that made our 2-hour flight seem like 2 minutes. While our conversation showed that we disagreed on some aspects of politics, our discussion about diversity was absolutely instrumental in my advocating for that cause.

Why do former politicians usually only show true humanity, humility and their softer sides when they deliver their concession speeches? Is their daily debt to the party system that's gifted them power so compromising that they can't be their true selves when in power?

Vroom vroom

Slamming bourbon and Cokes on a flight from Melbourne to Brisbane while dishing out social media marketing advice to V8 Supercars hero Mark Skaife was a highlight for this petrolhead. In a conversation from which my only 2 regrets were not capturing a selfie with the great man and losing the boarding pass he'd signed for my son Sam, Skaife was a fun co-pilot as we winged our way to Brissie. We left the plane, shall we say, not unrefreshed. I can only imagine the look of excitement in the cab driver's eyes when he saw Skaife, a national V8 Supercars icon, getting into the back seat of his Camry. Talk about performance anxiety!

The bodyguard

While on an overseas trade delegation, I lapped up rockstar treatment most of us mere mortals will only ever dream about. Well, it wasn't really a musical rockstar I was travelling with, but an influential CEO of an international company whose identity must remain under wraps. Such was his wealth and reputation that he was a target for kidnappers whenever he left the confines of his heavily guarded corporate headquarters or home compound.

He's a busy man who values every moment. For that reason, my discussions with him were carried out in his chauffeur-driven limousine over 2 days between his other meetings as I travelled between cities with him and his personal entourage of an armed guard and 2 maids.

Not only is he impressively wealthy, but he is also wildly obsessive, such that his toothbrush, cosmetics and clothes must be set up in a specific way when he travels. His maids travel with him and are on hand to recreate his home experience in each hotel suite. He literally walks out of his clothes at each day's end and into a perfectly ironed and placed new outfit the next morning.

Despite all of this, a nicer man you could not meet. It was a wild experience for a few days, but the thought of being a target for kidnappers and being shielded by an armed security detail 24/7 did little to float my boat.

A "moyo" moment

I've been blessed to have been able to play a part in assembling a team of Eddie Berenbaum from Virginia and Brad Inman from Inman News to reunite the beautiful Ekofo family from the DC Congo with their US-based son, the most magnificent and big-hearted Billy Ekofo.

On an emotion-charged stage in front of 4,000+ people in San Francisco, our collective efforts orchestrated a surprise reunion for Billy with his family after being separated for 14 years by political turmoil. This moment ranks as one of my life's most special. That I could play a small role in arranging flights and visas and facilitating that reunion for my beautiful friend fills my cup daily.

Watching Billy in a teary, warm embrace with his mother, father, brothers and sisters still gives me chills whenever I recall that day. Kudos to Heather Elias for first reaching out to me and Brad and to

Eddie Berenbaum for taking my calls. A most magnificent "moyo" moment. (*For the record, "moyo" is an African word that means life or heart and soul in Swahili and the DC Congo.*)

Peter with Billy 'Moyo' Ekofo

The power of a hug

Throughout my career, I've received inspiring feedback that has touched my heart. In one case, a special young lady and I were both brought to tears, and it's a moment that still makes tears well in my eyes today.

I'd spoken at a university campus outside Geelong for my inspirational friend Hayley Mitchell. As I left the stage, the applause was warm, and I felt good about my presentation. Walking to the back of the room, I caught sight of a young lady making a beeline in my direction out of the corner of my left eye.

I braced myself and quickly reflected if I'd said anything inflammatory or inappropriate in my session. Suddenly, she was upon me. Uncontrolled tears flowed, and she battled to contain her emotions to speak. She calmed as I handed her the only clean tissue in my pocket. Her words still move me today:

"Peter, my grandfather died a year ago. I loved him and miss him so much, and what you said today reminded me so much of him."

My heart swelled and tears flowed.

Next she continued, "I never got to say goodbye to him. Would it be okay if I gave you a hug?"

At that moment, we shared a warm embrace that fuelled our hearts with some homemade chicken soup for the soul. It was an exceptional reminder that there's something special about the human spirit and our ability to make a difference in others' lives.

We parted company later that afternoon and haven't spoken since. I have a standing offer to drop by the young lady's office when I'm next in rural Victoria. Likewise, she has a standing invitation to call me anytime. Even if neither of us follows through with our respective offers, sometimes all we need to know is that we have a tribe we can come home to.

Challenge accepted!

Through the mid-Peter Brewer 2.0 period, I was fortunate to build a friendship with the inspiring Brad Inman, who features in a few stories in this memoir. Brad is free-thinking and uncompromising. Money can't buy his opinion. He tells it like it is and rarely holds back. We share some common values around challenging the status quo and not tolerating the kind of people Brad describes as "chuckleheads".

Our mutual respect, significantly aided by the support of Laura Monroe (another gem), saw me added as an ambassador for the US-based Inman powerhouse events and publishing empire in 2011. Our association was mutually beneficial and lasted until the havoc of COVID. In those 10 wonderful years, I spread the word Down Under for Inman, and Inman spread the word about me, increasing my profile not just in Oz but also in the USA. I love a win-win relationship. It's a value that every great negotiation should be underpinned by.

I'm okay with people being sceptical. Hey, we're in the real estate profession. There's no shortage of BS to wade through in search of the truth. And despite every man and his dog proclaiming another street or suburb record almost daily or boasting about their new Porsche or Rolex every other day, there are a lot of people caught swimming naked when the tide goes out. So, I figured it was reasonable to receive a challenge from the Chair of an organisation I was involved with. Wearing his best shade of scepticism, the Chair said, "Let's see how good you are. I'll believe you're fair dinkum if you can get Brad Inman to Zoom into one of our Board meetings."

Peter with Brad Inman and Tara

Now, anyone who knows me knows there are very few challenges I'll shy away from. If the challenge in some form hints at bringing the level of my influence or credibility into question, then challenge accepted!

The mission began. My goal was not just to get Brad Inman to Zoom into a board meeting – that would be lame. Instead, I became laser-focused on getting Brad on a plane to Brisbane and having him stand onstage and deliver a keynote address at our organisation's next annual conference.

I am delighted to report that the great man did exactly that. What's more, he did it at his own expense!

I have enormous respect for the gentleman who posed this challenge to me. From recollection, I'm not aware he ever verbally expressed I'd far exceeded his challenge. However, I do recall the wide smile on his face when I captured a happy snap of Brad and him standing together in the boardroom.

If you're a cake lover like me, you'll agree there's always gotta be icing on the cake. For me, it came as Tara and I delivered Brad back to Brisbane airport for his return flight home. Unprompted, Brad asked me to turn my video on as I stopped the car, and I dutifully followed the master's orders. For the next 90 seconds, he delivered one of the kindest, most generous and warmest testimonials I could ever wish for.

Relationships matter. Kindness matters. Choose your friends and use your influence wisely. They'll take you almost anywhere you want to go.

Do you believe in fate?

The year was 1991. In fact, it was August 30, 1991, to be exact. A Friday. It was the day we settled on purchasing the family real estate business from my parents. About 2 weeks out, I put plans in place for a party to celebrate Mum and Dad's retirement and to usher in the soon-to-be heavily indebted, nervous new guard. It was scary going into the level of debt required to purchase that business. I remember joking with the bank about whether the bank or we should be more worried on the day we signed the loan papers.

The first person on my list of invitees for the party was Ray Milton, the then-president of the REIQ. Ray had been a good friend to the family, an amazing spokesperson and advocate for the profession and someone I have always respected. I reached out to personally invite Ray and still recall my genuine delight at receiving a call from his office to confirm he'd agreed to drive from the Gold Coast to attend the event and say a few words.

Even today, I look at the photo of me standing with Ray and feel humbled that he took the time to travel to share in the transition of our family's business.

Was I inspired? Yes. Is Ray's 50+ year contribution to the profession legendary? Yes. Did luck, good planning or fate see me become Chairperson of the REIQ 3 decades later? Who knows?

Whatever the driver, I'm forever indebted to Ray for agreeing to attend our small soirée and taking a genuine interest in my real estate career. The REIQ and the real estate profession are richer for Ray's selfless contributions. Perhaps the kindness he showed this young fella lit a flame in me to contribute to our wonderful institute just as he had all those years before me.

Final Curtain Call... but the Show Goes On

The good, the bad and the despicable: A lesson in humility

According to Justice Michael Lee, "An autobiography usually reveals nothing bad about its writer except his memory." His observation has been a guiding principle as I've put these reflections together. In a world where social media often presents an idealised, "bright and shiny" version of life, it's crucial to be honest about the less glamorous, "shite and briny" realities.

My extensive experience across all facets of the real estate profession, from grassroots to boardroom, has given me a unique perspective. True empathy, I believe, comes from walking in another's shoes – a principle not always understood by those in leadership positions. I've witnessed behaviour that still leaves me incredulous, including incompetence and outright fraud. While I won't name names to avoid legal issues, I can share some concerning observations.

One significant issue is the low barrier to entry for non-profit board and executive roles. This often leads to well-intentioned but unskilled individuals, and sometimes those with less noble motives, gaining positions of power and trust. This can range from minor infractions, like a local club treasurer using funds for personal expenses, to more serious breaches of trust involving significant sums of money. It becomes deeply personal when narcissistic and psychopathic individuals undermine the work of honest, hardworking leaders who genuinely want to serve their members and customers.

These individuals often exhibit a fascinating dichotomy. Despite their subpar performance, they demand ego-inflating titles, personal chauffeurs and business-class flights to luxury destinations, all at the organisation's expense. They revel in company-funded fantasy lifestyles, attending sham events and indulging in fine dining, while the balance sheet tells a very different story. Anyone who dares to question their actions or spending is quickly silenced. But history has a way of revealing the truth. My father often said, "The big wheel of life has a habit of turning, Pete. Just bide your time. Their day will come."

My career has also brought me into contact with some highly influential figures. One "industry god" I'd once revered shattered my admiration for him within 3 seconds with his arrogance at a chance meeting one Sunday morning. Excited at the opportunity of a one-on-one chat, I offered my expertise on a topic I was well-versed in. He promptly dismissed me, saying, "Peter, I meet 80 people a week like you."

His highly dismissive response was in stark contrast to his own advice to "treat every person the same way you'd expect your mother/father/sister/brother to be treated." His ill-chosen words and arrogance immediately banished him in my eyes.

Actions have consequences. It reminded me of the quote most attributed to Marcel Proust: "You should never meet your heroes."

I hope this "misguided messiah" reflects on his actions one day and realises that his arrogance towards me was the catalyst for the demise of his broader industry agenda. His story serves as a powerful reminder that words matter and have lasting impacts.

"It's nice to be important, but it's more important to be nice."

John Templeton

A lesson in forgiveness

Families are complicated things, and ours was no different. No one gives your parents a manual on managing their relationship, let alone adding a couple of pesky, demanding kids to the equation.

Most couples make it up as they go based on personal values, perceived societal expectations and, more often than not, "monkey-see-monkey-do" reflecting their own childhood experiences. Our family unit wasn't immune to challenges.

Sadly in life, some people struggle to contain difficult emotions and frustrations, and sometimes those struggles manifest in less than ideal ways behind the closed doors of a family home.

Broken objects can be replaced, but broken hearts rarely ever heal.

My own wonderful mother came from the world of show business. She believed that no matter what might be happening behind the curtain, the show must always go on. Through each challenge in her life, she'd bravely dust herself off and go on with the show. The world today is different. A family's relationship challenges were managed very differently 60 years ago. Support networks and resources for families encountering family and domestic abuse were often limited or non-existent.

Fortunately, with some support, a difficult period passed in our family. It was a sad, unnecessary and unfortunate chapter. Things happened. Lessons were learned. Life moved on. But that is not always the case for every family. Every 9 days, an Australian woman loses her life at the hands of a current or former partner. To sweep the conversation under the carpet would be disrespectful to the many who face the scourge of partner abuse every day.

As a society, we still have room for better. With my father's full support, my mother went on to provide much-needed safe refuge, food, clothing and counselling resources to assist women who were confronted by the DV scourge.

Physical and mental abuse against partners must stop. Each of us has a part to play in making those dark days a distant memory.

Dedicated to the memory of Carmel W.

Run to paradise

I'm sitting in 3F on a 6-hour flight home to Brisbane after a heartwarming week in Bali with my beautiful family.

Family – say no more

I've been listening to The Choirboys classic "Run to Paradise" on my AirPods. It's a banger of a song that's been a constant companion at the penthouse and the "other" house times of my privileged life.

It's kinda fitting that it inspires some of this final chapter.

After the *annus horribilis* of 2023 and my fightback of 2024, my soul needed time to recharge, refocus and reconnect with the real world, particularly my family, who have been pillars of strength for me, especially over the last couple of years.

I needed time to just be. Time away from the craziness of a corporate world where egos and stuff-that's-seriously-not-important become the focus rather than making the most of our 3 score and 10 years.

I was on a mission to find me again.

I could think of no better place and way to do that than in the paradise, tranquillity and wildly contrasting madness that is Bali.

As I sit here, refreshed, replenished and deeply thankful after 6 days with family, I'm also chastising myself that it's taken me 34 years to hit the pause button on life's busyness and press play on the much more important family button. After all, they're the main reason I do what I do. Life and its distractions can surely make a meal of where our focus is best spent.

By my calculations, I've got around 321 Saturdays left at the time of writing this. (*I was tempted to type "God willing", but I feel like I voided the conditions of my contract with the Big Guy upstairs long ago!*)

Having recently been diagnosed with diabetes and with my untreatable atrial fibrillation, I'm today paying the price for a life of poor discipline and excess. The bullets I thought I could dodge now have me squarely in their sights.

Facing your mortality can be pretty confronting.

At 65, the bells are tolling louder than ever before, and it's way past time for this fun-loving larrikin to listen to their increasingly reverberating chimes.

VA50 will touch down on my beloved Australian soil in just a few hours. I'll disembark with a new and refreshed set of priorities.

In the Year of the Snake, I'll start to formally wind down my days with the REIQ. I've enjoyed the relationship for 36-odd years, with the last 9 years on the Board and 7 in the Chair. As its leader, I can honestly say I've had the most enjoyment out of any of my business accomplishments.

I can't adequately express what it means to me to have been given that honour, especially given my humble beginnings and against all odds wagered on my life's likely success by Wynnum State High's school guidance officer. I'd like to think that Merv Miles, the author of the school reference that described me as "an independent type of lad with potential", would appreciate that I've defied the odds and actually reached some of that potential.

I've promised myself and others that when I walk out the door of the REIQ, I won't be the tone-deaf, annoying guy who hangs around beyond his time. My predecessor, Rob Honeycombe, gave me some golden advice. He told me not to follow what he'd done in the role but to put my mark on the grand institution during my time. I'll let history and others determine whether I did a good job.

I'll walk away comfortable in my skin and forever appreciative of the opportunity. I'd be less than honest if I didn't confess that I will be waving a copy of our impressive balance sheet and arguably the highest member satisfaction levels that the REIQ has had in many decades in the general direction of those who made my early days hell. They know who they are. History has already determined their legacy.

Having attempted retirement at 49, where I'd made the rookie mistake of not having a hobby, special interest or something to keep me occupied to fill the void of time, I'm a bit wiser this time. With my remaining free trips around the sun, I'll be trading professional time to savour more magical sunsets in my caravan at Noosa, marvel at more sunrises at Byron and camp on more farms to get some fresh cow pads on my RMs. I can't wait to spend more time swapping lies around the campfire, on sandy beaches or in dry and even flooded riverbeds with my mates of almost 60 years.

I want to spend more time writing. I'm really enjoying its therapeutic benefits. Truth be told, I've enjoyed writing some chapters and then immediately deleting them just for the cathartic value of venting.

I will be a fun, available Poppa B to my simply delightful granddaughters, Sydney and Gigi. I will be around to teach them and any future baby Brewers, fur or otherwise, the important stuff in life. Stuff like not copping crap from anyone, being prepared to play their own kind of music and sing their own special song and the importance of barracking for the mighty Maroons.

I'll teach them that, "You can't wait until life isn't hard anymore before you decide to be happy." In other words, don't sweat the small stuff because, in the scheme of life, it's mostly *all* small stuff.

I've been gifted two incredible children, Sam and Lauren. They both have and expect high values. Both possess an unwavering moral compass. Their work ethic is amongst the most dedicated

I've witnessed. Both practise a love for the environment, a strong commitment to social responsibility, community volunteering, respect for their bodies and self-care. As young adults, they continue to demonstrate a deep love for family. Somehow, despite my continuing foibles, shenanigans and repeated *faux pas*, they still tolerate me, which is an honour I deeply appreciate.

Naturally, I have a strong bias towards my brood, but I'm repeatedly reminded of their impressive natures and behaviours by people who matter. Watching them both grow as loving partners and parents to children and fur babies in their own relationships is heartwarming.

I look forward to playing whatever bit part they have for me in the next chapters of their lives.

Six days ago, as we flew to Bali, I was emotional, teary, inconsolable and trying to figure out whether I could keep myself together in front of my family for a week. I've been carrying a lot of baggage for a long time, and I could feel it unpacking in a visually ugly way if I couldn't keep it together. I knew I needed some important treatment. My body and soul screamed for a good shot of some miraculous substance.

Luckily, the magical medical intervention I desperately needed didn't require a chemical cocktail with FDA approval. It wasn't banned in Bali and, in fact, is a naturally occurring substance the Balinese proactively encourage.

The concoction that worked the desired magic was sitting in Rows 3, 4 and 5 on my flight!

Six days in Bali, deeply immersed in love, laughter and the beauty of my family was the remedy for my ills.

It's funny how your life and perspective change when you open your eyes and heart, and your family and the universe wrap their warm, loving arms around you and give you a big, loving, physical and metaphorical hug.

I reflect on the warm words Sam whispered to me, accompanied by one of his trademark giant bear hugs, "We're making memories, Dad."

My mission was accomplished.

Peter Brewer 3.0 is officially in the design phase. I have immense trust in the development team that will oversee and steer its next evolution.

Is it too late for a revolution? Who knows?!

"Run to Paradise" has evolved from the tape deck in my 89 Ute to the CD player in my first home, and now on my Spotify list on my Landcruiser's CarPlay. Over time, there have been some significant changes on the highways we've driven together. I can't wait to see what gets added to the playlist and where the next journey on this amazing highway takes me.

Where will this "independent type of lad who has potential" pop up next?

God only knows, but strap yourselves in; I know it's going to be fun!

THE END

Acknowledgements

Cramming my very privileged life into just over 82,000 words has been a challenge. It's virtually impossible to acknowledge everything and everyone who's helped shape the man I am today. Maybe there's a sequel in the planning. However, it'd be remiss of me not to acknowledge 2 people for the important parts they've played in my life.

Michelle, my long suffering wife of 25 years until 2012, was a loyal and caring partner in life and business while also managing a busy family. She is a loving mother to her son Brendan, who has raised his family in the UK. She's a wonderful mum to our children, Sam and Lauren, and a perfect grandmother to her brood, both human and fur. She showed remarkable tolerance for my quirks, ambitions and obsession with business, for which I owe her unqualified gratitude and appreciation.

To my partner, Tara. Thank you for welcoming this rusty, bruised, battle-weary relic into your life and attempting a mammoth restoration project. It's never lost on me that you took the chance to travel 10,000 miles across the hemispheres to call Australia your new home to be with me. We've both had times and experiences that we're not proud of. But those experiences have given us the benefit of some amazing wisdom and the opportunity to be better humans, partners and friends. I'm incredibly proud of the career, friendships and life you've carved out here in Australia and your commitment to becoming a dinky-di Aussie. I'm also proud of the high level of respect that you've single-handedly earned across our profession. It's an impressive feat for someone who claims to be an introvert. Your commitment to me is concerning. But hey, I'll take it while I can.

This book started with the idea of sharing a few short life lessons that might help enrich my grandchildren's life journeys. Twelve months and 109,000 barely legible words later, I realised I had the genesis of something more than a few short life lessons to share with a wider audience. But how could a bloke who, at 65, still can't distinguish between a verb, adjective, noun and pronoun achieve this? *(And don't start me on Oxford commas!)* Could anyone really translate those 109,000 rambling words into English?

Enter the wonderful Phaedra Pym. I want to acknowledge Phaedra's incredibly detailed, forensic fact-checking and wordsmithing that put the final polish on *Running out of Saturdays*. Phaedra has not just wordsmithed my ramblings into reality; she's expertly helped this first-time self-published writer navigate the complex world of putting my story onto paper, Kindle and audio. Thank you, Phaedra, Eric and team. Blessings to you for your brilliance, patience and perseverance. This book would not have seen the light of day without you.

I also want to acknowledge the ongoing encouragement from my support crew, Samantha Mclean, Greg Cary, Tara Christianson and Lee Woodward, who continued to jab my ribs to see this passion project through. My goal was to sell one copy. At the time of going to press, we've already tripled that goal. Thank you for believing in me. You helped me believe in myself.

Author Bio

Peter Brewer, known to many as PB, isn't your ordinary "boy from the burbs". He's a dynamic individual whose life has been a remarkable journey of entrepreneurial spirit, strategic thinking and unwavering enthusiasm. Peter has consistently demonstrated an innate ability to identify opportunities and turn them into successful ventures.

From his first foray into business with a cash-only mobile seafood business in the Taxation Office car park to a significant and enduring real estate career, Peter's resourcefulness and adaptability have set him apart. His sharp business mind, coupled with a wily sense of humour, has allowed him to deeply connect with people from all walks of life across the globe.

Peter is often regarded as a man ahead of his time, constantly challenging the status quo and devising creative solutions. He believes in hard work, learning from mistakes, turning challenges into opportunities and seizing the day.

www.ingramcontent.com/pod-product-compliance
Lightning Source LLC
Chambersburg PA
CBHW061725070526
44583CB00024B/3008